IT'S Go-Time

Ben Stark and Chris Hunter share
INSIGHTS & STRATEGIES TO HELP YOUR HOME-SERVICE COMPANY SUCCEED!

With David E. Rothacker

Published by
Go-Time Publishing
1500 Central Park Drive
Hurst, TX 76053

Printed in the United States of America

For quantity purchase discounts contact QuantityPurchases@GoTimeSuccessGroup.com

ISBN: 978-0-578-75335-5

Library of Congress Control Number: 2020945658

The web addresses referenced in this book were live and correct at the time of the book's publication but may be subject to change. The publisher assumes no responsibility for the topicality, correctness, or completeness of information provided by any third-party websites that may be referenced in this book.

Some names have been changed to protect privacy.

In an effort to be as inclusive as possible, the authors have taken a gender-neutral approach to pronoun usage, employing *they, them,* and *their* when referring to non-specific individuals.

Illustrations and Cover Design: David Thompson
Editor: Jason Liller

Dedications

Ben: To my beautiful wife Kim who is the hardest working person I know. She works in the business, keeps me out of trouble, helps me with all of my projects, takes care of our home, guides our family to happiness and keeps all of our children and grandchildren in check.

Chris: To my wife Nickie. She is my encourager! Without her none of this would have been possible! I love you!

Dave: To Tom McCart for his steadfast belief in me! RIP Brother!

Foreword

The story is a familiar one. Something triggers a technician to quit his job and start a company. Maybe he eases into it by moonlighting. Maybe he takes a quick jump after getting angry with his boss. Regardless, he is now in the contracting business.

Yes, the technician is now a businessperson, except he's not. He is a technician pretending to be a businessperson. Four out of ten never make the transition. Sure, they manage to be self-employed, but they do not own a business. They own a job.

There is no shame in being a single-truck operator, there is only shame in staying one. The single-truck operation should be a phase on the way to something larger and more sustainable.

"What's your family going to do if you get in an accident or get injured?" I asked a proud single-truck operator at a trade show.

"Man, I don't think like that," he replied.

Of course not. He's not thinking like that because that is thinking about *others*. He only thinks about himself. He's selfish. It's all about him. It's all about his freedom. If something happens to him, his customers will find another contractor, but will his family find another source of income?

Another four in ten manage to grow . . . some. They plateau with the owner still on the truck. After a while, these contractors accept their lot. They stop trying to grow. Ironically, they often make less money than the single-truck operator because they have overhead the one-trucker never experiences.

It is a minority of contractors who grow past this, and an even smaller minority who blow it out before successfully selling their business and walking away wealthy. The successful contractors illustrate the prosperity that the industry can provide. Knowing prosperity is available, it kills me to watch so many others struggle.

Worse than the struggling contractors are those who resign themselves to living a life of scarcity rather than one of abundance. They constrain their lifestyle to what the business throws off when they should instead imagine the lifestyle they want and build a business to support it.

Why do most contractors struggle? They don't know anything else. Contractors may go to trade school, but there is no owner school. They are trained on how to turn a wrench, not on how to turn a profit. This book will help them understand there is a better approach, a better way, and a pot of gold at the end of their business rainbow.

Many contracting business success books are written from the perspective of one person's story. The authors share what worked for them. And while they can be invaluable guides, they still represent single perspectives. This book takes a different approach. It gives you the first-hand perspectives of Ben Stark and Chris Hunter, woven together through the storytelling ability of Dave Rothacker.

I've known Dave the longest. He was part of a brain trust of great contractors and industry writers in the Cleveland area. Dave was one of the early proponents of online contractor idea exchanges. He started Area51HVAC, an early online bulletin board. A voracious reader, Dave has always given back to the industry and has an ability to look at an ordinary situation in a different way. He often brings forth unique perspectives that make people stop and think.

Chris Hunter started as the guy moonlighting in HVAC while he worked for the phone company. Soon after he started his business, he joined the Service Roundtable and became a poster child for our approach. As Chris said numerous times, "I didn't question it. I just did it."

Chris did it as well as anyone in the country. He did quite a bit of innovating on his own, building a multi-million-dollar business in small towns in southern Oklahoma before selling it. Chris did this in a rural, low-population market, proving a successful business can emerge anywhere.

Ben Stark recently sold his third contracting company. Ben is a money magnet. He's got the Midas touch. Everything he does becomes successful.

I've also noticed that Ben—if you're old enough to remember these ads—is the E.F. Hutton of contracting. When Ben talks at one of our meetings, contractors listen. They listen because Ben is sage. He knows what he's talking about.

Chris and Ben have different personalities. On the surface, their approaches are different, though substantively they are similar. Their values are similar. Both became wildly successful.

Dave Rothacker does a great job bringing the experiences and approaches of both Chris and Ben together in this book. Dave helps the struggling contractor understand that there isn't a single, rigid approach to success.

This book is a manual on how to succeed in residential retail contracting. It is a guide that, if followed, can lead to wealth and prosperity. Read it. Study it. Live it.

Matt Michel
President, Service Nation, Inc.

Contracting Business Hall of Fame
The Air Conditioning Heating & Refrigeration News' Legends in HVAC Award

Contents

CHAPTERS

Introduction

*"Begin with the end in mind" is based on the principle that all things are created twice.
There's a mental or first creation, and a physical or second creation to all things.*
– Stephen R. Covey

Did you miss *How to Run an HVAC, Plumbing, or Electrical Business 101* back in trade school? Of course you did. Why? Because back in the day, that type of education didn't exist.

But once you became a technician you learned how to run a business, right? Of course you didn't. Why? Because other than learning how to treat people, either by a caring or a crummy boss, nothing in your experience taught you how to market, how to use financials, how to analyze KPIs, how to perform annual success planning, or how to lead others, among a long, long list of other business skills that you were probably never taught.

You know who else missed that class? Ben Stark and Chris Hunter, two of the most successful people in the business. They were once technicians who went on to start their own companies. Going from truck to business owner, they enrolled in the School of Hard Knocks. The book you hold in your hands is a story of transformation, a compilation of lessons learned and massive action taken.

Ben and Chris are giving entrepreneurs by nature. Due to their profound success, they felt a deep desire to give back to the industries that have been so good to them. Setting out to write a book, they reached out to me, Dave Rothacker, a writer with twenty-five years of management experience in the HVAC industry.

The three of us had taken a similar approach to business over the years, an approach that crystallized and came to life when Chris developed it into the *Go-Time Formula*. It's a process that, when followed, brings uncommon success. We break it down in Chapter 1, *Begin With the End in Mind*.

HOW TO USE THIS BOOK

It's Go-Time can be read cover to cover or it can be used as a reference manual, focusing on one chapter at a time. Like Ben and Chris did with Ron Smith's *HVAC Spells Wealth* and *More and New HVAC Spells Wealth*, we recommend that you do both.

The more you dig into it, the clearer the focus becomes on how all of the chapters tie together. Ben and Chris are more than just good marketers, they're proficient in all of the disciplines covered in this book.

We end each chapter with a *Go-Time Formula* exercise that reinforces lessons learned, and you can create your own Go-Time Formula whenever you seek to create, innovate, modify, change, or learn a different segment of the business, or when you seek to create, innovate, modify, or change a system, process, or procedure. Here's the best part: The Go-Time Formula applies to every aspect of life. If you want to improve or enhance any area of your life, career, marriage, you name it, the Go-Time Formula will help you get there.

A business is a complicated, changing, living, and growing organism. For every topic covered here, be sure to check into the *Go-Time University* for a deeper dive and continuous updates.

All of the books written on our industry barely make up a handful of sand in the desert of available knowledge. Check our *book recommendation* section for our favorite grains of sand. For a more comprehensive dive into each topic covered here and much, much more, visit the Go-Time University.

Begin With the End in Mind

One theme that courses through the book is *Begin With the End in Mind*. Create and build your business with the intent to sell it. Your business is like your house: When it's time to sell it, you fix it up and do all that you can to make it attractive and desirable so that you can ask for top dollar—and get it.

Remember this concept and keep it in mind as you read each chapter.

Leadership

Ben and Chris are strong leaders who have cultivated a style that's a combination of servant and transformational leadership. In an industry that has more of a leadership shortage than a labor shortage it's crucial that you, too, develop a style of leadership that works in your company. We discuss this in the chapter titled *Transformational Leadership*.

As iron sharpens iron, so one friend sharpens another.
– Chris Hunter, quoting Proverbs 27:17

When Challenge Arises

The COVID-19 pandemic struck as we were completing this book. In addition to the serious health issues, the virus turned the world of work upside down.

Challenge, change, and crisis are inevitable. It's our contention that strong leadership, a crystal clear and desirable vision that includes beginning with the end in mind, and effective systems, processes, and procedures all help to reduce friction as the company moves forward, regardless of the roadblocks that circumstance may place in your path.

Guest Authors

Three other experts have leant their hands to this book.

Matt Michel - Matt is the founder and CEO of the Service Nation, Inc., an organization that includes the Service Roundtable and Service Nation Alliance.

Matt has the distinction of being the youngest person elected into the Contracting Business Hall of Fame. An uber-talented author and distinguished leader, Matt has been an integral contributor in the evolution of Ben and Chris's careers (and mine too).

Angie Snow - Angie and her husband Ryan own Western Heating and Air Conditioning located in Orem, Utah. Angie is a Go-Time Success Group coach and also operates her own practice, Snow Business Coaching.

Angie brightens and enhances our CSR chapter with her 7-Star CSR program.

Mark Matteson - Mark is a gifted author and speaker. Known for the popular book *Freedom from Fear* and its follow up, *Freedom from Fear Forever*, Mark is a storyteller extraordinaire.

Mark pens a roadmap for how to get what we want out of life and business. It involves responsibility, introspection, effort, and hard work. He calls it *Righteous Responsibility*.

Two Voices, One Guide

Ben Stark

Chris Hunter

Ben and Chris are experts in their field; together, they possess a staggering amount of business knowledge and experience. If you've ever had the pleasure of speaking with or listening to them in person, you know that while they share similar business beliefs, their personalities and styles of expression are quite different. That difference is what brings this book to life.

It's more than a collective, homogenized, singular voice. There is more educational and emotional impact when we're able to relate the knowledge and experience discussed here, by two people, to the individual, so the advice of Ben and Chris is offered separately, compared, and contrasted, in a way that lets you choose the parts that resonate the most with you.

1. BEGIN WITH THE END IN MIND
2. VISION, MISSION, CORE VALUES, WHY
3. WHEN WORK AND LIFE COLLIDE
4. COWORKER DEVELOPMENT
5. RECRUIT, HIRE, RETAIN
6. THE GO-TIME SERVICE CALL
7. CUSTOMER SERVICE REPRESENTATIVE
8. KEY PERFORMANCE INDICATORS
9. MANAGEMENT
10. LEADERSHIP
11. FINANCIAL MANAGEMENT
12. MARKETING
13. SALES
14. SUCCESS PLANNING
15. ACQUISITIONS, ADDING DIVISIONS, SATELLITE LOCATIONS
16. TRANSFORMATIONAL RELATIONSHIPS
17. SELLING YOUR BUSINESS
18. SUCCESS PRINCIPLES
19. RIGHTEOUS RESPONSIBILITY
20. TRANSFORMATIONAL LEADERSHIP

Imagine that we're in a museum curated and staffed by Ben and Chris. Each exhibit, chock-full of knowledge, wisdom, and experience, represents a chapter in this book.

I'll be your guide as we walk through and talk with Ben, Chris, and our guests, taking in the awe and wonder of their transformation from technician to effective and successful entrepreneurs.

Grab your notebook and join us on this journey of transformation and success!

David E. Rothacker

If you are working on something exciting that you really care about, you don't have to be pushed. The vision pulls you.

– Steve Jobs

My end game is a business that provides a significant return on my hard work and investment. It works for me instead of me working for it. And it will provide the same for its next generation of leaders. It's a vehicle designed to achieve financial independence and freedom. It's Go-Time!

— Chris Hunter

Imagine that you're a sixty-three-year-old owner of an HVAC, plumbing, and electrical business. Your son is a computer scientist and your daughter is a journalist; they have no interest in helping with the company. Your spouse wants to retire in two years. What should you do with the business? You went from working for a large contractor to starting a one-man business to being responsible for a company with fifteen employees. With minimal financial guidance over the years, few systems and processes in place, and a couple hundred service agreements, selling your business will hardly finance three years of retirement. You're going to need a lot more than that.

If you could turn back the clock to those early years, when it was just you and your truck, you would have been wise to *begin with the end in mind*. The *end game* is what you plan to do with your business when you decide to either step away from it or transition the company ownership to someone else.

No matter which direction you choose, the smartest play is to run and grow your business *today* as if you plan to sell it in the end.

Think of your business as a 1967 GTO sitting in the garage. With a passion for digging in and restoring cars, you lavish attention, care, and original parts on it. You enjoy the process. Your end game is to sell the car. Do it right and you'll receive top dollar. Skimp and cut corners and you won't.

Don't you wish someone would have told you about building an end game when you first went into business? Don't worry; it's never too late to start!

Chris: When I first started this business my end game was staying away from the end of my rope and not reaching the end of the money in my checking account!

Chris didn't reach the end of his rope because early on in his business, he joined the *Service Nation Alliance (SNA)* to seek out trusted advisors and organizations. This is a core practice of Ben and Chris. It's a theme you'll see throughout the book.

> **Chris:** I first heard the term *exit strategy* from Matt Michel at an SNA bootcamp. I thought, *this is crazy*. I was there to learn how to make my business grow profitably! What did that have to do with preparing my business for an exit?
>
> Little did I know, it has *everything* to do with an exit strategy. What I learned is that if you build your business with the end in mind, it helps you operate with processes and systems that facilitate that profitable growth.

> **Ben:** I had a six-month break after selling my first company and satisfying the noncompete agreement. During this period, I built a ten-to-twelve-year plan for the life of my next company. It included a description of the company culture, a growth-based marketing strategy, manpower development, annual revenue goals, and a minimum profit goal for each year.
>
> I put it in writing and adjusted it for each annual planning session. It pushed us to over-achieve almost every year and I'm proud to say that we reached our original ten-year revenue and profitability goals by year eight. I then sold the company to a private equity group at the twelve-and-a-half-year mark.

Ben's strategy prior to the launch of his second company and throughout its lifetime is the essence of beginning with the end in mind.

THE GO-TIME FORMULA

Early in his career, with a passionate desire to learn, improve, and grow, Chris studied successful businesspeople and reflected upon their successes and failures. No matter what the endeavor, he noticed the first thing successful people do is *create*. Whether it be a system, a process, or even a company, successful people create something first. Then they launch their creation and continue to improve upon it.

Being the create-a-process, launch-it, improve-upon-it, and make-it-repeatable kinda guy that he is, Chris thought, *We need a success formula to guide us along.*

Because he's also a take-massive-action type of guy, Chris has been known for years throughout the industry for saying *It's Go-Time!* It didn't take him long to chisel an acronym out of the rallying *It's Go-Time!* cry and create the Go-Time success formula.

And the Go-Time formula isn't just for business. It can be applied to any area of your life!

For the balance of the book we'll recap each chapter with the Go-Time formula. Because the end game is so important and because we want to set the Go-Time formula tone in our book's foundation, we're bringing it to you front and center. It's Go-Time!

Guide your end game with the following steps:

 **Goals** – Begin with the end in mind -

 **Observe** – Seek advisors -

 **Take Massive Action** – Pursue operational excellence -

 **Inspect** – What gets measured gets done -

 **Modify** – Look for a better way -

 **Engage** – It's Go-Time!

GOALS — BEGIN WITH THE END IN MIND

Create a picture of your desired future business. What is the annual revenue? What is the net profit? How is it structured? Can it operate without you? Do you rent or own your office/shop? Describe your investments outside of the business. Where do you live? Describe your home. Envision a well-taken-care-of family. Envision your coworkers thriving. Why are you even in business in the first place? What is your goal?

Ben: Build a structured vision of where your company is going.

Chris: My end game is a business that provides a significant return on my hard work and investment. It works for me instead of me working for it. And it will provide the same for its next generation of leaders. It's a vehicle designed to achieve financial independence and freedom. It's Go-Time!

If you don't know where you are going, than you probably won't end up there.

— Forrest Gump

OBSERVE — SEEK ADVISORS

While not all who have built a successful business will share your end game, they have traveled a road of growth, personal learning, and business development. Most of these leaders are willing to share advice.

Both Ben and Chris's end games were illuminated after joining a contractor alliance.

For Ben it was the Contractor Success Group in the early 1990s, North Texas ACCA, and the Service Nation Alliance.

After belonging to the Service Nation Alliance for a couple of years, Chris received a call from a national franchise group with an offer to purchase his company.

Chris: I told them I wasn't interested. They came back willing to make a seven-figure offer. I kinda perked up and thought, *hmmmm, I'd better listen*. I called Larry Taylor and Ben Stark after that and I got some great advice from both of them. Larry said that any time there's that much money being offered you owe it to yourself to at least listen. At the very least it will be an opportunity to learn.

Ultimately, the offer wasn't right for me. But a light went on and I thought, *This business might actually have some value*. That was an a-ha moment and it got me thinking about the end game!

Trade conferences like Service World, the International Roundtable, and events put on by Nextstar, EGIA, ACCA, and PHCC are excellent environments to meet influential leaders. Your lawyer, financial advisor, and accountant are also great resources. Ask for referrals from them for other advisors. Your church, local chamber of commerce, and Rotary clubs are other potential sources of advisors.

The key is to venture forth into the world with your eyes, ears, and mind wide open. You might discover that your son's third-grade teacher's husband is the financial expert that you've been looking for.

Ben: Study the work of leaders within your industry. Learn about what makes them successful. Run these lessons through your vision and culture. Apply what fits. In the quest for knowledge, it's also important to give back to others as you move forward and learn.

Chris: I sought out the industry's best. Ben Stark taught me how to structure deals. He showed me at what level the investment groups start getting interested in a company. SF&P has offered invaluable advice regarding buying and selling companies. Matt Michel educated me on positioning the company to be attractive to investors. The Service Nation Alliance taught me about processes, procedures, financial statements, recurring revenue, and so much more. You'll see many more examples as we move forward in the book.

TAKE MASSIVE ACTION — PURSUE OPERATIONAL EXCELLENCE

Take massive action! Operational excellence begins with a detailed plan of annual growth and development (we call it the *Annual Success Plan*). It follows with care, attention, and detail—Exactly what you'd put into that imaginary 1967 GTO sitting in the garage.

Operational excellence happens through and with your coworkers. It thrives within the environment of a vibrant company culture. Set business goals and, along with your coworkers, set key performance indicator (KPI) goals for their work. Work towards these goals, achieve them, learn, and move forward with others.

"Wax on. Wax off."

This term originates in the movie *The Karate Kid* in which Mr. Miyagi, the karate teacher, teaches Daniel, his student, that the seemingly menial task of waxing a car has important implications in learning the art of karate.

In our industry, a clean and organized service truck leads to a more effective service technician which leads to increased profitability which leads to investment which leads to increased company value and worth. The greatest achievements begin with the simplest things. Wax on. Wax off.

A company is a living, breathing entity.
It is either evolving or dying.
— Angela Blanchard

Ben: We take a leap of faith and a plan starts to form in our mind. We write it down or sketch it out. Positive action is then best supported by attending to a structured timeline.

Chris: Taking massive action is the heart of the Go-Time formula. The pursuit of operational excellence is driven by acting on proven processes and procedures, and developing people. Small steps of taking massive action over time, coupled with success, equals the Big Mo: *Momentum*.

INSPECT — WHAT GETS MEASURED GETS DONE

You have a clear and concise picture of that freshly restored GTO. Your business end game is to sell the company. Although seeking advice is a lifelong endeavor, you now have enough information to create goals and move toward operational excellence.

Just as a hospital patient has their vital signs taken, the business owner must monitor the vital signs of their business. Work takes place and production happens. Are the outcome and results on track to meet the owner's goals and coworker's key performance indicators?

As managers plan on a daily, weekly, monthly, and annual basis, the results of the plan must be inspected. As the old saying goes, "What gets measured gets done."

Ben: A set of key point indicators alerts managers to both excellent performance and to get on top of small problems before they become big problems. A solid grasp on the financials allows clarity when monitoring and staying on top of your company's vital signs.

Chris: Experience is not the best teacher. I can have lots of experience doing something incorrectly. If I don't take the time to inspect and evaluate results I've learned nothing except how to repeat mistakes. *Evaluated* experience is the best teacher!

MODIFY — LOOK FOR A BETTER WAY

To improve we must modify! Running an HVAC, plumbing, and/or electrical business requires continual planning, implementing, and modifying. Daily, weekly, monthly, quarterly, annual—and beyond—planning is based on evaluated experience plus fresh intelligence.

Do you have a place to document and store the thoughts, ideas, aspirations, goals, visions, and dreams that go into your end game? When plans must be changed and modified, as they always do, are your notes accessible?

Planning is not the only thing that requires change and modification. If systems, procedures, and processes remain stagnant, your business remains stagnant. The same applies to high levels of other areas such as marketing and sales.

Keep a journal – A journal is an excellent place to tell a *story* about your KPIs, financial statements, and other measurables. It's a place to record the *why* behind the *what*. Why was March so different from February? Was it a utility rebate, the weather, or effective marketing? This is the why behind fluctuating monthly sales. A simple note in your journal makes future reference clear.

Ben: Always look for a better way. I had to remove people who were doing a good job because they couldn't keep up with the necessary change of a growing company. It's important that change fits your company culture.

Perhaps the greatest modification I had to make was going from a service technician mindset to that of a company owner. Keeping a daily business journal has helped me more than almost anything else. It's my record of what goes on and I often refer to it when I'm looking for answers.

Chris: Constantly look for ways to improve. Don't be afraid of change. Every day, when we leave, we want to leave it a little better than the day before. If done consistently it compounds over time. The net result is significant improvement. Modifying the plan means reflecting on the evaluated experience and tweaking it for improvement.

> *Today I shall behave as if this is the day*
> *I will be remembered.*
>
> — *Dr. Seuss*

ENGAGE — IT'S GO-TIME!

Your end game is in place and documented in your business journal. It's time to engage and execute!

As a business owner, it doesn't matter if you are sixty-five years old or twenty. It's never too late or too early to create your end game.

Ben: Engagement is the most important thing. Nothing happens until you stand on that ledge and take the first step. Jim Rohn, the greatest business leader in my life, once said, "It is the set of the sails, not the direction of the wind that determines which way we go."

Chris: Engage! Take massive action! Don't quit! Focus on why you are doing it and give it everything you have! Keep taking massive action and repeat the Go-Time formula!

Work willingly at whatever you do, as though you were working for
The Lord rather than for people. (Colossians 3:23 NLT)

DO YOU WANT A MONEY MACHINE OR A WEALTH MACHINE?

A money machine is a customer-churn-and-burn driven business. If you spend big dollars on marketing to keep the machine churning, but spend minimal dollars and effort on coworker and customer care, the business will burn. The average life of a money machine is three to seven years, depending upon market size. These companies often change names, completely dissolve, or their customer base is sold for pennies on the dollar due to high liability incurred.

A wealth machine is a customer/coworker-centric business. With the end in mind, these companies build systems, processes, and procedures that support operational excellence. The customer/coworker experience is nurtured to ensure long-term success. The wealth machine is often very profitable after five years and is often a desirable acquisition target for investment groups and competitors.

Chris: When I had the a-ha moment that I describe above, I thought, man, this business is more than just something I'm working in. As Ben says, "it's a living, breathing entity on its own that you can build to gain uncommon wealth." That's especially important when it comes to your end game. I want to invest in this to build a wealth machine!

Describe your end game.

____

____

____

____

____

____

____

____

____

____

Describe what your life would be like if you ran your business with the end game in mind.

Which successful people, who have been there and done it, will you reach out to for wisdom and advice?

Notes

Work willingly at whatever you do, as though you were working for The Lord rather than for people.

— Colossians 3:23 NLT

Chapter 2

"Nice work last chapter putting together your end game."

"What's that fellas?"

Ben and Chris are telling me that some of our readers didn't complete the chapter-ending Go-Time action points. Do you really want to continue without putting some thoughts together on an end game? Do you want to let Ben and Chris down? Remember, the only way to gain all that this book has to offer is to participate.

Ben and Chris achieved and continue to achieve a high level of business success by taking massive action. When they were in front of successful businessmen and women, as we are in front of them today, they listened, learned, and took massive action.

Chris: In the early stages of my business I read Ron Smith's book *HVAC Spells Wealth*. I knew how successful Ron was and I understood his phenomenal influence over the industries. Folks listened to Ron. Why in all of creation would I not follow Ron's guidance and direction? Well, I did. I took massive action on Ron's advice!

YOU HAVE AN IMPORTANT DECISION TO MAKE

We're only at the start of the second chapter and you have already reached an important fork in the road. While there is no such thing as a magic bullet for business success, this is as close as you'll ever come.

Ever wonder why there aren't more successful contractors out there? It's because ninety percent of contractors take the wrong fork.

Successful contractors follow the path of successful contractors. They listen to those ahead of them on the road. And, like Chris did with Ron Smith, they take massive action on their knowledge and wisdom. Even though it's not a magic bullet, the *results* are pure magic.

We're going to ask you to think long and hard about why you might choose not to do the single most important thing a business owner can do: Build an end game.

Don't be a ninety-percenter!

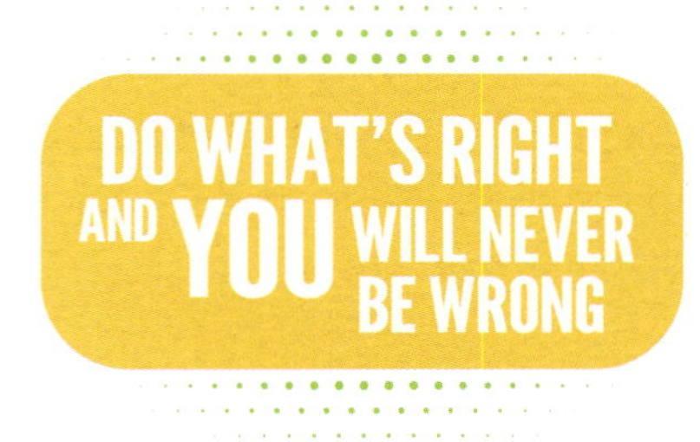

A YOUNG MAN'S LIFE IN THE BALANCE

Is it possible for the balance of a young man's health and life to be affected by the company he works for? If you're Chris "Pope" Popejoy, current operations manager at Hunter Heat and Air in Edmond, Oklahoma, that would be a big yes.

In the summer of 2011, Pope, at the age of twenty, started working at Hunter Heat and Air. A few months later, he started noticing shortness of breath, had chest pain, and was easily fatigued. The doctor told him that the pulmonary valve in his heart was failing. He needed open-heart surgery right away.

After the surgery, while still in the hospital, Pope began to stress. In addition to his health, he was concerned about his job and financial situation. Taking time off so soon after starting with a new company, would he even have a job to return to? What would Chris Hunter think of him?

To begin with, Chris Hunter paid extra to get Pope on the company insurance program early. Then he paid him for every week he was out of work. Chris not only visited Pope in the hospital, he took him to church and to medical appointments. When Pope started back to work, Chris hired Pope's friend to drive the company truck and perform all of the service technician's typical physical duties. Pope eventually recovered and today he holds an important leadership position in the company.

Of Chris Hunter, Pope says, "He taught me that if I always do what is right I will never be wrong."

Reading through this chapter we'll see how the manner in which Chris Hunter treated Pope is absolutely reflected in Hunter Heat and Air's vision, mission, core values, and WHY Chris is in business.

YOUR FRAMEWORK TO GET THERE

With your end game in mind, it's time to build a framework to get there.

> **Vision** – With the end game as your mark on the horizon, the vision is a brief, yet detailed statement designed to develop an internal view of the company's long-term culture and success plan.

> **Mission** – The mission is a statement that describes how the company achieves its vision.

> **Core Values** – The core values are how we carry out the mission. They are guidelines for our behavior and actions.

> **WHY Are You in Business?** – What is your purpose, cause, or belief? It is the source of your inspiration and passion. Why does your company exist? Why do you get out of bed every morning? And why should anyone care?

VISION

The vision is a big-picture view of your desired future. It's what your company is designed to accomplish and it's your blueprint for success.

The leader's job is to infuse hope and anticipation towards a better future by painting and casting the company vision. It's important for the leader to share the vision with their coworkers. Their vision turns into *our* vision.

A vision inspires and manifests a *what could be* spirit in the company, a sense of possibility. It instills meaning in the team's daily work. Without a vision, coworkers punch in, turn wrenches, answer phones, work on the computer, and punch out. *With* a vision they work together to build something in anticipation of an improved future.

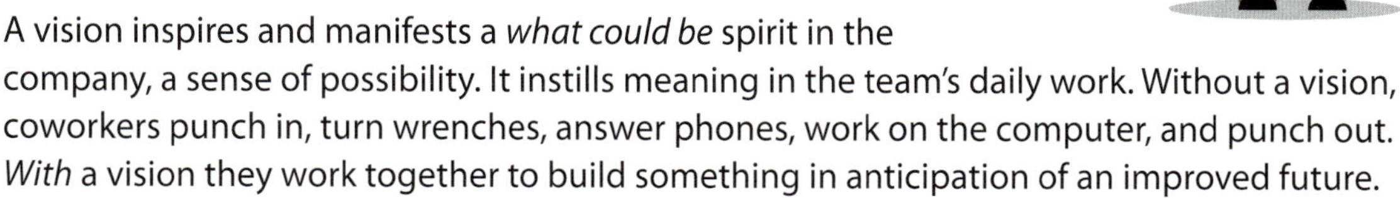

Ben: Vision is the blueprint to your success. I find most unwritten ideas are not acted upon. Putting your vision in writing allows you to set small goals on the way to the fulfillment of an idea. Defining a path from start to finish has always been my way through any successful project.

Chris: I must be intentional about taking time to cast the vision and share it with the team to make it *our* vision. If it's just *my* vision, the success of the business dwindles without me. If it's a shared vision with many people working towards it, success and legacy are attainable!

Sunny Service Vision – Our goal is to provide the ultimate customer experience by striving to exceed each customer's expectations. We will employ and nurture the development of our employees in the best environment while having fun and always maintaining a positive attitude. We are action takers, trainers, innovators, and hard workers. Through these actions we will be both feared and respected by our competition.

Hunter Heat and Air Vision – Get really good, develop leaders, and expand to neighboring areas.

MISSION

The mission is the lens through which the company operates as it works toward its vision. It reflects the WHY and purpose for being in business.

The mission is the reason coworkers show up each day. It reflects purpose and clarifies activities taken and not taken. The mission is also the public's window into the company's world. It should be built to be remembered.

As coworkers work toward the company vision, the mission galvanizes and focuses everyone's effort. It's the organization's North Star in the daily churn of business.

The annual success-planning event is an excellent time to review the mission and ensure it maintains relevance.

Ben: The mission of a company is a general marketing statement designed to promote the face of the company to the public. It's how you want the public to see you. It's the branding statement you follow knowing that it can be changed or adjusted as the company grows and develops.

Chris: Every company meeting starts with our mission, vision, and core value of the month. We give examples of how we live these, and we recognize team members for doing it well. We put our mission on our tee shirts, job trailers, office signs, and even a wrist band with the Bible verse that points back to our mission: *Work willingly at whatever you do, as though you were working for The Lord rather than for people. (Colossians 3:23 NLT)*

Sunny Service Mission – Creating customers for life by enhancing their lives. Cool home, warm heart, sunny service.

Hunter Heat and Air Mission – Keep customers comfortable. Save customers money. Commit to doing it better than anyone else. Honor God with our heart for the work.

CORE VALUES

Core values are foundational. They are the pillars upon which a company is built. Core values reflect how an organization behaves while carrying out its mission on the way to fulfilling its vision.

Core values reflect the collected belief of those within a company and they give direction to decision making. For instance, integrity is one of a company's core values. A coworker is confronted with a decision. Should they cut corners to get the job in quickly, or should they do the right thing? If they believe in the value of integrity, no corners are cut.

When an organization operates without core values, it allows an opportunity for less-than-desirable values to overtake its culture. When coworkers believe in a company's core values, a cohesive and unifying force develops.

Ben: A set of core values gives the company discipline to build a successful business. They drive coworker happiness, professionalism, and fulfillment. And they provide a framework to deliver world-class customer service.

Chris: Core values give the team freedom to operate and serve.

> ## People lose their way when they lose their why.
> ### — Gail Hyatt

<table>
<tr><td>Sunny Service Core Values</td><td>Hunter Heat and Air Core Values</td></tr>
<tr><td>

★ Integrity
★ Empathy
★ Professional
★ Family
★ Fun
★ Giving back

</td><td>

★ Integrity
★ Giving
★ Professionalism
★ Family
★ Communication
★ Efficiency
★ Faith

</td></tr>
</table>

WHY ARE YOU IN BUSINESS?

The WHY of why you are in business is your purpose, cause, and belief. Do you fix and replace HVAC systems? Do you simply pay people to work? Do you just buy products and services from others? Or are you determined to make a difference in the world by enhancing the lives of your customers, coworkers, and business partners?

A well-directed company owner's WHY affects customers, coworkers, and business partners. Customers who believe that you're out to enhance their lives don't simply call you to fix their A/C. They're engaging with you for the experience that your company delivers. Coworkers who believe what you believe don't punch in, jump on the hamster wheel, and punch out. They do much more than that. They bring their true and authentic selves to work because you've given them the opportunity to exercise their beliefs. And time spent with business partners is more than just transactional encounters. It's opportunities to build relationships that will grow towards a win-win synergy for both parties.

Why is your WHY important? No doubt you've heard a version of this parable: A traveler came upon three bricklayers. He asked each one what they were doing. The first said, "I am laying bricks." The second said, "I am building a wall." And the third said, "I am building a cathedral."

All three people were doing the same work, but the first had a job, the second had a career, and the third had a calling.

When your coworkers believe what you believe, they aren't simply fixing and replacing units. They are exercising their beliefs (and yours) toward their calling.

Ben recently sold Sunny Service, his third company. Sunny Service grew in one year what it took six years to achieve in his first company and four years in his second. He cites planning as the biggest difference. And planning based on vision, mission, core values, and your company WHY is a business's greatest force multiplier.

Ben: My quest in business has changed. After working for others for years I thought it looked easy and I could do it better. Of course, I was mistaken. After four years of mistakes, hard challenges, and barely breaking even, I knew I had to find a better way.

I joined a best-practice group and paid more money up front than I had made in business until then. What I discovered changed my life forever.

I learned to:

- ★ Stop working *in* my business and start working *on* it
- ★ Stop doing what my competition was doing
- ★ Start basing my pricing on overhead and profit demands
- ★ Become unique as a contractor in the local market
- ★ Utilize different marketing techniques than competitors
- ★ Offer different products and services than competitors
- ★ Develop best practices
- ★ Train staff on systems and processes and to become independent thinkers

I am in business to help design my own destiny and life and to help others grow.

> ### *What the mind of a man conceives and believes, the mind of man can achieve.*
> #### *— Napoleon Hill*

Chris sold Hunter Heat and Air in late 2018.

Chris: What is your life's purpose? What is your purpose for being in business? Sadly, most people never seek answers to these questions. I believe that knowing your purpose is the most critical thing that you need to address. Know your WHY and make sure everyone on your team knows it too!

In our workplace, the leaders' most important job is to discover his or her purpose in life in addition to our company WHY. That way, at the end of our lives, we can look back and see that it wasn't just a life in the rat race, but one that had an impact on many lives. A life with true significance.

I am in business to achieve my personal mission in life. The business is a tool to help accomplish that. I am in business to create and cultivate. I want to build something great and bring a lot of people with me on the success journey. I am in business to serve others. I am in business to leave a legacy. I am in business to impact the industry that gives so much to my family and my team for the better. We strive to leave it a little better than we found it!

REVIEW THE VISION, MISSION, CORE VALUES, AND BUSINESS WHY

As your business grows and evolves, some of these core components are likely to change. An excellent time to review the vision, mission, core values, and WHY is at the annual success-planning event that prepares the organization for the following year.

Write your vision statement

Write your mission statement

Write your core values

Write WHY you are in business

Notes

Owning and running a business is an all-consuming endeavor. With a vice-like grip on your time, mind, and back, is there anything left for family, friends, spirituality, health, fitness, personal development, social activities, community efforts, and giving back? When was the last time you took a vacation?

When confronted with this conundrum, most business owners think, *I need work-life balance.*

SAY NO TO WORK-LIFE BALANCE

Work-life balance is an unrealistic expectation. Author-businessman Dave Ramsey believes it should be called work-life ebb-and-flow. He says, "life balance isn't about doing everything for an *equal* amount of time. It's about doing the right things at the *right time*."

For Ben and Chris, ebb-and-flow equates to seasons in need.

Ebb and flow didn't exist in the early days of both Ben and Chris's businesses. It was more like all of their time flowed toward the season in need, shortchanging other important areas of their lives.

Ben: As a young man, I had a very difficult time with the balance of life. I didn't have a father figure and my mother was always at work. My education usually came by way of the school of hard knocks. I learned from personal mistakes and the mistakes of others around me. I also took knowledge from what worked well for others. Zig Ziglar, who was one of my mentors in the mid-to-late 90s, taught me about his *Wheel of Life*. It helped me organize and structure my life.

The first seven years in Chris's business were an out-of-balance work-life rat race. An event in 2013, however, changed his life and set his company on a new path.

Chris: I got fed up with my long-time back pain and had surgery. A month or so later I felt pretty good. Ignoring doctor's advice to take it easy, I lifted a beam and the pain came back, worse than before, and it required major surgery. I was going to be out of work for at least three months.

Panic set in! How would my business get by without me? Documenting systems and processes, I prepared like a madman in the weeks leading up to surgery. That surgery was one of the most difficult things I've ever been through. In recovery I was so sore I couldn't even think about the business.

Not skipping a beat, my team rose to the occasion and handled the business. In fact, they set records.

Larry Taylor, my Service Nation Alliance mentor, said, "Chris, your team has been doing great while you've been gone. When you go back to work, don't take back a single task that they've been doing."

Add this to the fact that my doctor said I couldn't lift anything now, and it forced me to build a team and work on the business. It freed me to pursue a better balance in my life, and it gave me the ability to be present with my family.

A LEARNING TRAJECTORY

Ben mentions learning from the school of hard knocks. In his first company, all of his time and attention were focused on the business, leaving practically no time for other areas of his life.

Aware of this, he devoted more time to family in his second company. But the wheel of his life was still not where he needed it to be. Non-work seasons were still suffering.

With Sunny Service, his third company, Ben made significant progress. The important takeaway here is his evolution of learning and the fact that you and I have the opportunity to learn from his over forty years of hard knocks, and the continuous modifications he's made throughout his journey of ownership.

A good part of Chris's wheel-of-life education came from the hard knocks of back pain and his faith.

There is a correlation to the attention both Ben and Chris put toward addressing their seasons of need and the ongoing evolution of building businesses that work.

WHEEL OF LIFE

Building Businesses That Work

This chapter is a microcosm of the entire book. Most business owners who are capable of addressing seasons in need, while not totally neglecting other areas of their lives, have an end game in mind. They have a vision for where they want the company to go, their purpose is woven throughout the fabric of their organization, the business mission is known to all, and their company adheres to a code of values.

They have systems, processes, and procedures in place in all departments, and they use them.

Ben: Building upon the systems and procedures that we developed in the first two companies, I decided to structure Sunny Service with an operations manager along with individual department managers. This allowed me to work on the business, not in it.

We continued to scour the horizon for products and services that allowed us to streamline and become more efficient. Great advancements have been made in today's service-management software. Companies like ServiceTitan, which Sunny Service uses, provide software that combines many functions of processes, record keeping, and systems that had to be done manually just a few years ago.

I teamed up with Chuck Morales, an outstanding instructor, and launched a technical-training school. It's now part of the Go-Time Success Group. Chuck trains all of the Sunny Service Super Techs and provides much-needed quality training for other business owners and companies within our profession.

> *To everything turn, turn, turn*
> *There is a season, turn, turn, turn*
> *And a time to every purpose under heaven.*
> *— The Byrds*

Ben's learning trajectory is a great illustration of how working on the business instead of in it allows owners to build businesses that work. And the further they move along that road, the more it allows them to work on their own Wheel of Life. In turn, this allows these leaders to model and coach coworkers to work on theirs.

Let's check in on the thinking that fuels the spokes on Ben and Chris's wheels of life. Based on this thinking, we'll then touch on coaching coworkers.

THE WHEEL OF LIFE

Ben:　Business and personal sections overlap. They ebb and flow. Whether you're an owner, manager, in the field, or in the office, there will be seasons when your professional plate is full, and times when it isn't. Do not neglect your personal life during the busy periods. Good communication with your loved ones paves the path for a necessary reduction in related activities. The same goes for community members and others with whom you're involved. When the seasons in need slow down, reverse your position. Flow toward your personal needs, allowing your professional needs to ebb.

CORE VALUES AND SPIRITUAL NEEDS

Ben:　The inner peace that comes from your spiritual beliefs allows a high degree of confidence and affects all other areas of the wheel.

Chris:　This is my core. I introduce myself as Chris Hunter, Christ follower, husband, father, grandfather, and business leader. Disharmony sets in when I mix this order up. Keeping my priorities straight is a must!

HEALTH, FITNESS AND ACTIVITY

Ben:　It's important to dedicate time for physical activities and to focus on proper eating habits. Regular medical checkups help to minimize long-term health problems.

Ben: As a young adult, I worked out in the gym a lot. I loved the outdoors and was an avid "river runner," traveling throughout the southern states, kayaking and canoeing. When my children got older we did more things as a family, like fishing, hiking, and camping. Because my job was so physically demanding, I never had to worry much about fitness.

Another thing that Dave Ramsey says is, "Work-life balance isn't about a 50/50 split. It's about being 100% present." Whether with family or at work, I try to be 100% present at all times.

Chris: Although I had some serious health concerns in my early twenties, it took a back injury and major surgery to open my eyes. Running hard will catch up to you. My health and fitness are now a priority!

This pivotal health event forever changed how I worked. As business owners, we are over-stressed and overworked. With little time and so much to do, we typically place health and fitness at the bottom of our list. This is wrong thinking! We need to reprogram our minds. Without good health and fitness, we cannot enjoy the other areas of our lives!

FAMILY AND FRIENDS

Ben: The nurturing of close relationships is critical. It's important to spend quality time together with family and friends. Find special places to go and enjoy activities in which all can participate.

The kids and I would spend time camping at state parks with family and friends. We'd load up for the weekend, take the dogs, and fish, hike, and cook out.

We'd choose parks that were close by. Sometimes, if work would call, I'd have to either leave the kids with friends for a couple of hours or I'd take them to Grandma's house for a couple of hours, run a call, and return to the camp and continue our weekend. Seldom did we have to cancel our plans. We always found ways to spend time doing things together.

Life is what happens to you while you're busy making other plans.

— John Lennon

Chris: To grow in this area we need to be intentional and to be present. It's about loving, not doing. This one above all others has generational impact, more so than money!

WORK AND CAREER

Ben: Early on in our career we think there's plenty of time to develop. We don't realize the cumulative effect of what's learned and developed today and its overall impact in the future. It's funny, but I always had a vision of where I wanted to be even before putting it in writing. When I eventually wrote it down, things began to work.

*Cards that Ben used to carry
in his wallet.*

Chris: As driven entrepreneurs or business owners, it's easy to let our work and career define us. Although it's important to hit this area with everything we have, it's equally important that we not let it solely define us.

For personal effectiveness, one of the most liberating things I've ever done was to work from home one day per week. I found I was getting more accomplished in that one day than if I spent forty hours a week at the office. Another possibility is to work from home early in the morning and come into the office mid-morning. These are great first steps for the contractor who struggles with working on the business.

FINANCIAL WELL-BEING

Ben: Early on, I read *The Richest Man in Babylon,* by George S. Clason, for financial guidance. I still use it today. I learned to pay myself first. This basic practice has allowed me the capital to act upon unique opportunities over the last forty years. You don't have to be an accountant, but you do need to understand accounting concepts and work with a trusted advisor.

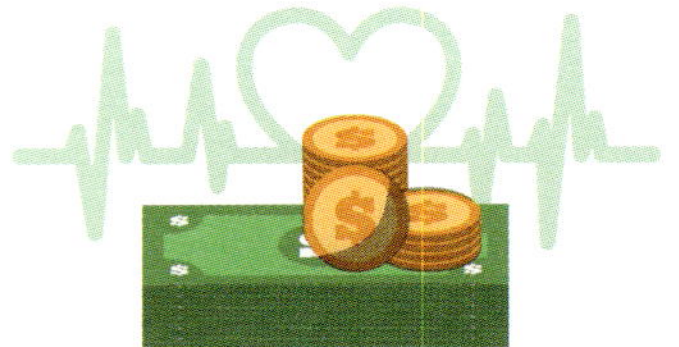

Chris: Money can't buy happiness, but when you don't have it, it's all you can think about. I've been there! My view on money is formed from my faith. I am managing the resources that God has blessed me with. Like any good manager, I want to provide a good return on my investment.

SOCIAL AND COMMUNITY

Ben: This is my most difficult Wheel of Life spoke. I do not make enough time to establish new contacts and do effective work in this area. It's something I'm working on. I recommend involving family and friends in your social and community work. While this economizes your effort, be careful not to cut either area short.

Chris: Leadership is influence. It's hard to gain influence unless you're social. Get out of your comfort zone and meet new people. Ask questions, learn, and give back value.

KNOWLEDGE, INTELLECT, AND EMOTIONAL INTELLIGENCE

Ben: I believe education surrounds us and, most of the time, it's free. To grow I use a journal in both life and business. I journal new ideas, systems, and processes. And I reflect upon past experiences for guidance and to make better decisions moving forward. The key is to take massive action and infuse it with passion!

I use emotional intelligence (EQ) to guide my behaviors and to help me relate to others.

Chris: The accumulation of knowledge helps you to grow in other areas of the wheel. You can't give what you don't have. Taking the time to grow and increase intelligence is what inspired the O for Observe in the Go-Time formula.

Without physical health, there is no wealth.

— Tony Robbins

WHEEL OF LIFE DESIGN: WHO CALLS THE SHOTS?

What or who determines where our focus, time, and effort flow in the Wheel of Life? Here are three sample directions:

Which Way the Wind Blows - With no priority, direction, or focus, we simply follow our or someone else's whims, fancies, and desires.

Stuff Happens - Sickness, disease, death of a relative or friend, divorce, job change, and/or when a loved one needs our attention are just a few things that can draw all of our focus, time, and effort into one spoke and away from others.

Intent - Calculated and planned, our focus, time, and effort are by design. If more time flows toward, say, health and fitness, we are aware of the spokes it draws from.

YOUR PURPOSE

Although stuff happens, in designing a healthy, although ever-changing, Wheel of Life, intention is the tool of choice. Intention is best deployed through the prism of purpose.

Ben's WHY/Purpose - *I am in business to help design my own destiny and life and to help others grow.*

Ben's companies were vehicles providing nourishment and growth for his family, his coworkers, and himself. When confronted with a Wheel-of-Life, spoke-changing decision, he runs it through his purpose filter. Will it provide more control over his destiny? Will it help others to grow?

Chris's WHY/Purpose - *I am in business to create and cultivate. I want to build something great and bring a lot of people with me on the success journey. I am in business to serve others. I am in business to leave a legacy. I am in business to impact the industry that gives so much to my family and my team, for the better.*

The same goes for Chris. When he is in a season in need, does the required activity serve his purpose? For instance, when he was preparing to sell his business, an enormous amount of his energy and time went into the effort. Knowing that the proceeds of the transaction would fuel every area of his purpose, he dove in and gave it everything he had.

Purpose is the North Star by which we navigate the Wheel of Life.

COMMUNICATION

When the flow of focus, time, and effort move in excess to one or more spokes in the wheel, it's important to communicate with others whose lives are affected by the change.

Family - Close family members should know your purpose. Ben and Chris's families are perhaps the greatest beneficiaries of their purpose. When the urgency of work calls, Ben and Chris communicate what's going on and how it ultimately ties in with the big picture. And of course, this also pertains to when the season in need is not work related.

A solid understanding of the Wheel of Life helps to coach family members when navigating their own Wheels of Life.

Coworkers - As an owner/manager in the company, all of your coworkers should know WHY the company is in business. What is its purpose?

Ben: One of our goals for Sunny Service, my third company, was for people to look forward to going to work. There's no way for me to fulfill the part of my purpose to help others, if our coworkers dread coming to work. The key is communication.

Coworkers communicate whether it's verbally or by body language. I've learned a lot about body language by studying emotional intelligence. When I spot a coworker who is down, or maybe just off, I listen, talk, and try to help.

Sometimes these issues involve more than one person. For instance, say there's scuttlebutt going around about a competitor who is trying to lure people away by paying a higher wage. In a case like that, we get back to basics with our communication. In meetings we'll talk about where the company is going and our mission. We try to develop an entrepreneurial mindset with our people by explaining why and how what we're doing is good for them.

> *Not in time, place, or circumstance, but in the man lies success.*
>
> **— Charles B. Rouss**

Looking across the growth trajectory of their careers and businesses, Dave Ramsey's ebb-and-flow description evolves for Ben and Chris. They turn to the season in need. Whether it's launching a new business, working through a scorching-hot summer, or preparing their company to sell, it's necessary and critical that their time, attention, and engagement be focused on that season along with the respect and communication from other areas.

Make use of the lessons that Ben and Chris have learned from experience and create your own Wheel of Life. Once created, continue to refine it and work it.

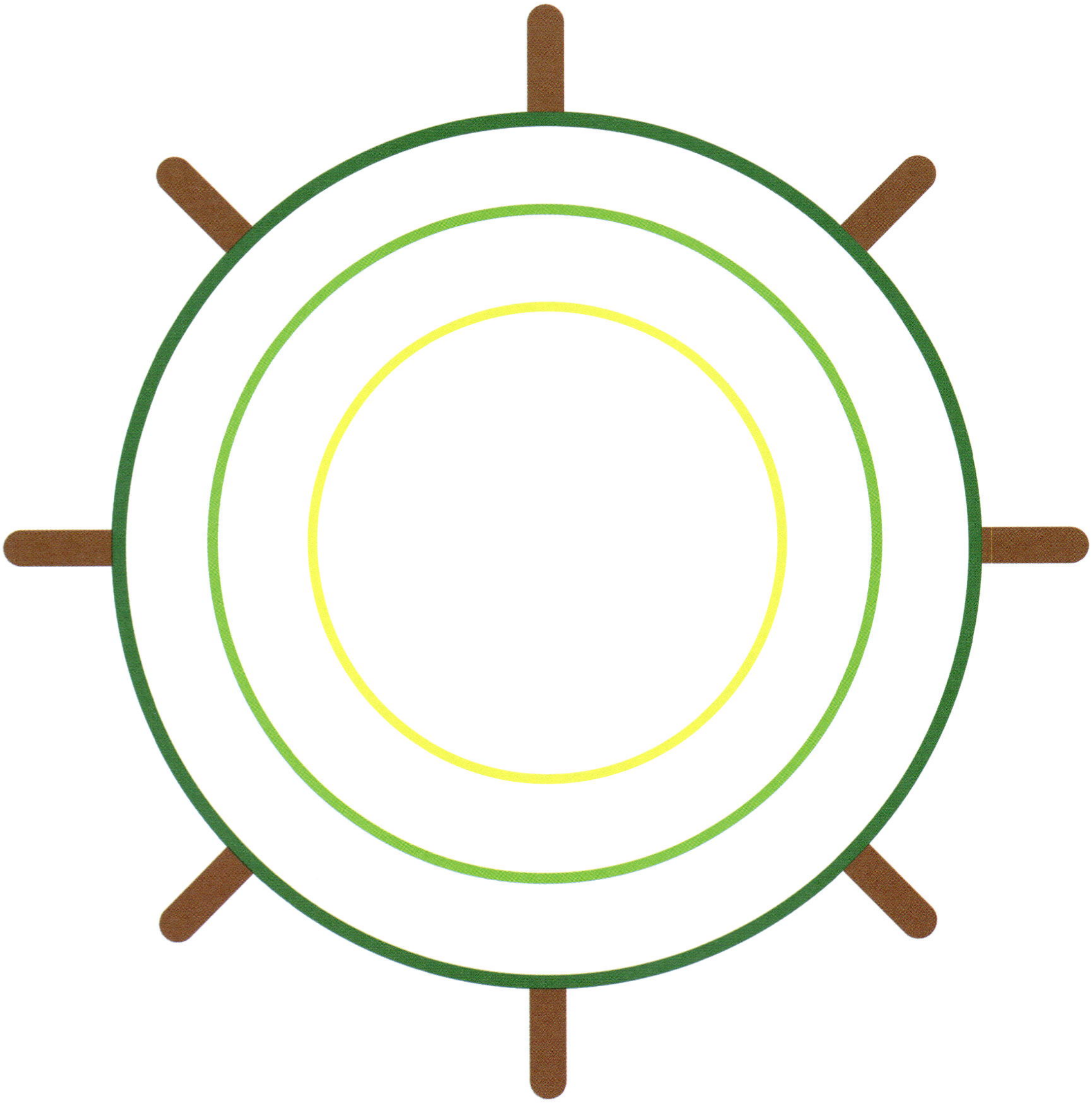

Goals – Create your own Wheel of Life.

Observe – Learn from others who turn to and engage with the season in need. How did they address the other spokes on the wheel at that point?

Take Massive Action – Move forward with what you're learning.

Inspect – Monitor your results. Review daily, weekly, monthly, and annually.

Modify – Your Wheel of Life will only work if you keep working on it. With intent, continue to make adjustments as you learn. This process never stops and that's a good thing.

Engage – Engage with your home and work teams. It's incredibly important to communicate your actions.

> *Lack of direction, not lack of time is the problem, we all have 24-hour days.*
>
> — Zig Ziglar

Build training into your products and services. When calculating pricing, put a percentage in for training, the same as you would for warranty reserve. Once the educational programs are up, running, and working, the percent put into warranty reserve can be reduced, thereby increasing profit.

Budget one half to one percent of total revenue or three to five percent of an individual's compensation package (not salary). Training is not an expense item, it's a production department and it increases profit.

— Ben Stark

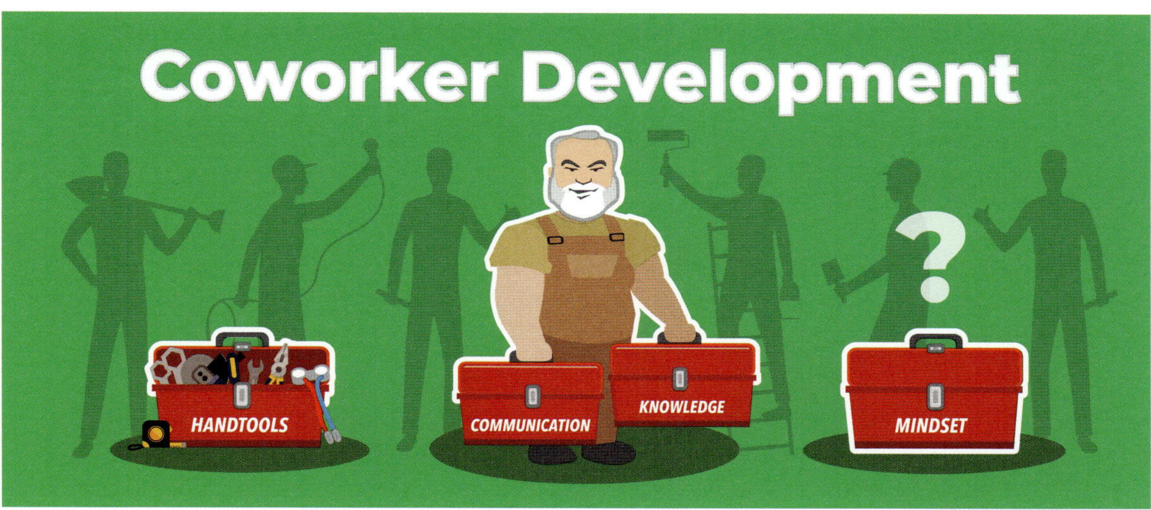

One scorching Texas July day, Freon Zone lost their top technician to an illness. Two weeks later, Bob the service manager and the rest of the team were at the end of their ropes when Pete walked through the door.

Pete was a tall glass of cold-iced tea. With twenty years of experience, he'd surely help get them out of the bind. A few weeks in, however, Bob discovered an all-too-common problem: While Pete did have twenty years on the job, it turned out that he had one year of experience repeated nineteen times.

The skeletons of companies that did not encourage their coworkers to learn, develop, and grow, and did not provide them with continuing education, are littered across the desert ghost towns of contractor ineptitude.

The desire to learn and grow, commonly known as a *growth mindset,* is one of the most important characteristics to look for in prospective hires.

Chris: How can one employee be incredibly average or even subpar at one company, yet do exceptionally well at another? It's the company leadership, culture, systems and, ultimately, its commitment to developing the team that makes the difference.

YOUR MOST IMPORTANT INVESTMENT

As an owner of a contracting company, the most important investment you'll ever make is *not* your building, not your trucks, and not your service-management software. The most important investment you'll ever make is in building your team and in developing its individual members.

Leadership and company culture, which we explore in other chapters, factor into team building. In this chapter we focus on the development of individuals.

WHO IS RESPONSIBLE?

No matter how you slice it, the company owner is responsible. As companies grow, individual department managers take over. At large companies, department managers often work hand-in-hand with a director of education.

Leadership should help coworkers find mentors. These are folks who have been there and done it. They are willing to share their knowledge and wisdom, and have demonstrated the ability to care for and about others. While it's desirable that the mentor work at your company, it doesn't always work out. Good mentors can often be found elsewhere.

IT'S AN INVESTMENT

Ben: Build training into your products and services. When calculating pricing, put a percentage in for training, the same as you would for warranty reserve. Once the educational programs are up, running, and working, the percent put into warranty reserve can be reduced, thereby increasing profit.

Budget one half to one percent of total revenue, or three to five percent of an individual's compensation package (not salary). Training is not an expense item, it's a production department and it increases profit.

TOOL BOXES

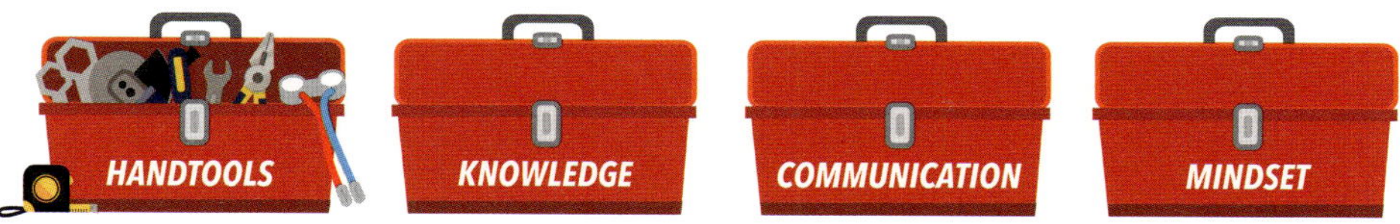

Ben: When it comes to technicians and installers, it's important to keep learning both simple and top-of-mind. I use a Tool Box analogy: Focus on filling these tool boxes with knowledge, behaviors, and tools sought by the very best of companies, and you'll be sought after and, more than likely, never have to worry about a high-paying job again. Use these same tools to create opportunity and wealth for your family and yourself.

The Hand Tools Tool Box - Develop a list of the hand tools, meters, and other gear that will assist everyone in every position in your company to complete their tasks in a timely manner.

   ★ Field Technicians, Maintenance, Service, Production
   ★ Customer Service, Opportunity Managers
   ★ Comfort Advisors
   ★ Accounting
   ★ Warehouse
   ★ Marketing

The Knowledge Tool Box - The training required for each person in your company to raise and fulfill the vision you have set for them.

   ★ Establish a training calendar
   ★ Knowledge of preparation and anticipation
   ★ Understand the "Problem Solving Process"
   ★ Knowledge of troubleshooting
   ★ Find answers using relationships
   ★ Learn how to complete tasks more rapidly

Train people well enough so they can leave, treat them well enough so they don't want to.

— Richard Branson

The Communications Toolbox - Learn to be comfortable when speaking with customers and other business associates to find answers to problems and concerns.

- ★ Discover your field of expertise
- ★ Build confidence through experience, study, and relationships
- ★ Ask open-ended questions
- ★ Listen. Take meticulous notes. Repeat answers
- ★ Be able to communicate the "Problem Solving Process"
- ★ It's not what you know, it's your ability to find and solve problems. Your ability to understand
- ★ Practice. Role-play. Repeat

The Mindset Toolbox - Prepare mentally. Think ahead. Positive mental preparation is critical to problem solving and customer satisfaction.

- ★ Passion to satisfy the customer
- ★ Completion of task as a craftsperson or communicator
- ★ Understand that troubleshooting is a process of sequential steps on the way to success
- ★ Be a mentor and lifelong student of the trade

STRIVE FOR THE COMPANY MISSION

A cared-for and educated workforce is critical to a successful company mission. Let's take another quick look at Ben and Chris's previous company missions:

Ben - Sunny Service mission – Creating customers for life by enhancing their lives. Cool home, Warm heart, Sunny service.

Chris - Hunter Heat and Air – Keep customers comfortable. Save customers money. Do it better than anyone else. Honor God with our heart for the work.

A company does not enhance their customer's lives or make a commitment to do it better than anyone else with employees who have one year of education and twenty years of experience.

A company's mission cannot be achieved with a workforce that doesn't develop and grow.

TRAINING FACILITIES

A serious commitment to education and development deserves a serious training facility. Build a lab that can accommodate product, technical, and safety education. Build a classroom to handle leadership, life-skills, sales, customer-service, front-office, soft-skills, and systems-and-process training.

Lab – Involve coworkers to build out the lab with system trainers and simulators. Use old equipment or equipment donated by business partners.

Classroom – Equip with easel pads and stands, white boards, or a white-board wall. Include large monitors and computers. Keep video equipment on hand to tape tech, CSR, and sales role-play. Invest in a green screen.

Library – Dig the VHS tapes, cassettes, DVDs, and CDs out of the closet, gather your books and operational manuals, and create a library. Develop a checkout system to track educational material.

SET DEVELOPMENTAL GOALS

We discuss technician-career pathways in the *Recruit, Hire, and Retain* chapter. Career paths are first brought up and discussed throughout the recruiting and hiring process. Then, as part of onboarding, developmental goals are established. Goal implementation, feedback, and coaching are the backbone of a good developmental program.

Chris: Coworkers fill out goal worksheets. Goals are set in the following areas:

★ Personal goals
★ Mind, body, and spirit

An investment in knowledge pays the best interest.
— Benjamin Franklin

★ Personal finances
★ Work (what I want to accomplish)
★ Places I would love to go
★ Three things I want to learn or that I enjoy learning about
★ Three things I want to do
★ Three things I would love to have

Once I have these I can assist other leaders to help their teams move forward and connect the dots between the coworker and the company. That's when the magic happens! That's what the team remembers. That's what pushes them on when it's hot and they're tired. It all goes back to connecting their WHY to their work.

Let's face it, a lot of people don't know how to grow. They need help. The goal-setting exercise and follow-up pushes them to take massive action. A goal sheet that isn't reflected upon and used is useless.

If I see someone who wants to be a better husband and dad, I am intentional about who I team him up with. I prefer to put him with a strong married man and father who is a great mentor instead of with a good tech who is single. This hasn't always been the case. I missed it before and I witnessed the negative consequences.

EDUCATIONAL CALENDAR

Ben also meets with coworkers to ask about and discuss upcoming educational needs. When classes are designed, and outside instructors are brought in, to address coworkers' expressed needs, it builds their confidence and shows them that management takes their concerns seriously. When classes are held out of town, add in a break and a little bit of fun and you'll create a training event that will enhance the effectiveness of your entire team while also building their morale and camaraderie.

Classes with Chuck Morales, Director of the Go-Time University and outside trainers are scheduled on an educational calendar. The following areas are covered:

- ★ Technical knowledge
- ★ Safety
- ★ Sales
- ★ Customer service
- ★ Communication skills
- ★ Life skills
- ★ Management
- ★ Leadership
- ★ Company processes, procedures, and systems

USE OUTSIDE EDUCATORS

When it comes to educating the HVAC, plumbing, and electrical workforce, whether it's office staff, management, field personnel, or CEOs, our first choice of course, is the Go Time University! **www.gotimesuccessgroup.com/**

Manufacturers – Use co-op dollars to fund education. Most manufacturers do a good job with training, especially on the latest technologies embedded in their products. Take advantage of interactive video and do remote training with your favorite manufacturer.

Use Other Business Relations – This type of training is low or even no-cost. It's a great way to stay on top of new products. Educating technicians on features and benefits is key to producing higher average service tickets. Local parts and supply houses are always offering training.

It's important to ensure outside training is of high quality and in sync with products and services offered by your company. When coworkers are awake, engaged, and learning, they're not asleep and burning your investment.

Trade Associations – Groups like the Air Conditioning Contractors of America (ACCA) and the Plumbing-Heating-Cooling Contractors Association (PHCC) are excellent choices.

> *It's only as we develop others that we permanently succeed.*
>
> *— Harvey Firestone*

Contractor Alliances – Ben and Chris are members of the Service Nation Alliance. They attribute a great deal of their success to the SNA and rate contractor alliances as the best source of leadership, management, operations, financial, sales, and marketing education! When owning their own companies, Ben and Chris would take team members to the two national Service Nation Alliance days each year along with Service World. It's a great opportunity to network and to learn from colleagues and peers.

> **Ben**: I've belonged to three contractor alliances over the years. When vendor rebates are factored in, membership comes at no cost.

> **Chris:** We can learn a lot from our peers. Several members of the Service Nation Alliance have sent team members to each other's shops to learn. The feedback is that it's been one of the best training experiences they've ever had.

MEETINGS

Never have a meeting unless you can have the meeting before the meeting. Chris learned this principle from John C. Maxwell's leadership training. It's proven highly effective in running meetings and rallying support for change.

Chris led the following types of meetings with the Super Techs on a regular basis:

Quick Team Meeting – Check in first thing in the morning and discuss the plan for the day, plus any issues from the previous day.

Sunday Leader Check-in – Because Mondays are so hectic, the leadership team checks in on Sundays. This might be a quick text or a phone call, just enough to look ahead and get everyone on the same page.

Leaders Meeting – A weekly meeting to discuss key issues, KPIs, financials, and planning. This twenty-to-forty-five-minute meeting is also used to educate the leaders on leading their respective teams.

Service Meeting – Technicians are involved in choosing training topics. Topics are assigned for them to study and teach their peers.

Company-wide Meeting – Held on the first working day of each month, this meeting is a celebration and the company's most important meeting. Praise and recognition are doled out in each key performance area by department leaders. The company vision, mission, and core values are reviewed. This time is also used for a fun team game or activity to reinforce a point.

IRON MEN EVENT

Following a few years in business, Chris became aware of the fact that problems at home become problems at work. He also discovered an aching educational need in the Super Techs: Life-skills training.

So Chris organized a Bible study group. In the beginning it was only him and a couple of others. When he decided to offer free pizza others joined in. Soon, one hundred percent of his Super Techs were onboard. In addition, he began to offer life-skills training on topics like how to be a better husband, fatherhood, personal finances, divorce, etc. The training evolved into life-skills training based on Biblical principles.

Word of the group got out. Others wanted to attend. So Chris opened his doors. Problem was, so many local tradespeople wanted to attend that he had to move it to the local fellowship hall. Based on Proverbs 27:17 (*As iron sharpens iron, so does one friend sharpen another*), Chris named the event the *Iron Men Group*.

Side note: One of the outside contractors that attended eventually sold his business to Chris.

As Chris's company began to open branches farther away from the home base, it became more difficult to get people in. The Iron Men event eventually ran its course and the company no longer conducts sessions. But the education it provided, the fellowships it developed, and the people whose lives it changed helped to make the Super Tech culture what it is today.

Chris: If you know what you are, what you stand for, and what your mission is, and you have fun doing it, you attract people to become part of the team.

Service Manager – "Training is expensive and hard to schedule. It seems like whenever we get someone trained up, they leave. Why put all that effort into training and then they leave?"

Owner – "What if we don't train them and they stay?"

Goal – Work with coworkers to set educational goals in technical, communication, customer-service, leadership, and life-skills.

Observe – Find and observe companies that have a great learning culture. Search for educational organizations that care for their members and clients. Spend time with individuals on your team and help them to discover their WHY.

Take Massive Action – Help team members connect their WHY to the team's. Assemble a comprehensive educational program based on needs. Help coworkers develop a personal-growth plan that focuses on all aspects of their lives.

Inspect – Regularly and systematically check in on the results. Offer encouragement and inspiration.

Modify – Work to improve the overall educational. Help individuals change their developmental plans based on inspection results.

Engage – Continue to repeat and work the plan. If you're not growing, you're dying. Always strive to develop your team and yourself.

Notes

Why do people stay at companies? Among other reasons, it's because they feel wanted, appreciated, recognized, and respected. This isn't mushy feel-good stuff. This is you staying in business and producing profitable revenue. This is what you do to thrive in today's economy. More importantly, this is what you do because it's the right thing to do!

— David E. Rothacker

Do you wonder why every fellow contractor you talk to has difficulty finding skilled help? Do you find yourself constantly turning away good, qualified applicants because you're overstaffed? Do you find a challenge in *continually* trying to come up with creative gifts for coworkers' twenty-five-year work anniversaries?

Of course you don't. It's a dog-eat-dog world out there and you're in the trenches just like everyone else. Finding, hiring, and keeping coworkers is one of the greatest challenges our industries face. Finding, hiring, and keeping the *right* coworkers is even harder.

While Ben and Chris have faced times when there weren't even any dogs to eat, they persevered in developing recruiting programs, built and rebuilt hiring processes, and fortified desirable cultures where their people can thrive.

Perhaps one of their greatest discoveries is bringing people on board who believe in their vision, purpose, and values. When coworkers get to punch the clock and remain themselves, when they get to exercise their deep held beliefs every day, and when they do it in a culture that supports and cares for them and others who share their ideals, you will *have* to start worrying about those gifts for twenty-five-year work anniversaries. And you know the best part? Coworkers in this position make your best recruiters.

    Chris: If you attract what you are, the team must be showcased because that is who you are!

So, based on company culture and who you are, you need to recruit and hire individuals who fit in with your team. These are the coworkers who not only have your back, they're gently nudging you forward. These are the coworkers who stay on and want to contribute.

RECRUITING

Other than developing leaders, recruiting and instilling a recruiting mindset is the most important job an owner has.

Ben: Recruiting is a continual effort to find coworkers who fit with your company culture or can adapt to it.

Chris: My recruiting philosophy is to go on offense. Start young and think like a college football coach. Appeal to what's most important to my target audience. They want a better boss, a brighter future, and a bigger vision. Most are looking for meaning and purpose in their work.

Customers look for companies with a large number of online five-star reviews. Guess who else does? Potential job applicants. They want to work for smart companies that employ coworkers who produce five-star ratings.

When Recruiting, Ben Looks for the Following Traits:

Frontline support, technicians, and installers need to be able to:

★ Be outgoing
★ Follow a script either on the phone or in front of customers
★ Adjust to the customers' personalities
★ Create solutions to customers' problems
★ Be system and process oriented
★ Adapt best practices
★ Grow their skills

Chris: We look for a great attitude, strong work ethic, and a desire to succeed. Hire for attitude, train for technical aptitude!

Like the Boy Scouts

Ben: I struggled for years to find the right people. One day I decided to look for an example of a successful organization that is outstanding at recruiting. When I was young, I had a positive experience with the Boy Scouts. Why did boys want to join?

After serious thought I had the answer: It was *merit badges*. Set a goal for a badge, work to achieve that badge, and take another step up the ladder to the next scout level. There was a crystal-clear line of progression and advancement to become an Eagle Scout.

Based on Boy Scout merit badges, Ben created the following program to inform recruits and provide internal structure and clarity for the road ahead:

Career Path to Success Program. (Name the levels here to fit your own company culture)

★ **One Star – The Recruit – Base Earning Scale**
Onboard and then set six-month to one-year goals
Establish set amount of training hours
Gain knowledge while working as a helper
Build a personal tool chest*
Cross train with other helpers and warehouse personnel
Assist in recruiting person to step into their role
Receive a bonus to mentor this recruit

★ ★ **Two Star – Maintenance Service Tech – Production Pay Plus Mentor Bonus**
Perform precision tune ups on recent equipment installs
Establish set amount of technical, customer service, and communication training
Increase personal tool chest
Cross train with experienced maintenance service techs
Learn minor service repairs in offseason
Mentor coworkers

★ ★ ★ **Three Star – Junior Service Tech – Production Pay Plus Equipment Spiffs**
Learn to diagnose and repair equipment
Assume on-call duties
Attend to higher levels of technical, customer service, and
 communication training
Continue to build personal tool chest
Cross train with dispatch, CSR's, and senior techs
Start to work as senior tech in offseason for a set amount of hours

> *When people are financially invested, they want a return. When people are emotionally invested, they want to contribute.*
>
> **— Simon Sinek**

★ ★ ★ ★ **Four Star – Senior Tech –Team Leadership Status - Bonus When Team Meets Goals**
Is proficient in all aspects of the residential-service business
Establish set amount of home performance, airside, and light-commercial training
Personal tool chest includes home-performance, and airside test equipment

★ ★ ★ ★ ★ **Five Star – Master Tech – Trainer and Home Sales Compensation**
Establish and begin management-training program
Establish and begin sales-training program
Prep for department or company-wide bonus programs

*A personal tool chest is one part valued collection of tools, meters, and test equipment; one part acquired knowledge, relationships, and wisdom; and one part confidence-building, relating to, and communicating with others; and it's one part mindset—positive mental preparation critical to problem solving and customer satisfaction.

Ben: We put the Career Path to Success on poster boards and place it in training areas. We continually discuss it in coaching and review sessions.

Access to company mentors is critical to a coworker's career-path success. To keep a vibrant mentor program, reward the mentor with a slice of the green tech's success. It may be as simple as one half to one percent of what the mentee makes on a production basis.

THE ASSIST

Legendary professional hockey player Wayne Gretzky famously said, "Skate to where the puck is going, not where it has been."

The overwhelming number of skilled-trade business owners skate to where the puck has been. Think that's an exaggeration? How many companies do you know that have a written career path for service technicians and installers? How many:

★ Brand recruiting and mentoring into their culture?
★ Require recent hires to assist in the recruiting process?
★ Build mentoring into their processes?
★ Offer a mentoring bonus?

Ben's service tech career path is a bullet list of actions that fit on one piece of paper. It isn't a list that he simply sat down one afternoon and cranked out. It took over forty years to build it. That's forty years of experimenting, doing, experimenting, learning, modifying, and doing again. That's forty years of tribulations, perseverance, and delight. That's forty years of knowing where to hit that hockey puck.

The question is, will you skate to where the puck is going? Or will you skate to where it's been?

WHERE DO YOU RECRUIT?

Company Website

The company website is one of the most powerful recruiting tools available. It's also one of the first places prospective coworkers or recruits go when they hear about your company. Create a career page to address all of their concerns and provide easy access to it. Don't make visitors jump through hoops trying to find it. Place a career link on the top of your home page.

Prospects and recruits need to know why they should work for you. The best-case scenario is that they agree with your vision, purpose, and values. This means they believe what you believe. And when they get the opportunity to exercise their beliefs, ultimately helping others, you'll have a committed and dedicated coworker. This is one reason the company owner should shoot a video explaining their vision, purpose, and values and insert it on the career page.

Not all companies have their vision, purpose, and values figured out. Most serious company owners, however, understand that the key to profitable business is through well-supported and cared-for coworkers. While it's necessary to list company benefits, perks, and amenities on your website, the more important part is to speak to your prospect's inner needs and desires. Like Chris says, "They want a better boss, a brighter future, and a bigger vision. Most are looking for meaning and purpose in their work."

Include a video on the career page of present coworkers talking about why they love working at your company. https://youtu.be/7y-Dqg5s2w0

Make it Mobile

To begin with, your entire website needs to be optimized for cell phones and other smart mobile devices. This is an absolute must.

Most forward-thinking companies have a job application on their career page, and most people use their cell phones more than their personal computers. Consequently, most people are not going to complete that job application on their cell phone.

The key is to have a mobile-friendly form that captures a small amount of information. If the applicant is intriguing, you can have them fill out the entire application later on in the recruiting process.

Social Media

As an owner, Chris and his team used social media like a valued and trusted Sawzall.
One day, Chris was reading Joseph Hobson's Facebook page. Chris noticed that Joseph, a local HVAC technician, was going through a family-related challenge. He also noticed Joseph's smile and overall positive attitude in addition to his work ethic. Joseph worked early mornings unloading trucks for UPS as well as being a tech.

Chris messaged Joseph with encouragement and offered prayers.

A couple of months later, when Chris was in dire need of a technician, he reached out to Joseph's wife, Lacey, on Facebook. Explaining that he was an HVAC contractor, he asked if they were looking for anything more in life. It just so happened that Joseph's hours had been cut and they were indeed looking for more.

Today, Joseph is the GM of Hunter Heat and Air's Ada location overseeing a staff of ten coworkers.

Chris and Joseph both tell this story, which also represents *faith*, one of the company's core values, on video. https://youtu.be/pPBwQszQhlA

By reaching out to Joe, Chris shows us how to proactively use social media. Another way to showcase your company's culture on social media is to include pictures and videos from training, holiday parties, cookouts, get-togethers, and fun activities.

Whether you're in the office or out on a job, use live Facebook video. Capture what it's like to work at your company. Ask questions, interact with people, and make it fun.

LinkedIn - All business owners should have a LinkedIn account. A common response when you tell someone this is, "Why should I have one; I'm not looking for a job."

And while that's true, prospective coworkers *are* looking for jobs. What better way to show off what you and your company are all about? Demonstrate your WHY, vision, mission, and core values. Write articles about them. Relate them to the company culture. You're looking for people who believe what you believe. Appeal to them via your articles!

AREA SCHOOLS

Consider giving career day talks at your local public schools. Not only will you educate students, you'll educate teachers as well (Some might even be prospective customers or coworkers).

Chris: I visit trade schools, high schools, and even grade schools to talk about our profession. When people serve our company well, I notice! Two of our comfort consultants served our company as former salespeople. Now they sell for us.

CULTURE BOOK

Chris: The Service Nation Alliance helped us to build a company Culture Book. It's a smart and beautifully designed communication piece that contains:

- ★ Company vision, mission, and core values
- ★ Amenities and benefits
- ★ Vacation and holidays
- ★ Awards gained

In addition, it showcases our focus on company communication, individual health and wellbeing, personal development, fun, and giving back. It demonstrates the commitment we make to our people. We pass the Culture Book out to prospective coworkers to show them what we're all about.

We continually train our leaders on what to look for in potential team members and the recruiting process.

Ben: Where will your new coworkers come from in five years? Get into the schools and talk about your trade. Perhaps some companies and industries in your area are rapidly declining. Find ways to touch and educate individuals looking for more. We refer to it as forward-thinking.

PEOPLE ARE LOOKING FOR MORE

Ben and Chris are on the lookout for people in their communities who provide superior customer service. Most supermarkets, restaurants, and retail stores offer limited career opportunities. The HVAC, plumbing, and electrical professions are in a position to offer much more. And people are looking for more. As Chris said, "they want a better boss, a brighter future, and a bigger vision." People want meaning and purpose in their work.

Be a better boss. Do you think managers in retail operations really care about their coworker's lives? As an owner or manager in our industries, you have a golden opportunity to make a real difference. Soak in and drink up Joseph Hobson's story. Offer people more.

COMPANY HEADQUARTERS

Your office, shop, warehouse, and satellite branches are open books. They tell a story about you, your team, and your company to anyone who walks in.

What does a prospective coworker think when they walk into a disorganized and messy office? To be real, probably not much. Why? Because it's what they've seen in most offices and shops. It's what they know.

Now, imagine when that prospective coworker walks into a clean, organized, and well-run office. A friendly receptionist greets them with a warm and inviting tone. A facility tour reveals:

- ★ Dedicated training and educational areas
- ★ Organized dispatch, CSR, and sales areas
- ★ Organized parts and job-staging areas in the warehouse
- ★ Organized tool and equipment bullpen
- ★ All coworker's pictures and vision boards on one wall
- ★ A clean lunchroom with a full kitchen
- ★ Dedicated truck-washing area

Your organization is going to stick out like a lemonade stand in the desert. The type of facility we describe here tells prospective coworkers how much you care about your people. It tells the sharp ones how much you care about your customers. Who *wouldn't* want to work there?

JOB FAIR

Hold a job fair at your office or shop. Not only is this a great chance to show off your facilities, it's a super-great chance to show off your coworkers. Bring in folks from all departments to inform, educate, and answer your guest's questions.

Have your top installers and service techs there showing off their vehicles and talking with guests.

Hold twenty-minute mini training sessions to provide a taste of your educational programs and training.

Make it a fun event by holding a raffle and giving away tools and meters. And, as is the case with any premium company event, bring in good food.

Create an atmosphere for your guests that simulates what it might be like to work on your team, and be sure to collect contact data and email addresses so that you can keep in touch with prospects.

In preparing for a job fair later in the day, Chris and his team shot a guided video tour of his facilities. It was a great way to entice interested parties to attend.

OFFER A CAREER

In addition to the Career Path to Success program Ben talks about above, smart companies have structured programs to take an inexperienced person off the street and start them off on a brand-new career.

Commonly referred to in the industry as *fast track programs*, this type of education provides the new coworker with the basic fundamentals to get the job done.

> *Treat a man as he is and he will remain as is. Treat a man as he can and should be and he will become as he can and should be.*
>
> — *Johann Wolfgang von Goethe*

For example, a new maintenance tech is trained to interact with the customer and how to perform a basic tune-up on a furnace and condenser.

Other positions like Comfort Advisor and CSR, are often fast-tracked as well.

THE BOTTOM LINE

People want to be on winning teams. They want to work for and with winners. Strive to be that company everyone talks about and wants to work for. Follow Ben and Chris's lead, foster a culture of development, growth, and improvement, and do right by your people. Prospective coworkers will find you.

HIRING

A Google search on *the cost of a bad hire* reveals some interesting insight. The overarching theme of the first thirty search results is *surprise*. People are surprised by the extreme cost and detriment of hiring the wrong person. Most of the articles address "true meaning" and "true and hidden costs."

Financially, bad-hire cost estimates range anywhere from fifteen to thirty percent of a person's annual pay. While this is staggering, it might not even be the worst part. The non-financial costs of extra stress and decreased morale on existing coworkers, in addition to lower productivity, will absolutely gut a company.

WHAT ARE YOU LOOKING FOR?

What qualities, traits, and characteristics are you looking for in new coworkers?

Character - Does your applicant have the right character to fit in with your company culture? While the interviewer begins to get a feel for the person's character in the first interview, a great place to start, and perhaps avoid an undesirable prospect, is social media.

In recruiting, Chris looks for a great attitude, strong work ethic, and the desire to succeed. Traits like these, and others that are not so desirable, tend to surface in the applicant's social media accounts. Be sure to check them out.

Growth Mindset - You want coworkers who are passionate about developing and growing as individuals. What have they done in the past to advance their careers?

Team Oriented - Does the person work well with others? Are they supportive? What have they done in the past to help fellow coworkers?

A Desire to Serve - Most techs like to fix things. The key is to find the ones who relish the fact that they can improve a customer's situation, or even life, by engaging their talent and skills.

DON'T PASS ON THEM

Ben: If an excellent job applicant crosses our path, we hire them. It doesn't matter if we don't have an open position. We hire, then we increase our marketing and/or budget as needed. With the industry labor challenges, our job is to manage the situation and act in the best interest of our companies. Oftentimes that involves upgrading a position or moving a less-qualified person to a different role.

The One Thing

There is one thing that successful business owners do to overcome bad hires that others do not. Establish and use a hiring process. In other words, do not use shortcuts. And whatever you do, don't wing it!

HIRING PROCESS

Website Application Form - The online application makes it easy for job applicants to apply. Provide a means for uploading applicants' resumes as well.

Analyze Resumes From Various Online Job Sites - Scan resumes for desirable applicants.

Perform Social Media and Online Candidate Research - If you're considering a prospect, check out their social media presence. You'll most likely discover if they might or might not fit in with your culture.

State Background Checks and Drug Testing - In addition to conducting criminal and driving background checks and drug testing, make sure you state this practice in recruiting and public media messages. One, it weeds out undesirable candidates, and two, it informs customers and potential customers that your coworkers are top-quality people.

Phone Interview - Conduct a phone interview and determine whether or not you want to bring the applicant in for an onsite interview.

Onsite Interview - Invite the candidate into the office for an interview. Remember, you are selling your organization as much as the applicant is selling their potential. Give them the full tour, showing off your facilities.

> **Chris:** The owner or other significant leader should conduct the interview. It's critical to get the right people on the bus. We involve the team leader in the process and, if the situation is right, we involve other team members as well. Every time a new coworker is added it changes the team chemistry. We must be careful and deliberate to make sure it changes for the better.
>
> We use a structured and calculated interview process that relies on open-ended and clarifying questions.
>
> We also attempt to involve the spouse in the interview process. If we can win the spouse's approval on a desired candidate, it's a done deal!
>
> As with recruiting, we continuously train our leaders on the hiring process and technique.

Technical Test - Whether it's a service technician or installer, test for technical aptitude. Design a basic mechanical aptitude test for those who may be put through a fast-track type of program.

While it's important to check an applicant's technical aptitude, there is one critical factor not to overlook. Some very good technicians are not good test takers. If the other criteria line up and the applicant bombs the test, take a good hard look before you eliminate them from consideration.

Personality Assessment Test - Understand the candidate's personality and behavioral tendencies by administering a personality assessment test. *DISC Profile* is an example. It checks for how people respond to challenges, how they influence others, and how they respond to rules and procedures.

Second Interview With Other Company Leaders - Have the would-be candidate's manager or other leaders in your company interview the candidate. This helps to make sure positive and/or negative tendencies are not missed in the initial interview.

Include Significant Other - When hiring a married candidate, it's good to take the couple, along with the department manager and their spouse, and *your* spouse, out for an informal dinner or spousal interview. Do this after the second interview.

Although it seems as if you're hiring one person, with married couples you're usually hiring two, albeit unofficially.

> ★ Will there be support at home?
> ★ Will there be a problem at home? (Author Dave Ramsey says, ". . . the spousal interview might help you discover if the person is married to crazy, if they are, stay away.")
> ★ Does the spouse share similar values?
> ★ Talk about your vision, your WHY, and company values
> ★ Demonstrate your belief in taking care of coworkers
> ★ Gain the spouse's confidence
> ★ Gain *your* spouse's opinion

ONBOARDING

Onboarding is the process that a company uses to bring a new hire on board. Paperwork is completed and a thorough indoctrination to the company is performed. It happens during the new team member's first week.

Chris: Onboarding takes place in our main office and never on a Monday morning. We have a team member who champions the established process.

The key to getting off on the right foot is to make clear what is expected of the new team member. We show a video that explains where the company has been and where it's going. We paint a picture of the future for them to see how they will fit in and flourish.

We provide crystal-clear expectations for every position. If a team member wants to move on and become a leader, the cost and higher standard that must be achieved are in plain sight.

Each new team member is assigned a mentor.

Chris: Give new hires a ninety-day probationary period. Inform them that your company is on probation with them as well. There are few obligations from both sides during the trial period.

It doesn't work out, dig in and really understand why. You and your team, along with the candidate, have put in significant time and effort to this point. But if it doesn't work out, part ways.

Make it Special

Chris's team sends flowers to the new team member's wife welcoming them to Hunter Heat and Air. This makes a fantastic and positive impact on the new hire's spouse.

RETENTION

The costs of recruiting and hiring coworkers are astronomical. Combine that with lost production, training, administrative and other costs which aren't easily seen, and the smart business owner understands the value of retention.

Why Do People Stay?

Buy Into the Vision, Purpose, and Company Values - Coworkers have confidence in the leader. And they have confidence in the leader's vision. That vision represents something positive for them personally.

It's a common theme in our book: Coworkers who buy into the owner's WHY feel that it's their purpose, too. And when people get to exercise their purpose and values every day, it no longer feels like work. They're not working for a wage, they're working to fulfill their own heart's desires.

Coworkers Want to be a Part of Something Larger Than Themselves - Whether it's helping others and giving back to the community, being a part of an innovative team on the leading edge of their field, or being an integral part of a nationally renowned company, people crave to be involved with efforts bigger than themselves.

Coworkers Are Challenged, Using Their Skills and Talents, Developing, and Learning - According to Wikipedia, a state of flow is when people are in a "mental state of operation in which a person performing an activity is fully immersed in a feeling of energized focus, full involvement, and enjoyment in the process of the activity."

A commercial-service tech who is given a steady diet of residential clean-and-checks will become disenchanted, lose focus, and probably quit.

Your people don't necessarily need you to provide all of their training. They *do* need you to be involved in educational and career planning. They need you to care and they need you to be in the game.

Feel as Though They're Making a Contribution - Coworkers need to know that they're doing important work and that it's important to the success of the company.

Feel Wanted, Appreciated, Recognized, and Respected - This isn't mushy feel-good stuff. This is you staying in business and producing profitable revenue. This is what you do to thrive in today's economy. More importantly, this is what you do because it's the right thing to do!

Believe in Their Managers and Have Mentors Within the Organization - People leave managers who don't guide, coach, and care about them. This means they leave your company. Magic happens when coworkers trust and believe in their manager.

People often get thrown off by the title *mentor*. A mentor doesn't have to be deeply committed, responsible, and part of some elaborate, complicated program. A mentor is simply someone who has already been down the road you're traveling. They know what's ahead for their coworkers, and they offer caring advice and guidance.

Lots of people would like to help but they don't know how to get started. Coach them along in this role.

Believe There's Room to Grow and Places to Go in the Company - This goes in part with the company vision and purpose. It's something that needs to be continuously communicated.

Best Benefits and Amenities in the Area - If you want the best, you have to pay the best. Period. Cut corners and *you* lose.

Transparency and Communications - Be an open book, be real, and be honest. Openly discuss the numbers. What do they mean to your coworkers and what do they mean to the company? Consistently communicate expectations, wins, positive and negative customer stories.

> *Do not hire a man who does your work for money, but him who does it for the love of it.*
>
> — **Henry David Thoreau**

Love Company Culture - This is an accumulation of all of the above. They are part of something bigger than themselves, working with real teammates who feel the same way and are treated with respect, care, and appreciation while being recognized for their efforts.
A key to a successful and thriving business is to keep coworkers engaged. When your people are engaged they find meaning in their work, find the work challenging, and can feel how they make a difference in the lives of others.

Extra Measures

Sometimes an owner must resort to other measures to retain their people. At one point, Ben had competitors siphoning away his coworkers by offering large signing bonuses.

Ben: Even though I had spent a significant amount of money training my coworkers and had kept them working during slow periods, I began to lose some to competitors.

I decided to combat these actions by developing our Spring Retention Program. The goal was to at least keep our people until mid-September. We thought it was worth up to three-thousand dollars per coworker to not have to retrain and develop new techs.
If they signed on with us they received:

- ★ $1,000 company-funded training package
- ★ $800 tool account
- ★ $800 cash bonus or paid time off
- ★ Two-day fishing trip

Chris: From a business point of view, the days of "what can you do for me?" are long gone. It's about what we can do for our coworkers.

Chris believes that for businesses to succeed, coworkers must continue to develop and grow. Hunter Heat and Air focuses not only on technical and customer-service skills, they focus on life skills. The company strives to develop the worker and to develop the individual and family man or woman as well.

The Super Techs stay on because of that and because they are both appreciated and recognized. They are cared for and they care about their work, customers, and company.

Goals – Set goals to build and develop processes in recruiting, hiring, and retention.

Observe – Research how other companies are doing this. Take classes at the Go-Time Success Group.

Take Massive Action – Put processes in action.

Inspect – Evaluate the effectiveness of each process. Is it working? Why or why not?

Modify – Tweak and adjust the process.

Engage – Move forward, treating this process as a continual loop of high-energy goal-setting, learning, action-taking, evaluation, modification, and engagement.

Notes

____

____

____

____

____

____

____

____

____

____

The service technician is a problem solver. They've been invited into the customer's home to solve a problem, reduce hassles, save time, improve comfort, reduce energy bills, and make their lives better.

— Ben Stark

The Go-Time Service Call is the heartbeat of electrical, plumbing, and HVAC operations! It begins with the customer's call for help and it ends with, "Thank you for your business, Mrs. Jones."

From the incoming call to completion, the Go-Time Service Call is process-oriented, checklist-guided, and repeatable by all.

THE INCOMING CALL

Your CSR answers the call for service and immediately seeks to earn the customer's trust and loyalty. She does this by empathizing with the customer's problem and by conveying confidence and care.

The CSR then asks the customer if they have a club membership. If not, they'll present a thumbnail of the benefits and quote service-call fees.

Ben: We use sort of a DEFCON analogy when charging for service-call fees. We call it *Dispatching for Profits*.

SLOW

MODERATE

BUSY

Green – Business is slow. We need to keep the trucks on the road. Waive or discount service-call fees.

Yellow – Business is moderate. Offer a discount to move the call to the next day.

Red – It's busy. Calls are booked out several days. Full price on service-call fees.

Ben's company uses green, yellow, and red-colored magnets on dispatching boards in the dispatching office. If the CSR sees that it's a red day, they schedule and charge accordingly.

Chris: We charge a dispatching fee. This is the cost to get a professional technician with a fully stocked truck on the road, and it's a line item in the CSR's flat-rate repair screen. There are three different levels of diagnostic fees depending on how involved the troubleshooting is.

We call after hours *Hero Time*. It's a chance to outshine the competition. We don't charge overtime to our customers; overtime expenses are built into regular pricing.

SERVICE-CALL POSITIONING

What level technician is dispatched? The intent is to place the technician with the appropriate technical and communication skills on incoming service, precision tune-up, and problem calls.

DESCRIPTION	PRIORITY	RATING ★
Existing Club-Membership Customer		
Service Call: who to send-	M	3 to 5-Star Tech
Precision Tune Up (PTU): who to send-	M	2 to 4-Star Tech
Problem Call: who to send-	H	4 to 5-Star Tech or SM
Existing Customer Equipment Over Eight Years Old		
Service Call-	M	4 to 5-Star Tech
PTU-	M	3 to 5-Star Tech
Problem Call-	H	4 to 5-Star Tech or SM
New Customer Equipment Over Eight Years Old		
Service Call-	H	4 to 5-Star Tech
PTU-	M	3 to 5-Star Tech
Problem Call-	H	4 to 5-Star Tech or SM
New Customer New Equipment		
Service Call-	M	3 to 4-Star Tech
PTU-	M	2 to 3-Star Tech
Problem-	H	4 to 5-Star Tech or SM
Existing Install Customer (Less Than Eight Years)		
Service Call	M	2 to 3-Star Tech
PTU-	L	2 to 3-Star Tech
Problem-	H	3 to 5-Star Tech or SM
Light Commercial		
Service Call-	M	4 to 5-Star Tech
PTU-	L	3 to 5-Star Tech
Problem-	H	5-Star or SM

Tech Ratings ★ ★ ★ ★ ★

1-L	Helper	Low Technical, Low Communication
1-M	Helper	Low Technical, Mid Communication
2-L	2-Star Level,	Mid Technical, Low Communication
2-M	2-Star Level,	Mid Technical, High Communication
3-L	3-Star Level,	Mid Technical, Low Communication
3-M	3-Star Level,	Mid Technical, Mid Communication
3-H	3-Star Level,	Mid Technical, High Communication
4-L	4-Star Level,	Mid Technical, Low Communication
4-M	4-Star Level,	High Technical, Mid Communication
4-H	4-Star Level,	High Technical, High Communication
5-M	5-Star Level,	High Technical, Mid Communication
5-H	5-Star Level,	High Technical, High Communication

RUNNING THE GO-TIME SERVICE CALL

The Go-Time Service Call is based on a repeatable process. Each step is essential and fits like a puzzle piece into the next.

1. Preparation
2. Arrival
3. Introduction
4. Purpose of Call
5. Transitional Statement
6. Tune-up/Service Diagnostics
7. Presentation of Recommendations
8. Completion of Call
9. Obtain Next Call

To begin the process of a successful service call, the technician must prepare for excellence before departing for the customer's home.

Successful people do what unsuccessful people are not willing to do. Don't wish it were easier; wish you were better.

— Jim Rohn

PREPARATION

Personal Hygiene

- ★ Pressed and clean uniform; shirt tucked in
- ★ Well-groomed; hair combed; company-logoed hat
- ★ Professional shoes
- ★ Free of tobacco and other offensive odors
- ★ Smile

Paperwork & Credentials

- ★ Have appropriate paperwork to complete the call. This includes invoice, club membership form, recommendation/option form, energy-rating card, equipment and thermostat stickers
- ★ Wear company ID badge

Mental Preparation

- ★ Positive attitude!
- ★ Put aside stress and personal problems to mentally prepare for a successful service call
- ★ Never share personal problems with the customer
- ★ Review past service history on this customer
- ★ Understand the nature of the call. Review instructions specific to this customer, like "unfriendly dog" or "pet boa"
- ★ Smile

Communication With Customer

- ★ Notify customer at least thirty minutes prior to arrival

Arrival

- ★ Arrive on time or five minutes early
- ★ Park clean truck in driveway after receiving permission from customer
- ★ Exit vehicle within thirty seconds of arrival
- ★ Put on a smile, exit vehicle confidently with clipboard and shoe covers in hand

INTRODUCTION

- ★ Knock on customer's door
- ★ Take two steps back from door to give the customer space
- ★ Greet customer with a smile and a pleasant demeanor
- ★ Introduce yourself while handing customer two business cards
- ★ Put on shoe covers

Purpose of Call

- ★ Confirm purpose of the call
- ★ Give the customer a brief overview of what you will be doing
- ★ Ask customer to show you the thermostat

While Standing at Thermostat, Ask:

- ★ Is this where you normally set your thermostat?
- ★ Which room is the most uncomfortable room in your house?
- ★ Who in your home suffers from allergies?
- ★ Approximately how much is your high summer electric bill?
- ★ Approximately how much is your high winter utility bill?
- ★ Are there any plumbing or electrical problems you would like us to check?
- ★ Do you have any other concerns?

Ask customer to show you the work areas. This sets the stage for the customer to see what has been done and how the area improved following service. This is one of the best ways to earn trust and loyalty.

Attitude, not aptitude will determine your altitude.

— Zig Ziglar

THE PIVOTAL QUESTION

The technician establishes credibility and the desire to help and be of service to the customer. The *Pivotal Question* is a critical moment in the Go-Time Service Call that takes the pressure off of the tech to *sell*.

HVAC, plumbing, and electrical companies provide a wide array of products and services to homeowners. Naturally, company owners want their technicians to educate customers about them. A frequent response to putting this in play is, "I am not a salesman!"

The Pivotal Question removes what is traditionally thought of as sales from the equation. Ask the customer this question after they've shown you the various work areas:

> *I'm going to check your system now. I'll be looking for anything that could shorten the life of your system or cause excessively high utility bills. If I find anything, would you like for me to make a list and share it with you or just go ahead and fix it?*

TUNE-UP/SERVICE DIAGNOSTICS

Follow Detailed Checklist Procedures for:

- ★ Air conditioning/heat pump system tune-up
- ★ Heating system tune-up
- ★ Electrical system tune-up
- ★ Plumbing system tune-up
- ★ Service-call diagnostics

Based on the Pivotal Question and your subsequent work, keep a written list of items that can be recommended to the customer while performing the procedures listed above. Take pictures to aid in visual explanation.

Take pictures and videos to be stored in customer file for code-work verification, equipment operation, service-call analysis, technician training, and examples to be shared internally for most excellent work.

PRESENTATION OF RECOMMENDATIONS

It's critical for the technician to understand that their recommendations will:

- ★ Fix your customer's problems
- ★ Save your customer money
- ★ Save your customer time and hassle
- ★ Improve your customer's comfort

The service company does not want to sell anything the customer does not want, need, or cannot afford. Never assume a customer can or cannot afford something. To make that assumption is disrespectful. Treat every customer the same.

Prepare Recommendations

- ★ Technician to compile a list of recommendations in the service vehicle
- ★ Ensure each recommendation has an associated price
- ★ Prepare and complete invoice in software or on paper
- ★ Include model and serial numbers of serviced equipment
- ★ Organize pictures for presentation
- ★ Write neatly

Present Recommendations

- ★ It's important to keep in mind that the customer requested these recommendations by responding to the Pivotal Question.
- ★ In case we haven't mentioned it, remember: *Smiling is important!*

Technician to Include the Following Points Prior to Making Recommendations.

- ★ My job is to show you what is wrong with your system
- ★ My job is not to sell you anything
- ★ I don't want you to buy anything you don't want
- ★ I can fix as little or as much as you want

Walk Through the List of Recommendations With the Customer.

- ★ Use non-technical language to educate the customer
- ★ Use pictures, videos, diagrams, parts, etc.
- ★ Demonstrate how recommendations will solve a problem, improve comfort, save time, and/or save money and hassle
- ★ Listen carefully to the customer
- ★ Answer their questions thoroughly

Ask the Customer: Do I need to charge you full price or do you have a club membership?

Explain the benefits of a club membership. Demonstrate the cost of repairs with a club membership and without. See Chris's video here: https://youtu.be/7q5SAJiyypM

If it's an Older System, Explain to the Customer: The typical life expectancy of a system is ten to fifteen years. Your system is in that ballpark and is closer to the end than the beginning. If this were my home, I would start planning and budgeting to replace the system.

ENERGY-SAVINGS GUIDE

The technician prepares a repair estimate on an old system. To help the customer decide whether a system replacement might be wise, the technician contrasts the cost of the repair plus repair estimates over the next five years plus overpayment in utilities against a new energy-efficient system and its related utility savings over the next five years.

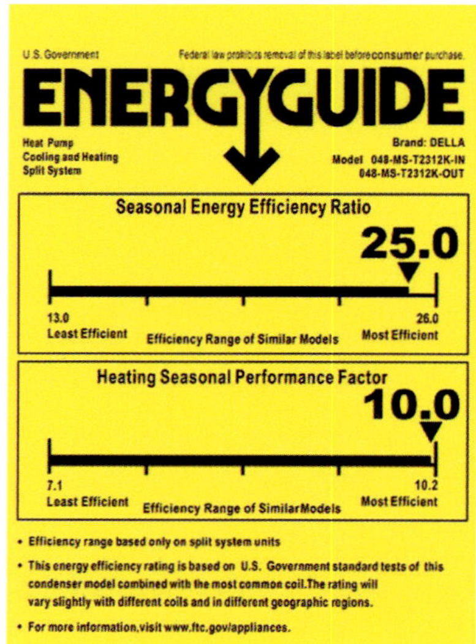

If the technician is equipped to offer a system replacement, they proceed. If not, a lead is turned over to the comfort advisor.

Obtain signed authorization for recommendations to proceed.

COMPLETION OF CALL

Return to Equipment

- ★ Install and/or repair accepted recommendations
- ★ Pack up tools and clean/vacuum work area
- ★ Cycle system
- ★ Visually inspect outdoor/indoor equipment one more time
- ★ Place company stickers on equipment and thermostat
- ★ Go the extra mile. Do the unexpected
- ★ Finalize invoice

Return to Customer (With a Smile)

- ★ Ask customer if they want old parts
- ★ Show customer completed work
- ★ Schedule future service date if recommendations cannot be completed
- ★ Collect payment
- ★ Provide customer their copy of the invoice
- ★ Ask customer for permission to take pictures for social-media marketing
- ★ Take pictures
- ★ Explain the importance of a company review and ask, if they are completely satisfied, would they please help you out and complete a Google review. Also, ask if they would let their friends and family know about your service. Ask to place a yard sign.
- ★ *Thank the customer for their business!*

Obtain Next Call

Return to the vehicle and promptly leave the customer's home, parking down the street. Contact the office for the next call. The reason for this is twofold: One, the company vehicle gets more neighborhood exposure. Two, the customer might need to leave home and would feel trapped by the service truck in the driveway.

STRIVE FOR FIVE-STAR REVIEWS

Chris: We have a favorite restaurant that we go to weekly. The food is good, and the people are friendly. The receipt always comes with a review request. I never fill it out. Why? Too much effort, I guess.

One day our waitress asked if I would do her a huge favor. The wait staff was in a contest for reviews, and reviews are also how the

The time to repair the roof is when the sun is shining.

— John F. Kennedy

company judges individual performance. She said it would mean a great deal to her, if I was satisfied with her service, to leave a review and mention her name. Now that she had asked and explained, I left a five-star review, mentioned her name, and left a compliment about how much I enjoyed the food and her service.

Right then and there it clicked! The key to generating positive customer reviews is to teach our technicians to provide awesome service, to genuinely ask for the review, and explain why it's important.

Next, make it easy for the customer to fill out the review or they will not do it.

Finally, make five-star reviews a big deal within the company. Read them aloud at company meetings, post them on the company's Facebook page, and on the owner's personal page. This shows public appreciation for the customer taking the time to do it and for the technician who earned it. What gets recognized gets repeated!

COMMUNICATE, COMMUNICATE, COMMUNICATE!

Chris: The parts-ordering update is a potential weak link in the chain of customer communication. Staying in touch with them during the process can make or break a situation that is already bad. Help to soothe the customer's anxieties by staying in touch.

REMINDER POINTS FROM BEN

★ Only complete repairs and recommendations after receiving the customer's written authorization.

★ Document declined repairs and recommendations on service tickets.

★ The service technician is a problem solver. They've been invited into the customer's home to solve a problem, reduce hassles, save time, improve comfort, reduce energy bills, and make their lives better.

★ We do not continue to add refrigerant to leaking systems. Educate the customer why you need to locate and repair the leak.

★ The sources of most customer complaints and service callbacks are easy to identify. Most often they are:

     ☆ Water leaks
     ☆ Undersized return air
     ☆ Failure to cycle system before technician leaves home
     ☆ Charging refrigerant into a leaking system
     ☆ Customer feels pushed or sold-to

THE PERFECT SERVICE CALL, THE GO-TIME SERVICE CALL

The origin of the Go-Time Service Call has the same roots as Joe Cunningham's The Perfect Service Call. Joe, Ben Stark, and others worked on the genesis of the "Call" nearly three decades ago. Although no single person invented the "Call" mega credit must be given to Joe for carrying the torch, maintaining high industry visibility and excellence, and evolving it as time moved on.

Goals – Set goals for call taking, dispatch, the Go-Time Service Call, and handling leads. Remember, the effort surrounding the service call should be checklist-guided, process-oriented, and repeatable. Strive for an experience that is great for the customer, technician, and company.

Observe – Seek out companies that deliver an exceptional service-call experience. Look for above-average service tickets, maintenance conversion ratios, five-star customer reviews, and leads set.

Take Massive Action – Practice and role-play the Go-Time Service Call. And then take it to the field and put it in play. Continue to practice it.

Inspect – Evaluate the Go-Time Service Call. Monitor CSR calls, dispatching software reports, online reviews, and happy calls.

Modify – Company growth necessitates change. Continue to course correct based on inspection and feedback.

Engage – Be disciplined. Stay with the process and strive for a repeatable, consistent, and awesome customer experience.

Notes

When do I need to add a receptionist, CSR (Customer Service Representative), and/or a SC (Service Coordinator)? The day before your wife starts looking for a divorce attorney.

— Chris Hunter

Chapter 7

I'M NOT IMPORTANT, I JUST ANSWER THE PHONE.

The following fictitious story represents a theme that Ben and Chris have encountered and addressed over the years.

> Pete, the owner of Chilly Willy Air, was showing a local businessman around the office. Pete introduced each coworker and described their position.
>
> "This is our Opportunity Management Center. Our CSRs and service coordinators play important roles in maintaining Super Tech service. They are critically important!" Suzy overheard Pete. "I'm not important, I just answer the phone."
>
> With the grace of an Olympic balance-beam specialist recovering from a near fall, Pete looked at Suzy and said, "Without you and your teammates here, this company doesn't exist! Every new customer talks with you first. If they don't like you, they won't like our company. If they don't like our company, they won't do business with us and we would soon run out of customers. We would have to close our doors."
>
> "Wow! I never thought of it that way," Suzy replied.

Over the next few days, Pete noticed an increased enthusiasm, confidence, and a whole lot more smiles out of Suzy.

Of course Pete and his leadership team had some work to do . . .

HOW AN OPPORTUNITY MANAGEMENT CENTER (OMC) EVOLVES

"When do I need to add a receptionist, CSR (Customer Service Representative), and/or a SC (Service Coordinator)?"

The day before your wife starts looking for a divorce attorney.

Countless businesses start off with the owner-technician handling all areas of the business. When he begins to spend more time on the phone than repairing systems, he hires his wife or girlfriend. Technicians and installers are added as business increases. Soon, the office duties are too much for the wife/girlfriend and they bring in help.

Staffing rules of thumb, used just a few years ago, are now outdated by technology. Back in the day, the cellphone alone changed the single-truck owner's entire landscape. And those weren't even smart phones.

Today we have sophisticated mobile service software like ServiceTitan, digital call scheduling like Schedule Engine and companies geared to handle back-office duties, like Contractor in Charge and Out of the Box Technology. Your office-staffing options are endless.

Chris: When I first started the business, I was the main technician, installer, salesperson, bookkeeper, service coordinator, and CSR person. I was the janitor, too!

Business got crazy. I couldn't keep up with the calls, not to mention everything else. If a person isn't careful, this is the stage when customer service and company reputation start to suffer.

I finally brought on an office person and proceeded to dump the phone answering, bookkeeping, service coordination, CSR duties, and personal assistant to the owner on her. What could possibly go wrong?

As we grew past fourteen trucks, we added a third CSR. The need to separate the dispatch and CSR at some point will come. As I studied best-practice companies, I noticed all the larger ones operate this way. The company now has dedicated CSRs that do inbound and outbound call taking and making. Service coordinators handle between seven and twelve trucks each.

The bottom line is the CSR and service coordinator roles are always evolving with company growth and technology. Use the Go-Time formula and keep repeating the chase for excellence in the OMC.

Ben: Early on we had CSRs who also handled the service-coordinator role. Cross training was essential. The roles split as we got larger, but we continued to cross train. Our OMC grew to over ten people working from 8:00 to 8:00, seven days a week, in multiple shifts.

WHERE SUPER TECH SERVICE STARTS

You can have the most talented and gifted service technician on the planet, but if he or she doesn't have the right tools, all of that special talent is neutralized. The same goes for CSRs and service coordinators. 21st century OMC coworkers need an excellent service-management software program. The Hunter Super Techs and Sunny Service both use ServiceTitan.

Ben: The CSR is one of the most important front-line positions in a contracting company. The first impression is the lasting one. We empower the CSR to make decisions that are best for the situation at hand, even if it means adjusting the price.

CSRs are opportunity managers. The core responsibility of their position is to keep the service technicians and comfort advisors fueled with work. A critical link in the chain of company success, the CSR is where Super Tech service starts.

WHAT MAKES A GOOD CSR?

Callers want to feel the CSRs enthusiasm, empathy, and desire to help. That and the professional tone helps to build the foundation of a successful customer relationship.

Chris: Marie was our go-to waitress at our favorite restaurant. Her brother, Juan, was a Super Tech at one of our satellite branches. We always talked about Juan and his work, until one day Marie said, "I'd make a great Super Tech!"

> *I have learned to imagine an invisible sign around each person's neck that says, 'Make me feel important!'*
>
> *— Mary Kay Ash, Founder, Mary Kay Cosmetics*

She eventually came aboard as a maintenance technician. She caught on quick and did a phenomenal job! She booked her own calls one day per week, and ran calls the rest. She was so good at it that she wanted to explore being a CSR/service coordinator.

The time Marie spent in the field helped a ton! She understood time requirements, parts, types of repair, and the technicians. Marie is also bilingual and that's huge.

Always be on the lookout for great service. A person with an outgoing, friendly personality and a desire to serve can pretty much succeed in any position in this field, especially the CSR role.

Ben: The CSR position is sales-oriented, not task-driven. We look for:

★ An energetic and positive personality
★ Ability to empathize and to read people
★ Well-spoken and communicates with confidence
★ Ability to handle rejection and reset

Chris: If necessary, our CSRs waive or refund dispatch fees. Beyond that, problems and complaints go to our customer-service manager. I'm not a fan of having CSRs handle complaints. I want them to remain happy and confident in our services and team. If they handle problems, they might start to develop a hesitancy and maybe even lose respect and faith in our departments.

CSR KPIs — KEY PERFORMANCE INDICATORS:

★ Calls taken, calls made
★ Leads
★ Percentage of leads booked
★ Club memberships sold
★ Club memberships renewed
★ Emails captured
★ Happy calls

Ben expects his CSRs to book three calls per tech per day and two sales calls per day per comfort advisor. Ben and Chris recommend keeping KPIs to between three and four at one time. CSRs at both companies strive to book eighty to ninety percent of the incoming leads.

Ben: If the CRSs are converting forty percent of total incoming calls to booked customers, the company would need twice as many leads as the department that converts eighty percent of the calls. With the cost of getting the phone to ring today, that's a big deal.

Chris: I used a company to monitor all incoming calls. They provided recordings of these calls to help their clients continue to grow. It's amazing how many red-hot leads get drenched in an ice bath when first encountering the CSR. It's even happened with my own team.

I spent a day with Ken Goodrich, CEO of Goettl Heating and Air Conditioning, at his Las Vegas location. Ken's CSR department is a well-oiled machine. He even had a coach walking the floor training new CSRs and helping others. There were scripts on all the desks, multiple screens, and one big screen with daily revenue requirements and progress. At one point I heard a manager come in and say they needed calls. He instructed the CSRs to waive the dispatch fee if they needed to book calls.

WHAT MAKES A GOOD SERVICE COORDINATOR?

A good service coordinator (SC) has nerves of steel; the blended disposition of a grandma, mom, and drill sergeant; the finesse of an orchestra conductor; and the ability to navigate through a hurricane while multitasking with a smile.

The CSR and SC roles require many of the same talents, skills, and characteristics. The main difference is that the SC works directly with, and supports, the service technicians. And no other position in the service department wields as much control over profitability as the SC. Like a basketball point guard, the SC distributes the ball to the person who is in the best position to finish the play.

Working with and supporting service technicians requires a special personality. A SC's bad day, left unchecked, will transfer directly to the technicians. And the SC cannot let one service technician who has a bad day affect their relationships with others. Navigating around stress is a must.

> *I've learned that people will forget what you said, people will forget what you did, but people will never forget how you made them feel.*
>
> *— Maya Angelou*

A Good SC:

- ★ Is trustworthy
- ★ Has a positive and enthusiastic personality
- ★ Has a calming personality
- ★ Has above-average communication skills
- ★ Thrives in a fast-paced environment
- ★ Can be stern when necessary
- ★ Doesn't rush technicians
- ★ Understands department goals
- ★ Has an above-average knowledge of local geography

DISPATCHING FOR OPPORTUNITY

Opportunities abound in HVAC, plumbing, and electrical companies. The end goal is to make sure customers receive the best service. That happens by matching the right technician with the appropriate call.

Depending upon their training and natural ability, some technicians are better equipped to turn over leads or sell replacement systems. These techs are dispatched to homes with older systems.

> **Chris:** The Hunter Super Techs have a system that matches service calls to a technician's selling ability. For instance, if you are a level-3 selling tech, you would be dispatched on systems twelve-years-old or older. The same strategy pertains to maintenance calls.

SC KPIs

- ★ Calls dispatched
- ★ Total service-department club memberships sold
- ★ Total service-department leads turned in
- ★ Total service-department systems sold
- ★ On-time percentage
- ★ Service-department revenue
- ★ Service-department gross margin

LIKE A NASCAR PIT CREW

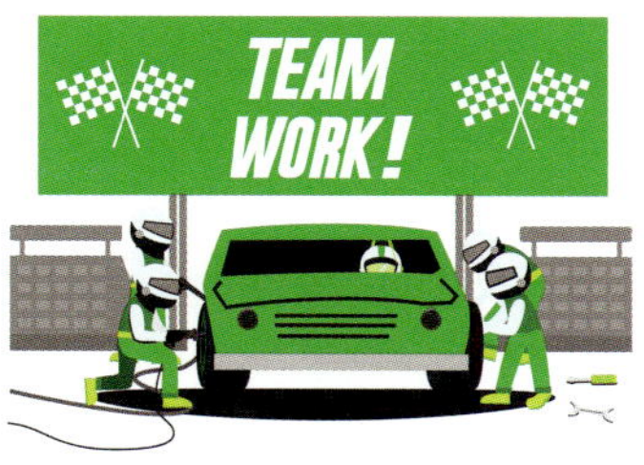

At Hunter Heat and Air, CSRs and SCs support Super Techs like a NASCAR pit crew. The same empathy shown toward customers is channeled toward the Super Techs.

Chris: To demonstrate support for the Super Techs, CSRs and service coordinators chose to do something special for one tech every week. They make gift bags, bake cookies, and include a thoughtful card. Heck, sometimes they even throw in balloons! Imagine being a tech and finding that in your truck. They also get together and make breakfast for our team on the mornings of company meetings.

A Story That Brings This Special Relationship Together *and Then Some*

One day a customer received notification that Super Tech Dylan Smith was dispatched to her home for an A/C repair. Her bad day had suddenly gotten worse. She'd gotten a flat tire and didn't have a jack. She wouldn't be able to meet Dylan at home. She'd have to reschedule. Laura, a service coordinator, called Dylan with the update. Dylan then called the customer and asked for directions to her location and said he'd be there shortly to help.

As Dylan was changing the tire, another Super Tech customer noticed the truck and stopped. She approached the customer in distress and said, "I use the Super Techs for my HVAC, plumbing, and electrical needs. If you're not using them, you should. And this, pointing to Dylan, is who they are!"

The evangelizing customer then took a picture of Dylan changing the flat and posted it to Facebook.

Dylan finished and drove to the customer's house and repaired the air conditioner. By that time the customer's husband had arrived at home. He heartily thanked Dylan for his kind effort.

After the repair, Dylan went on to his next customer, never mentioning to anyone else what had just happened. But Laura did. She gave Dylan a big shout-out on the company's private Facebook page.

CONNECT YOUR CSRs AND SERVICE COORDINATORS TO OTHERS IN THEIR ROLES

Ben and Chris have each connected their top CSRs and SCs with top CSRs and SCs at other companies. They exchange knowledge, information, and ideas. These are invaluable learning experiences that offer indirect therapy. Stress can be dialed back when one talks with others who walk in their shoes. Another side benefit is that friendly competition keeps everyone on their toes.

CSR AND SERVICE COORDINATOR EDUCATIONAL REQUIREMENTS

- ★ Products and services offered
- ★ Ride-a-longs with techs and comfort advisors
- ★ Weekly and daily coaching
- ★ Sales
- ★ Communications
- ★ Personality assessment

CSR EDUCATIONAL REQUIREMENTS

- ★ Using scripts
- ★ Service management CSR software
- ★ When not to use scripts
- ★ Role-play and practice

SERVICE COORDINATOR EDUCATIONAL REQUIREMENTS

- ★ Basic knowledge of HVAC, plumbing, and/or electrical systems
- ★ Service-management dispatch software, including reporting
- ★ Basic knowledge of repair times
- ★ Excellent grasp of the area geography
- ★ Vendor knowledge
- ★ Parts knowledge

CROSS TRAIN

As we mentioned, when companies are small, it's necessary for one person to handle the CSR and SCs responsibilities. But as companies grow, these duties are split. Ben and Chris are strong advocates of cross training these positions.

Have your CSRs and SCs ride along with your technicians and have your technicians spend a day in the CSR and SC's chair.

MARKETING — DEPARTMENT ROLE

It's vital for the marketing department or company owner to communicate when ads and specials hit the airwaves. One sure sign of a poorly run program is for the CSR or SC to answer the phone, "I'm not aware of that special Mrs. Jones." This wasn't particularly difficult in the old world of newspaper ads and direct mail. In the fast-paced world of social media and website offers, much more care and diligence are required.

Educate your CSRs and SCs on the cost of leads. With call tracking, the CSR can see the lead source and know how much it cost to generate that call. For instance, when a pay-per-click call comes in, they know that cost could be anywhere between twenty-five and a hundred and fifty dollars. This way they are more aware of the cost of making the phone ring and how important it is to book the call.

TEN IDEAS TO ENERGIZE CUSTOMER SERVICE

1. **Hire schoolteachers for CSR roles in the summer.**
2. **Book the next maintenance call while the tech is performing maintenance at the customer's house.**
3. **Monitor weather for extreme and mild conditions. Have backup and contingency plans in place.**
4. **Monitor technicians' scheduled days off while booking future calls.**
5. **When techs troubleshoot the whole house and/or system, CSRs can follow up those invoices for future work.**
6. **Keep a CSR on call. Pay on each booked call.**
7. **Send handwritten thank-you notes to customers.**
8. **Keep a mirror on each CSRs desk.**
9. **Encourage CSRs to build a vision board to keep on desk.**
10. **Peer review each other's calls. Ensure accurate classification and quality.**

Goals

- ★ Provide an excellent customer experience
- ★ Book ninety percent of the inbound leads
- ★ Fill service, maintenance, and comfort advisors' schedules
- ★ Place the right personnel in the right place at the right time for the ultimate customer experience

Observe

- ★ Observe well-run CSR departments in other companies
- ★ Explore professional education for CSRs

Take Massive Action

- ★ Enroll your CSRs and SCs with Go-Time Online University classes taught by Angie Snow
- ★ Implement the scripts
- ★ Train on how to book calls and how to overcome common objections
- ★ Create written policy on how to address problem areas
- ★ Follow up on past service call recommendations
- ★ Make happy calls

Inspect

- ★ Measure calls taken and made
- ★ Spot check and review CSR call recordings
- ★ Measure inbound/outbound booking rates
- ★ Measure club memberships sold and renewed
- ★ Measure percentage of leads booked
- ★ Count happy calls

Modify

- ★ Adjust the scripts and/or processes to meet ever-evolving customer needs
- ★ Continue to make systems more efficient and more simple

Engage

- ★ Keep taking massive action and improve
- ★ Make decisions, put them into play, and follow up in a timely manner
- ★ Create contest and awards for call booking percentages, club memberships sold, and outbound appointments booked
- ★ Connect CSRs with top CSRs from other companies to exchange knowledge and ideas

Angie Snow and her husband Ryan own Western Heating and Air Conditioning in Orem, Utah. Angie is a Go-Time Success Group coach and also operates her own practice, Snow Business Coaching.

When it come to the role of CSR, Ben and Chris talk about the importance of the role, how the role evolves from wearing many hats in small businesses, and what to look for in good CSRs and critical KPIs. Angie, on the other hand, zeroes in on the role's function. It's a perfect complement to Ben and Chris's outlook!

WHY SEVEN STARS? 

Because five stars are not enough. We all strive to be the BEST company and provide the BEST service! I'd like to suggest that five-star service is the expected standard. If your company doesn't meet expectations in any way, then you would probably get less than a five-star review.

We don't want to simply meet standards. We want to be *memorable*. We want to get and keep customers for life. We want to provide service that is worthy of *seven* stars! It takes a team to create seven-star customer service, and as a team we must start with the end in mind, and envision what seven-star customer service looks like.

How do you do this? Ask your team these three questions:

1. What do our customers expect?
2. What are they getting?
3. How do we exceed their expectations?

Which companies exceed our expectations? Costco will accept any returns, no questions asked. Starbucks, where everyone knows your name and your drink. Chick-fil-A, where leadership and positivity are part of the main course. Think of a few others and then determine what you need to do to add your name to that list.

As a team, we all play a part in providing seven-star customer service, but it's the CSR that the clients encounter first. The CSR has only seven seconds to make a great first impression. Do they sound confident, knowledgeable, trustworthy, clean, and honest? Like it or not, a customer will form impressions of your company based on the CSR's voice, tone, pace, vocabulary, and enthusiasm. No pressure, right?

CSR is a performance job, period. A CSR must be able to perform on the phone. A CSR must be able to make a good impression. If they don't, the client will go elsewhere.

Wise owners understand this. They invest thousands of dollars a year in marketing and branding to get the phone to ring. Many companies track their cost per lead (and all should). Companies spend anywhere from fifty to three hundred dollars per lead, per phone call. It is critical that CSRs are able to turn these leads into booked calls. Once they've done that, then the rest of the team gets to work their magic. The CSR has set the ball in motion for the rest of the team.

Here is my suggestion for every owner: Invest in your CSRs. Give them the training, coaching, and tools they need so they can represent your company with confidence. Invest in them like you would your technicians. Do not underestimate their value.

The seven-star CSR program that our company follows is a seven-step process that goes beyond five-star service and expectations. Your customers will be delighted to speak with your seven-star CSRs. It's about the experience. And the experience starts with your CSRs.

SEVEN-STAR CSR PROGRAM OVERVIEW:

Step 1 – Build a Relationship of Trust

People like to work with people they know and trust. A CSR gets to start building that trust right away. Most clients are vulnerable and concerned. They want to know that calling your company was a good decision. Your CSR can start building trust in a number of ways. Here are five important ones:

1 – Greet. A friendly greeting that thanks the client for calling and offers to assist. Always go for the gold when making your first impression on the phone.

2 – Connect. Make a connection. Relate, empathize, and seek commonality.

3 – Project Empathy. Use your voice to calm and reassure the customer. Tone, pace, vocabulary, and inflection are all part of this.

4 – Listen. Respect the client by listening to them, not cutting them off, and then restate what they say to prove that you're listening. Absolute focus on the customer is key.

5 – Validate. Let them know that they made a great choice by choosing your company and you are going to take care of them.

Step 2 – Gather Information

CSRs need to gather information about the system and the client so that the company can take the proper actions. What type of service do they need? When do they need it? Are they in our service area? If CSRs do not ask the right questions, they could be setting your technician up for a disaster. Believe me, I've seen it!

The cool thing about gathering information is that there are things that a CSR can do to not only book the call, but to determine the opportunity that lies within the call. By asking a series of questions, a CSR can quickly determine the RIGHT technician for that call. What's going on with the system? How long has that been happening? What's the age of the system? Where is it located? How many units do you have? By simply asking questions, we can set the technician up for success.

A CSR is not supposed to diagnose the problem over the phone, only gather the information so the technician can be prepared and ready to go. When the right technician is sent to the call, the issue can be diagnosed or a potential lead can be set. This step is crucial for efficiency and profitability.

A seven-star CSR also knows how to gather the contact and billing information that ensures clear communication and ease of process.

Step 3 – Positive Word Choice

Every word that comes out of your mouth begins as a thought. To improve our language and word choice, we must change our thoughts. It begins by being conscious of the language we use. Are the words negative or positive? Many CSRs from all industries use phrases like "No problem," "Bear with me," "Don't hesitate," and "I can't get anyone out until Friday." Do you see the negative words? *No, problem, bear, don't, hesitate, can't.* While the message is probably not intended to be negative, the words are, and they can tap into the mind in a negative way. For example, if someone says it's *no problem* or *not a big deal,* then one could assume or question that it possibly *was* a big deal or a problem. To alleviate any doubt, simply say "You're welcome" or "My pleasure." Those are positive and they will never plant a negative seed. Tell a Chick-fil-A worker "thank you" and the reply will always be, "My pleasure!"

This is a simple thing that CSRs can change when they're conscious of the words they say. Habits are hard to break. Start now.

Step 4 – Add Some Sugar

We've got the basics down now, but how do we make our calls so delightful that our clients *enjoy* speaking with the CSRs? We add some sugar!

The sugar I refer to is the value that comes *only* when doing work with your company. Why would I want *your* company to service my home? Why *your* technician? What makes *your* service so great? Could your CSRs answer those tough questions? They may not be questions that customers actually ask, but you better believe they are thinking them.

Seven-star CSRs answer those unasked questions by using value statements throughout the call. They don't use them in a boisterous or braggadocious way, they just work them into the natural flow of casual conversation.

Instead of saying "A technician will be there at 2:00," they could say, "Mark is one of our most highly trained and certified technicians, and he will arrive in his fully stocked van at 2:00." You could go on and build value by explaining more about what he'll do while he's there, and what the client can expect.

Adding sugar gets the clients *excited* about working with your company!

Step 5 – Offer Solutions

The answer is always *yes*. When a client calls in and needs help with something, "Yes, I can absolutely help you with that." On every call, CSRs have an opportunity to find a solution. Even if the CSR doesn't know the answer, they have people in their company who do, and they can find a way to answer, resolve, or fix anything. Believe it!

But what if the answer is no? For example, the schedule is completely full, and they need service today. A CSR can still say, "Sure, I'd be happy to help," then gather the appropriate information. Based on the opportunity at hand, this could be a job that you'll want to get on your schedule right away. If you need to, you can adjust the schedule and fit them in.

I've had CSRs that have turned clients away because of a full schedule, without even finding out what kind of an opportunity the client represents. They already said no. The answer is *never* no. The answer is, "Let me gather the information so I can help you."

The same answer applies when dealing with an upset client who has a problem. I believe there is no such thing as a problem, only a miscommunication or a misunderstanding. When you take this stance, then any problem can be resolved by gaining clarity.

CSRs must first go to the level of the client. What is their perspective, and what do they understand about the situation? Once a CSR has determined what their understanding is, they can create a bridge to the solution through proper communication and helping the client see the right solution. CSRs feel empowered when they know that every problem can be solved.

Step 6 – Nurture the Client Relationship

Seven-star CSRs refer to their customers as *clients*. A customer is someone who makes a one-time transaction. A client is someone who has a long-lasting relationship with your company—a customer for life! There are sure-fire ways to turn a customer into a long-time client, beginning with what happens after the service call. Is there a follow up? How do we know that they are completely satisfied?

Seven-star CSRs have a process that keeps them in touch with the client after the service has been provided. They know what communication method the client prefers, whether it's a phone call, a text, or an email. It's important to make sure that the expectations were, in fact, met, and that the client is completely satisfied with the service they received. The only thing better than a satisfied customer is a loyal client.

A loyal client will be your advocate and your cheerleader. They will feed your business with referrals, reviews, and continued business for life.

Step 7 – Ask for the Review

Whose job is it to ask for a review, anyway? The technician? The CSR?
The answer: It's *everyone's* job. So what stops them from asking? Fear. Fear of rejection, fear of offending, and fear that the client might not be happy with the work. That's the wrong mindset.

If you have provided amazing service that is worthy of a seven-star review, then why not ask for it? When I have received service that goes beyond my expectations, I *want* to give something in return. It's called *the give-receive cycle*.

The key to making this cycle work is to ensure that your company truly has given amazing service. Before a CSR or technician asks for the review, ask if they are satisfied and happy with the service. If they say yes, then ask them to give your company a review, and give them three reasons to do it:

> 1 – It provides wonderful feedback for your company so that you can continue to improve.

> 2 – It helps your technician get recognition for a job well done.

> 3 – It helps other consumers find a service company that they can trust.

See how easy that is? It will take some practice, but the CSRs and technicians who practice this give-receive cycle will help gather more reviews . . . which means a better reputation . . . which means more work . . . which means everybody wins!

Seven-star CSRs do not become seven-star CSRs overnight. It's a process that takes practice. It's a process that takes consistency. With continued practice, role-playing, and call evaluations, a CSR's performance can and will improve. CSRs will gain a seven-star status along with a sense of increased confidence; more booked calls; and loyal, raving clients.

What are you waiting for?

Notes

I have been tracking a consistent ten to twelve KPIs for over twenty-five years. I adjust manpower, marketing, cash flow, and vehicles accordingly. This keeps me ahead of the game. Otherwise, problem recognition slows, and we lose momentum. And once momentum is lost, it's very hard to get it back.

— Ben Stark

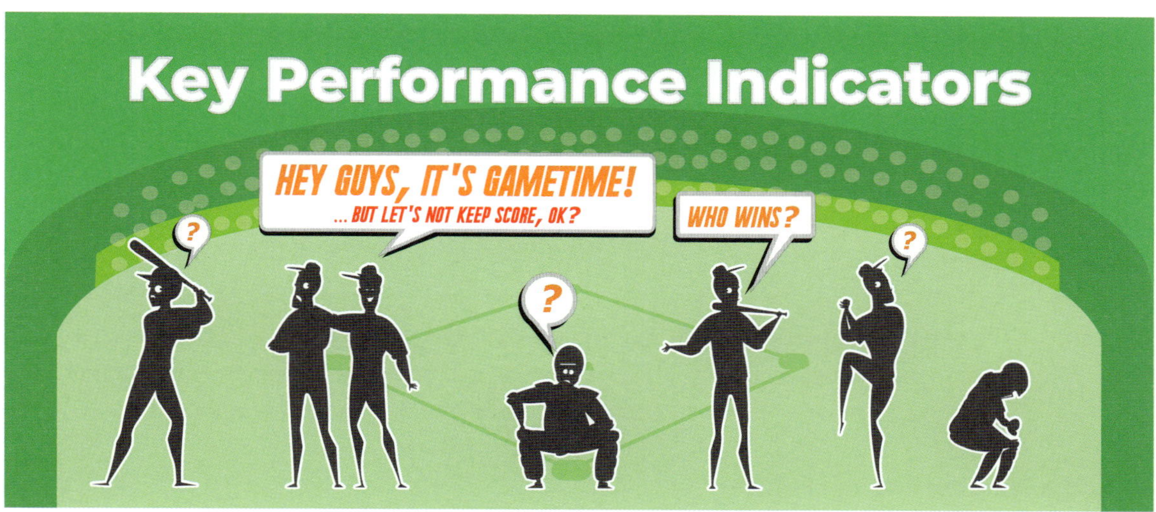

Imagine that you're at a baseball game and it's a slugfest. The visiting team scores four runs in the first inning and the home team scores five. It goes back and forth like this the entire game. Coaches strategize how to both score and stop runs. The game ends with a walk-off three-run homer in the bottom of the ninth inning. What a game!

Now imagine you're at a game and no one's keeping score. With nothing on the line, the players go through the motions. The fans quickly lose interest and go home. To an empty stadium, the announcer says, with tongue in cheek, "Thanks for coming out to watch a complete lack of effort and action today." Why even play the game?

What happens when no one keeps score at your company? How will you know if your coworkers and company are on target to hit the goals that will move your company forward? Making progress is one of the greatest motivational forces in the universe. If, that is, those involved can see the progress being made.

KEY PERFORMANCE INDICATORS

KPIs allow the business owner *and* their coworkers to keep score. They're a way to measure performance against operational goals and national industry benchmarks. KPIs are how you chart your progress —or lack of it.

For instance, a baseball player's batting average is .275. His goal is .300, which is also an industry mark of excellence. Knowing that his average is .275 allows him to make performance modifications. Maybe he'll hire a coach to help him adjust his swing.

A service technician's average ticket goal is three hundred and fifty dollars or more, which is also a non-performance-pay national industry benchmark. By keeping track of the score, he (and his manager), know that his average revenue per day is three hundred dollars. This triggers the team of manager and coworker to analyze the tech's performance and begin to make adjustments.

A Window Into History . . .

Ben: The habit of establishing, recording, and keeping KPIs is like writing notes in a journal. It gives management a view into the coworkers' and company's growth and development over time. A manager can analyze both individual and department progress.

. . . And a Window Into the Future

Ben: I have been tracking a consistent ten to twelve KPIs for over twenty-five years. I adjust manpower, marketing, cash flow, and vehicles accordingly. This keeps me ahead of the game. Otherwise, problem recognition slows and we lose momentum. And once momentum is lost, it's very hard to get it back.

BEN'S HVAC KPIs

- ★ Service labor ≤ 20%
- ★ Maintenance labor ≤ 18%
- ★ Residential replacement labor ≤ 9%
- ★ Sales-closing rate ≥ 50%
- ★ Company gross margin ≥ 45%
- ★ Replacement equipment + materials ≤ 35%
- ★ Maintenance equipment + materials ≤ 10%
- ★ Service equipment + parts ≤ 18%
- ★ Total marketing cost ≤ 10%
- ★ Total operating expenses ≤ 35%
- ★ New club memberships added to base each day ≥ 3.5

It's important to remember, as we've noted throughout, the values of the KPIs will change depending upon the business owner's demographics and business intent.

Numbers are not a substitute for leadership. What's important is how you use them.
— *Jack Stack*

A Window in the First Place

Chris:　When I first started in business, I had one KPI (even though, at that time, I had no idea what a KPI was). Did I have enough money in the bank to make payroll? I first learned about KPIs after joining the Service Nation Alliance.

We Started Slowly With the Following Three KPIS:

Service, Maintenance, and Install Average Tickets - We started by using industry benchmarks. Boy was that eye-opening! We had no idea how bad we were. It forced us to closely examine our labor rate, pricing structure, gross margins, sales, and service-call procedures and systems for successful service calls and system replacements.

Perhaps one of the greatest benefits from this exercise was that it allowed us the opportunity to create a hybrid performance-pay system that rewards Super Techs for just doing their jobs. In our system, we started with an hourly pay and simply added a performance element, like spiffs on specific items, commissions for replacement equipment, five-star reviews, average ticket, and so on.

In the home, we look for ways to help keep the customer safe, comfortable, and to save on energy bills. Super Techs simply present solutions as options, no selling involved!

We Then Concentrated on These KPIS:

Conversion Rate on Maintenance Agreements - Converting regular service customers to our club membership is a top priority. It helps maintain consistent company growth and provides steady year-round work. A company with year-round work attracts top talent. This KPI is structured into our performance-pay plan. When Super Techs hit their KPIs, they benefit financially.

Service and Install Labor Percentages - This KPI measures our efficiency, pricing, and sales competency. Tracking labor percentage allowed us to implement performance pay for our installers. Because installers weren't getting spiffs while working in hot Oklahoma attics with difficult-to-install high-end equipment, no one wanted to do the work. After we implemented performance pay, *everyone* wanted to be an installer! The company wins and the coworker wins.

> **In business, numbers talk. But it takes people to make those numbers talk.**
>
> **— Larry Taylor**

Chris and his team's intention to track these KPIs were the catalyst to greater all-around efficiency and performance.

Chris: In order to track these KPIs, we had to get our record-keeping ducks in a row—and let me tell you, they were all over the pond!

While we knew our company's overall labor percentage, we had no idea where each department stood. The number one, and most important action we took was to departmentalize our entire operation.

Check this out: You're flying a plane and the entire instrumentation panel goes dark. Although the plane is still in the air, and you still have control over it, you have no idea about direction, fuel, and other critical details. Why fly your company blind?

So we departmentalized. Cool, let's check the labor percentages! But we didn't have a system in place to track where labor was spent, so we found a payroll company with an app to track labor. Later on, we took care of this need through ServiceTitan.

The point is, when you commit and take action to improve your operation, you'll find other areas in need. It's like you get the fuel gauge working, but you need the rest of the instruments to reach your destination.

START WITH SMALL STEPS

Listed below are the KPIs and business-performance metrics that Ben and Chris used. At first glance it might seem like an overwhelming amount of items to track. No worries. Take a breath and start with the average tickets, conversion rate on maintenance agreements, and the labor percentages.

By taking small steps, you can set up, refine, and make a hardcore habit out of the reporting process. As Chris discovered, the more care and diligence that you put into tracking, the more you will learn about what affects sales, performance, and profitability.

Business-Performance Metrics — Target

HVAC Service and Maintenance
	Target
Service labor	≤20%
Service cost of goods sold, parts and supplies	≤18%
Service gross margin	≥62%
Percent of total sales	25
Average calls needed to generate replacement lead	≤10
Maintenance labor	≤18%
Maintenance cost of goods sold, parts and supplies	≤10%
Maintenance gross margin	≥60%
Percent of total sales	15
Average calls needed to generate replacement lead	≤18
Callbacks	≤1%

Plumbing Service and Maintenance
	Target
Service and maintenance labor	≤21%
Cost of goods sold, parts and supplies	≤15%
Callbacks	≤1%

Electrical Service and Maintenance
	Target
Service and maintenance labor	≤21%
Cost of goods sold parts and supplies	≤15%
Callbacks	≤1%

HVAC Residential Replacement
	Target
Replacement labor	≤9%
Equipment and materials	≤35%
Gross margin (after support wages and commissions)	≥45%
IAQ and home performance	≥65%
Percent of total company sales	60
Warranty expense	≤2%

Marketing–Sample Budget
	Target
Target Range	6-10%*
Branding	25%
Call to action	50%
Internal	25%

Leadership–time spent
	Target
Recruiting, retaining, and building career pathways	30%
Developing best practices	30%
Vision and company direction	30%

Other
	Target
Average revenue per team member per year	≥$170,000
Club membership conversion	≥35%
Club Memberships per million dollars of service sales	≥1,000
Five-star reviews per tech per day	≥40%
EBITDA	≥10%
Operating cash and or credit days of operating expense	≥20%
Overhead as a percent of sales	≤30%
Field-to-office ratio	3 to 1
Company annual growth rate	≥10%

Percent will vary depending upon marketing needs.

Residential Field Staff KPIs — Target

HVAC Service Technician
	Target
Average ticket	≥$350
Leads set per service call	≥20%
Closed calls	≥85%
Service-call-to Club Membership conversion rate	≥30%

HVAC Maintenance Technician
	Target
Average tune-up ticket	≥$175
Leads set per maintenance call	≥15%
Closed calls	≥50%
Tune-up-to-Club Membership conversion rate	≥70%

Plumbing-Service Technician
	Target
Average ticket	≥$450
Closed calls	≥92%
Service-call-to-Club Membership conversion rate	≥30%
Tankless water heater leads	≥15%

Electrical-Service Technician
	Target
Average ticket	≥$500
Closed calls	≥85%
Service-call-to-Club Membership conversion rate	≥30%
Generator sales leads	≥15%

Comfort Advisor
	Target
Replacement system (average install ticket)	≥$8,500*
Sales-closing ratios (on average)	≥50%
Technician lead	75-85%
Current non-Club Membership customer	55-65%
Club Membership customer	70%
Self-generated	65-80%
Marketing lead	25-35%
Commission	9%
Annual sales	≥1.5 mill

*This figure fluctuates highly per market area. Adjust accordingly.

Customer Service Rep (CSR)
	Target
Call-conversion ratio	≥80%
Non-Club Membership conversion ratio	≥20%

Bookings per day
	Target
1. Service and maintenance calls per tech	3
2. Sales leads per comfort advisor	2
3. Happy calls	≥60%

Service Coordinator (SC)
	Target
Percentage of productive time booked per day dispatched	≥50%
Total service dept. Club Memberships sold	≥30%
Total service dept. leads turned in	≥20%
On-time percentage	≥95%
Maintenance calls booked per maint. tech	4 per day

KPIs CHANGE

KPIs change. Whether it's when a one-truck owner adds a tech, a three-million-dollar company increases to seven, one company acquires another, or technology advances (and it always does), KPIs need to be adjusted.

There's also another reason.

To get a handle on this, we need to go back to May 6, 1954 when Roger Bannister ran the first under-four-minute mile. For decades, runners couldn't crack the four-minute mark. Yet once Bannister did it, others broke it too.

A similar phenomenon occurred in the HVAC industry when Charlie Greer and Tom McCart became the first comfort advisors to break one million dollars in annual sales. Once they did it, others did it too.

Someone has to break the barrier so that other may follow. Why? For one, it provides psychological reassurance. Knowing that a feat has been accomplished means that it can be accomplished again. When it comes to the trades, other factors involve advances in technology, education, and coworkers striving for improvement.

It's important to understand what drives the change in metrics and to adjust for growth! When setting KPIs, be sure to account for the local economy. All things considered, a contractor operating in rural Indiana faces an altogether different economy than one operating in big-city California.

You can also learn a tremendous amount by studying great companies, especially if they're in your industry. Pick an overachiever, a superhero, and find out what it measures — just ask.
— *Jack Stack*

PUBLISH INNER COMPANY KPIs

One of the most powerful ways to get results with KPIs is by making each coworker's performance public on an ongoing basis. When a technician sees other techs with better performances, their competitive juices kick in. No one wants to be the low man on the totem pole. An amazing aspect of this practice is that performance begins to improve with minimal management effort.

Companies publish KPIs on whiteboards, video monitors in the warehouse and tech areas, and on service-management software, available on computer tablets. If you're using whiteboards and your service management software isn't capable of publishing coworker KPIs, take pictures of the whiteboards and send them to all coworkers.

KPIs GO SOCIAL

Both Ben and Chris cite the Service Nation Alliance (SNA) member dashboard as being instrumental in their business success. Members are grouped with non-competing companies of similar size. Information is confidential to each group. KPIs and operational metrics are entered into the dashboard each month. Historical detail is one click away.

Online discussions are based on the data. "How did you reach that number?" "Your average service ticket has increased over the last eight months. Why?" "Your average installation is below average. Why?"

The practice of discussing KPIs with non-competing contractors is priceless.

A useful metric is both accurate, in that it measures what it says it measures, and aligned with your goals. Don't measure anything unless the data helps you make a better decision or change your actions.

— Seth Godin

Do you monitor, track, and use KPIs on a consistent basis? Or are you stuck on the hamster wheel of daily chaos, leaving no time to keep score?

Make a commitment today to start keeping score! Manage your business using KPIs and Business Performance Metrics.

Goal – What are your coworkers' KPIs? What are the company's? What are yours?

Observe – Do you have access to other contractor's KPIs? Do you belong to an alliance that facilitates access to member's KPIs and operational metrics? Do you pursue KPI education?

Take Massive Action – Do you make KPIs public within the company? Are your coworkers aware of their KPIs? Do you coach based on results?

Inspect – Do you or your managers monitor and evaluate KPIs on a weekly basis? Do your coworkers monitor each other's KPIs?

Modify – Do you make adjustments based on individual KPI results? Do you adjust based on performance and growth requirements?

Engage – Proper KPI engagement can lift morale, brighten your culture, and drive your business. Have you bought in? Are you moving forward with KPI management?

Notes

The single biggest decision you make in your job — bigger than all the rest — is who you name manager. When you name the wrong person manager, nothing fixes that bad decision. Not compensation, not benefits — nothing.

— Jim Clifton, Gallup CEO

Do you remember the managers in your career? Whether it was at McDonald's, the local grocery store, or Bob's Heating and Cooling, it's a good chance that you do. Even when we have a hard time remembering where we were earlier in the day, why is it that we can still paint such vivid pictures of the bosses in our career?

Two reasons: One, the manager contributed to our success. Two, the manager stymied, stifled, or delayed our success.

If you played sports, you probably remember your coaches for the exact same reasons. Why do we have especially strong memories when it comes to bad bosses? Thinking back, we conjure visions of the Wicked Witch of the West. Is it possible that we've simply had more bad ones than good ones?

The Gallup organization owns the world's largest database on the subject of management. According to the 2017 State of the American Workforce Report, only thirty-three percent of workers are engaged on the job. Why?

To help answer this question, let's look at what the Gallup data says about why workers leave their jobs:

- ✔ Limited career-growth opportunities
- ✔ Poor pay and benefits
- ✔ Bad manager or management
- ✔ Toxic company culture
- ✔ Poor job fit
- ✔ Jealous boss

Every one of these reasons can be traced back to the manager or owner. As Marcus Buckingham famously said in *First, Break All the Rules*, "People leave managers, not companies." Buckingham's book is based on Gallup research.

While these points can all be traced back to the manager, Gallup didn't include *jealous boss*. That was Chris's idea. Wait till you hear his story!

Chris: I got fired from McDonald's when I was sixteen years old. Although my actions directly led to my termination, it was what transpired leading up to it that provide my lesson for how not to lead.

My shift leader and I went to the same high school. I was well-liked and he wasn't. He had it out for me from day one. Because we'd never had a confrontation or anything, I think he was jealous.

Case-in-point: He wrote me up for having facial hair, which was against the rules. Ha! I was lucky if I had two whiskers! He just continued to needle and give me a hard time. It all came to a head when he refused to give me the night off when the Dallas Cowboys played in the Super Bowl. He knew what a Cowboys fan I was and did it out of spite. I didn't go to work that night and got fired.

That was a challenging job, but I loved working with the people. Well, everyone but the shift leader. I learned a lot about customer service, processes, and how *not* to lead.

MANAGEMENT EVOLVES

Fifty years ago, management was all about command and control. *This is your job. This is how you do your job. Don't like it? Go home! Don't like it and don't want to go home? You're fired!* That began to change in 1982 when Thomas J. Peters and Robert H. Waterman, Jr. published their seminal book, *In Search of Excellence*. They introduced a more autonomous, entrepreneurial business model that, among other things, focused on values and productivity through people.

Back in the day, an HVAC manager might have dealt with some training, conflict resolution, bailing a tech out of a technical jam, and the annual coworker review. In recent years the role has evolved.

Today we see companies built and operated on the owner's purpose. Coworkers are also driven by purpose and meaning in their work. Pure gold, which we discuss in the "Vision, Mission, Core Values, WHY" chapter, is found when the owner's and coworker's purpose intersect.

Coworker development is a priority. In addition to technical and soft-skills training, companies are offering programs to develop their coworker's mind, body, and spirit. If you don't offer your people life-skills training, the guy at the other HVAC company will.

Coaching has replaced managing and bossing people around.

Annual reviews are slowly becoming relics of a distant age. Ongoing and frequent conversations, both structured and casual, are filling the feedback and communication needs of today's workers as coaching replaces managing (managers still manage processes and systems, though, just not people).

Strengths-based cultures are taking over the landscape. Leaders are focusing on their people's strengths instead of their weaknesses.

People are seeking meaning and fulfillment while exercising their values and beliefs in the workplace. They seek companies that allow them to live their most authentic lives 24-7. We're not in Kansas anymore, folks!

FROM TOP TECH TO SERVICE MANAGER

Ben: Managers are often raised from the ranks of field technicians. They are promoted because they are accomplished techs. While that might seem like a great way to reward these technically minded people, there is nothing in their job that prepares them to be a manager.

Chris: I promoted my top service technician to service manager. I couldn't wait for someone to help me with the scheduling and technical questions, customer complaints, sales estimates, truck issues and, of course, the techs who just wanted to tell me about their day or the latest job they'd been on. Along with business cards, I gave him a nice pay raise. I had high expectations!

> *Management is about getting things done through other people; it doesn't get any more basic than that.*
>
> — **Rosa Say**, *Managing with Aloha*

Chris: Things didn't work out so well. I'd taken my top technical guy out of the field. Leads, sales, and club memberships declined. To make matters worse, the other techs were calling me with technical problems *and* problems with their new service manager. As a matter of fact, I was now fielding more calls than before.

The problem? My top tech was an alpha male with limited leadership skills. I had thrown him into a position that required him to lead and influence his coworkers. That's an entirely different skill set than what made him a successful technician.

Putting him partially back in the field, while still running the department, I tried to work things out. It got worse. We both agreed it would be best for him to go back to his old position full time. That didn't work either. When you take a top producer, put them in management, and then back in the field to be an equal once again with his peers, bad things happen!

Due to a bad choice in the first place, poor training, and not properly communicating expectations, this whole move was a total bust. My top tech wasn't a bad person. He was just a victim of me trying to put a square peg in a round hole.

TEAM LEADER

The old expectation of a company's top technician placed in the service-manager role was *sink or swim*. And if that person started to swim, his stroke barely kept him from drowning. Barely drowning is not the type of performance a competent business owner needs from their managers.

A team leader is a perfect steppingstone between technician and any management position. Training that will help make the team leader a competent manager can begin while he's still performing team leader responsibilities.

Typical Team Leader Responsibilities:

- ★ Perpetuates the company vision, mission, and core values
- ★ Custodian of the intended company culture
- ★ Information and cultural conduit between field and management
- ★ Conducts weekly team meetings
- ★ Coaches and mentors team members
- ★ Performs ride-a-longs
- ★ KPI and department goal implementation
- ★ Assists team members in developing life skills
- ★ Conducts sales and technical training
- ★ Provides technical support for team
- ★ Provide soft-skill support for team
- ★ Forecasts work and communicates with dispatcher
- ★ Monitors and controls overtime
- ★ Performs customer service

Next, we're going to take a peek into management functions that Ben and Chris created. While a detailed journey into these noble practices is beyond the scope of this book, we share these to highlight the steps that our two leaders have taken to develop their people.

THE SUPER TECH SERVICE MANAGER TRAINING PROGRAM

The following is an outline of the service manager's training at Hunter Heat and Air. This window provides us with a view into both the importance and sophistication associated with a service manager's role. Use this as a checklist to verify your own service-manager training curriculum.

> *The moment you feel the need to tightly manage someone, you have made a hiring mistake. The best people don't need to be managed. Guided, taught, led—yes. But not tightly managed.*
> *— Jim Collins*

TRAINING TOPICS

Choosing a service manager—job description

Time management—personal and team

Leadership skills—John C. Maxwell's Leadership Gold and The 21 Irrefutable Laws of Leadership

Transformational coaching

How to be a real success

Financials

How to get to the numbers

Managing KPIs

Staffing demands

Laws of teamwork

Training programs

Meeting structure

Dispatching

Holding people accountable

Mentoring

Steps to a service call

Onboarding procedure for new coworkers

Club-membership management

Pricing

Systems and processes

Forecasting

Vehicle inspection and setup

Inventory management

Purchase-order system

Troubleshooting

On-call scheduling

Customer service

Team-member conflict resolution

Customer-conflict resolution

Performance evaluations

Terminations

Recruiting

Pre-employment testing

Interviewing

Quality control—callbacks

Sales training—how to train the team

Sales training—how to bring in outside resources

Training budget

Management of shop time/down time

Setting up a job board

Individual training on the above list is available at The Go-Time Success Group Online University: www.GoTimeSuccessGroup.com/

THE COWORKER REFERENCE MANUAL

Ben has created and developed a series of manuals that guide and serve both the coworker and their manager at Sunny Service.

The following are descriptions of what's included in each position's manual.

The Service-Tech and Maintenance-Tech Field Manual

Company mission and vision statement

Job description

The Go-Time Service Call—step by step procedure to provide a consistent customer experience

Troubleshooting questions—designed to solve problems before calling the manager

Troubleshooting diagrams—electrical, plumbing, and refrigeration problem-solving charts

Creed of a Craftsman—points of pride a technician lives by

Paperwork process diagram—instructions on paperwork documentation

Truck inventory requirements—tool and parts requirements

Warranty policy—how to handle callbacks and warranty issues

Production or Lead Install Manual

Company mission and vision statement

Job description

Job start and flow procedure—install job planning

Drawings of job expectations—how we install system components

Creed of a Craftsman—points of pride an installer lives by

Paperwork-process diagram—instructions on paperwork documentation

Truck-inventory requirements—tool and material requirements

Sales-Manager Policy Manual

Company mission and vision statement

Job description

Five-Step Sales Presentation Review

Third-party article file

The complete sales system process

Referral program outline

Customer-Service Representative Manual

Company mission and vision statement

Job description

Productivity expectations

Bonus plan

Incoming-call scripts

Outgoing-call scripts

Cross-training objectives

Individual training on the above list is available at The Go-Time Success University www.GoTimeSuccessGroup.com/

SYSTEMS AND PROCESSES

If there is one thing that both Ben and Chris are *fanatical* about it's developing, installing, maintaining, and evolving systems and processes. Inspired by Michael E. Gerber and his *E-Myth* series of books, the lads are on a par with the best McDonald's restaurants when it comes to organizational procedures and effectiveness. As a matter of fact, Ben is a certified *E-Myth* instructor.

Chris: Whenever we ran into a problem, instead of panicking about the fire, stomping it out only to have it reignite later, I asked, "What step in the system broke down?" or, "Do we have a system for that?" We took immediate action on the issue and the system.

We apply the same principle to coaching our Super Techs. Ninety-nine percent of the time, the typical *no-charge* service call is the result of not having a system in place or not using the system we had. If the tech follows the Go-Time service call system, the office follows the dispatch-for-opportunity system and then follows up with the debrief system, the odds of a no-charge are drastically reduced.

Here's an Example From Our Install Department

Whenever we had a wrong-equipment snafu on the job, it always came back to the perfect estimate system not being executed. One time, an installed furnace continued to give us fits. I mean replace two brand-new furnaces fits, throw money out the window fits! And to dump the entire saltshaker into our open wound, it was a very influential customer.

Eventually we discovered that it was a propane system and, continually, we failed to install a conversion kit. I know, *DUH!* Our perfect estimate form did not have a box for fuel type or whether or not a conversion kit was needed.

Of course we installed the conversion kit. But we also adjusted our form.

USE THE GO-TIME FORMULA

Chris: Whether or not we were creating or modifying a system or process, we used the Go-Time formula.

We set the goal. Then we observed how other successful companies did it. Next we took massive action and put it into play. We inspected the results and modified them as necessary. Finally, we engaged wholly with the system and moved forward.

In regard to the furnace snafu that I describe above, we tried many different versions of the perfect estimate system. When we hit the propane conversion kit speed bump, we continued to inspect and modify the system by including the fuel-type and conversion-kit boxes.

We continue to use the Go-Time formula for perpetual improvement!

Problem Solving/Solution Finding

Over the years, Ben developed and used the following formula to solve problems:

- ★ State the problem
- ★ Define the problem
- ★ List or state possible solutions
- ★ State best long-term solution
- ★ Develop action plan
- ★ Implement the plan—take action
- ★ Set time to revisit and follow up the plan

Develop Decision Maker Skills

- ★ Research the past in the context of the decision
- ★ Hone questioning skills
- ★ Apply decision-making to future events
- ★ Use logic to analyze situation
- ★ Decision-Making Process
- ★ Identify the purpose of the decision
- ★ Gather information
- ★ Brainstorm with principals
- ★ Involve principals to judge and evaluate alternatives
- ★ Select best alternative
- ★ Execute

> *Human beings have an innate inner drive to be autonomous, self-determined, and connected to one another. And when that drive is liberated, people achieve more and live richer lives.*
> *— Daniel Pink*

INTO THE FUTURE

Ben: Our industry is quickly moving into the future. Modern tools and software allow unprecedented ways to monitor and measure coworker productivity. The use of financial metrics and data have increased in sophistication, particularly in terms of departmental segregation. The modern manager must adapt from the days of technician stardom to that of an engaged coach who manages by the numbers and by the heart.

Ben has invested decades in refining the structure of management in his companies and developing individual managers. The following list is a culmination of wisdom that, over the years, has been tested in the fires of reality.

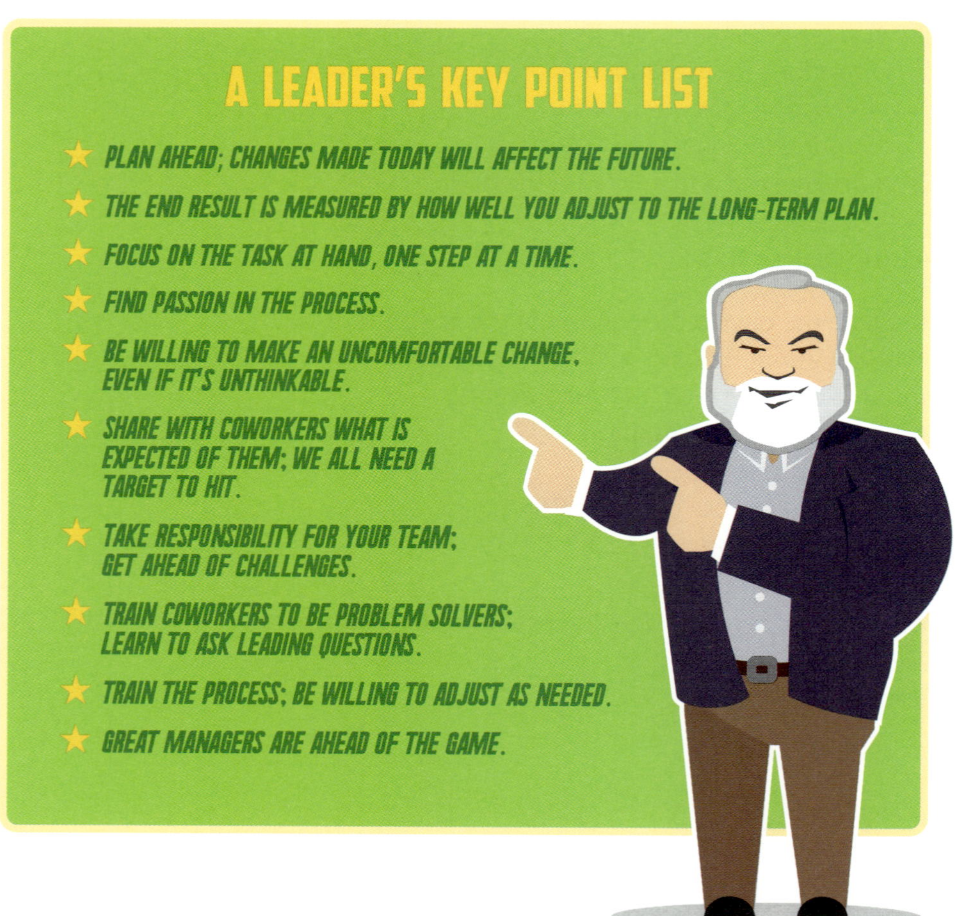

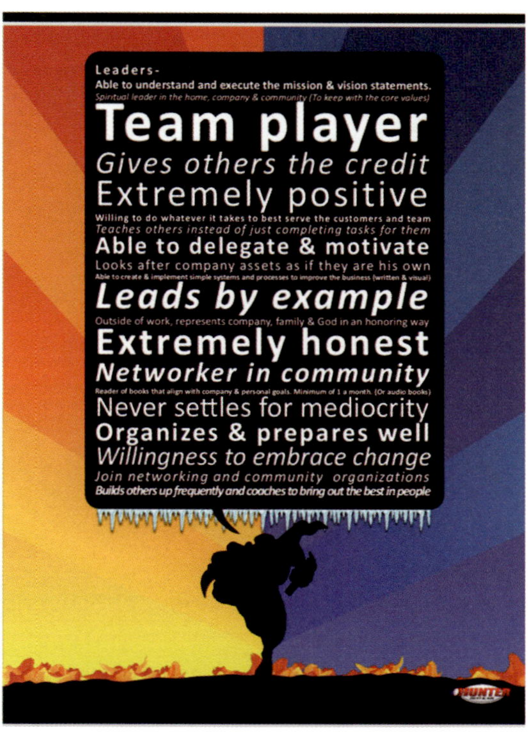

Chris – This graphic, which hangs on the Super Tech's walls, describes what we expect out of our managers.

Chris: What kind of manager are you? Your legacy is formed with every decision, new hire, coaching session, and even termination.

It's an honor to be a manager in the home-service industry! Management is a position of great influence. Managers are entrusted with the care and guidance of their coworkers' jobs and careers.

> *The best executive is the one who has sense enough to pick good men to do what he wants done, and self-restraint enough to keep from meddling with them while they do it.*
>
> *— Theodore Roosevelt*

Goal – Craft a plan of development for your managers that includes financial literacy and soft-skills competency.

Observe – Study other owners who have a strong management system and strong managers. Engage in Go-Time training.

Take Massive Action – Move forward with the plan.

Inspect – Monitor and measure your manager's effectiveness.

Modify – Coach your managers.

Engage – The company leader sets the tone. Be the example you want your managers to become.

With great power comes great responsibility.
— Spider-Man

Notes

There are five nonnegotiable characteristics that every effective leader must have: a sense of calling, an ability to communicate, creativity in problem solving, generosity, and consistency.

— John C. Maxwell

Think leadership. Quick, who comes to mind? Larger-than-life characters like Abraham Lincoln, John F. Kennedy, Mother Teresa, or Martin Luther King Jr, right? Or perhaps it's businesspeople like Jack Welch, Bill Gates, Steve Jobs, or Sheryl Sandberg.

Leadership is influence, and the people we just mentioned are some of the most influential in history. We tend to associate leadership with the John F. Kennedys of the world without recognizing the everyday leaders who walk and work among us. Even worse, we don't recognize ourselves as leaders.

This may not be a problem if you work on an assembly line, drive an over-the-road truck, or are a forest ranger. You are not. You are the owner or manager of an electrical, plumbing, or HVAC business. Coworkers put their trust in your ability to provide avenues for income, benefits, meaning, and hope. They trust in your ability to build the necessary infrastructure, systems, and processes to keep the company moving forward. They trust in your ability to oversee an operation that serves the customer. And perhaps most importantly today, they trust in your ability to facilitate their growth and development.

YOU ARE A LEADER

You are a leader. Whether or not you want to be an *excellent* leader is up to you. Sadly, many are not aware of this choice. Here's a fictional tale of two contractors and how they handled the challenges of leadership.

Joe

Joe quit working for a large HVAC contractor and started his own business. With one truck, Joe was the salesman, tech, installer, phone answerer, and CEO. Business took off. Joe started hiring. Five years later he had ten coworkers.

Those first five years were a blur. Joe's shortcomings hit him like a runaway freight train. He had been a technician, not a sales-and-numbers guy. To keep his head above water, he needed to learn how to intelligently present and offer his services. And he needed to learn how to keep track of his revenues and expenses.

Joe pursued training in sales and financials. He felt that that he needed help in marketing, but with so many urgent things going on, he never took action and he never looked back. He had no such feeling about leadership.

Joe's idea of leadership was telling his coworkers what to do. Because he couldn't keep the same ten coworkers together for more than six months, Joe's days were filled with giving orders.

Joe was a positional leader. This means Joe's ability to get things done through his people came from his position as company owner. People gave Joe their backs because that's what they were paid to do.

Tom

Tom quit working for a large HVAC contractor and started his own business. With one truck, Tom was the salesman, tech, installer, phone answerer, and CEO. Business took off. Tom started hiring help. Five years later he had ten coworkers.

Those first five years were a blur. Tom's shortcomings hit him like a runaway freight train. He had been a technician, not a sales-and-numbers guy. To keep his head above water, he needed to learn how to intelligently present and offer his services. And he needed to learn how to keep track of his revenues and expenses.

Tom knew there were successful HVAC contractors out there. One day he read a story in the *HVACR NEWS* about a contractor who had just won an award and was two hours away. Tom called Larry, who owned an eight-million-dollar operation, and they met for coffee.

Larry taught Tom that in order to get stuff done he needed to inspire his people, not tell them what to do. He told Tom about *servant leadership*. Larry also advised Tom to join a contractor alliance and to pursue sales and financial training.

The servant leader chooses to serve first. He strives to address and act on his coworker's high-priority needs. The act of tending to these needs is what leadership is all about. It energizes and stimulates the leader to continue, nurturing and developing more servant leaders along the way.

Tom embraced servant-leader training and inspired his coworkers. Although he coached and guided, he no longer told. Inspired, Tom's coworkers bought in. No one jumped ship. As Tom developed his leaders, he found more and more time to work on marketing and other areas of need in his business.

As a servant leader, coworkers gave Tom their hearts in addition to their backs. To them, work didn't feel like traditional manual labor. It was working together with purpose for a common cause.

Not Quite a Real-Life Example

For obvious reasons, Joe is not real. But you know Joe. Maybe you were Joe. Maybe you *are* Joe. No worries. It's never too late to change!

Tom's character reflects upon Chris and his early journey. These were the formative days of the Go-Time formula.

THE LAW OF THE LID

It never occurred to Joe to pursue leadership training. He thought it was for corporate big shots, not owners of HVAC companies. Joe's ability to lead was limited by his personal experience with managers and owners of companies that he worked for. One of the reasons Joe started up his own business was because he thought he could do better than his former bosses. He didn't. He had no reference to what "better" actually was. Joe hit the lid on his

Leadership ability is the lid that determines a person's level of effectiveness. The lower an individual's ability to lead, the lower the lid on his or her potential. The higher the leadership, the greater the effectiveness.

— John C. Maxwell

potential. And without any leadership training, his ability to lead was neutered. Who in their right mind would want to work for Joe?

On the other hand, Tom's ability to lead continued to grow. He pursued leadership education like John C. Maxwell's curriculum, continued to locate and learn from other leaders, and continued to develop leaders within the Go-Time Success Group. As a matter of fact, Chris, the real-life Tom, is a John C. Maxwell certified coach, trainer, and speaker.

THE NUMBER-ONE CAUSE OF CONTRACTOR FAILURE

The Law of the Lid explains why most contractors either close their doors, operate at a loss, or with minimal profit.

True leadership is about serving your people. For your coworkers to maintain and thrive you need to be able to . . .

- ★ Establish a compelling vision
- ★ Lead with purpose
- ★ Assemble the right team
- ★ Guide the company culture
- ★ Learn and utilize financial, sales, operations, and marketing education
- ★ Build systems and processes
- ★ Create business alliances
- ★ Develop your people
- ★ Develop your leaders
- ★ Develop yourself

And you need to be able to run your business with high enough profits to keep the company evolving and to pay you what you deserve. It starts with leadership and continues with leadership development.

Remember what Maxwell says, "The lower an individual's ability to lead, the lower the lid on his or her potential. The higher the leadership, the greater the effectiveness."

CULTURE

A thriving, engaged culture built on purpose is critical, especially to younger generations.

People want to:

- ★ Make a difference in the workplace
- ★ Work for an organization committed to making a difference
- ★ Belong to a cause greater than themselves
- ★ Work toward purpose
- ★ Be acknowledged and respected for their efforts
- ★ Work for a growth-minded organization

All companies have a culture. Whether it's a positive and growing culture, or a negative and toxic one, it's up to the owner.

A TALE OF TWO APPRENTICES AND HOW THEY WERE INFLUENCED BY CULTURE

Scott

Scott graduated from a vocational technical school. He found an ad on Craigslist and applied at ABC Air. The service manager, desperate for a warm body, hired him on the spot. He assigned Scott to ride with Bill, a senior tech. Bill was an apprentice once. He learned by keeping his mouth shut, fetching his senior tech's tools and dodging pipe wrenches. When he failed to dodge a pipe wrench, he never forgot the lesson. Bill was old-school.

Excited to learn, Scott asked Bill a lot of questions. Bill didn't use pipe-wrench training but, aggravated, he told Scott to keep quiet and watch. He also told him to keep quiet in front of the customer. Scott's main priority was to make sure no tool or mess got left behind.

Scott got every single hard and nasty job. Bill held the license and reminded Scott of it at every turn. Bill bragged about continuously hazing Scott to the other senior techs, who did the same thing with their apprentices.

> *Culture is a set of living relationships working toward a shared goal. It's not something you are. It's something you do.*
>
> **— Daniel Coyle**

Scott soldiered through the abuse. He came home every night beaten down. With zero enthusiasm it was hard to get up for work, yet he did. He continued fetching tools throughout his apprenticeship program until one day . . .

Scott got his journeyman license and was assigned his very own apprentice. Like Bill, Scott didn't throw pipe wrenches, but Scott did everything else like Bill, too. The cycle continues.

Zach

Zach graduated from a vocational technical school. He'd heard good things in the community about XYZ Air so he checked out the company website. He was drawn to the coworker page where he noticed a picture and bio of each coworker. Zach applied and got an interview with the service manager.

The service manager explained why the company was in business. He talked about the company mission, its core values, and painted a crystal-clear picture of where the company was going. The picture involved coworker growth and development.

Zach got the job. His first day was devoted entirely to orientation. He learned about the company's policies, processes, and procedures. He got a company identification badge, his picture taken for the website, and business cards. The service manager assigned Zach to ride with Rob, a senior technician.

Rob immediately took Zach under his wing. He encouraged Zach to talk about his wants and needs and to ask questions. Rob explained and modeled the concept of servant leadership. On the job, Rob involved Zach with diagnostics, customer interaction, upgrades and repairs. Rob talked highly of Zach in public and around the other senior techs, as they also did with their apprentices. Zach's confidence escalated, and he went home each day energized. Rob and the service manager supported his growth and development, sending him to paid training and events.

Zach eventually got his journeyman license and was assigned his very own apprentice. Like Rob, Zach taught, encouraged, and supported his apprentice's growth and development. The cycle continues.

People are not born leaders! And a growth-and-development culture doesn't happen on its own.

TRUE LEADERSHIP SEPARATES

Why are some contractors successful while others seem to agonize like an armless bandit trapped in quicksand?

Successful contractors recognize early on that leaders are not born. Leadership is a skill that, like brazing, must be learned and developed. A healthy and vibrant culture begins with the leader's intent to serve others.

This explains why, in part, two contractors in the same town, with a similar talent pool, capital, and resources, have such different levels of success. One is continually growing with a double-digit profit percentage, and another is stuck on a plateau of quicksand.

Leadership is measured by a growing and profitable company combined with a healthy culture.

LEADERSHIP POSSIBILITIES

Ben and Chris have two distinct and different personalities and communication styles, yet each shares the similar, passionate fire of servant leadership! It is the foundation upon which their leadership is built and a core reason for their business success.

The passionate care and support that Ben and Chris have for their coworkers permeated every inch of their former organizations and is evident in their individual philosophies.

An exciting possibility here is that there is more than one way to provide positive influence and one need not be a John F. Kennedy or a Bill Gates to do it.

Influence is not bringing your coworkers around to your truth, it's bringing them around to their own.

— Chris Hunter

OUR LEADERSHIP BELIEFS

Vision - Vision is a big-picture view of your desired future. It inspires and manifests a *what could be* spirit in the company. It's the model for the blueprint and processes that drive the end in the Begin With the End in Mind journey.

WHY - The WHY of why you are in business is your purpose, cause, and belief. It's a profound sense of why the company does what it does. It gives meaning to coworkers, customers and transformational relationships. Manifested in energy, it helps coworkers rise to the occasion.

Trust - Trust is the rock upon which leadership is built. It neon signs respect, integrity, consistency, authenticity and belief. To instill trust, be trustworthy.

Add Value - Serving others is the pathway to advancing our leadership. By adding value to others we help them move forward, instill confidence, enable them to be a part of something bigger and help them make a difference in the world by helping them be more of who they can be.

Influence - Leadership is influence. People follow those they believe in. Positive influence by way of adding value to others, is the most powerful benefit of leadership.

Develop Leaders - The only way to grow and truly make an impact on the world, is to develop leaders. And the only way to lead developing leaders is to grow as a leader yourself.

Inner Circle - Your inner circle is a group of trusted and diversified confidants. These folks are experienced, compatible, successful, trustworthy and determined to make a difference in the world. Their wealth of knowledge and character help to raise your self-expectations.

Connection - Leaders connect with a person's heart first and then their head. Connections lead to relationships and positive relationships move people to get on board. First connection, then positive relationships and then? Make a difference and change the world.

Legacy - A positive legacy determines whether or not a leader was successful. It's the footprints we leave behind us in the world. Live the way you want your story to be told. At some point in your journey, give back to others and your industry to make more of an impact.

Bottleneck - We rise from the bottom of the bottle towards the top. At some point we all arrive at a bottleneck - the point where our leadership abilities stop. The only way to navigate this narrow passage is through development and growth.

Take Massive Action - When opportunity arises take massive action! Once the elements of education have been separated from our failures, take massive action! The only way forward, the only way to move ahead of the pack and the only way to arrive at our vision is to take massive action.

Contact the Go-Time Online University for more on leadership training:
www.GoTimeSuccessGroup.com

THE MOST IMPORTANT SKILL

The most important connection between a growing and vibrant company and its leader is the ability of its leader to lead. Leadership is the most important skill for a company owner to pursue, develop, and have!

The bottom line in leadership isn't how far we advance ourselves but how far we advance others.

— John C. Maxwell

Goal – Set short and long-term leadership-development goals.

Observe – Continually monitor and observe other business leaders leading their organizations.

Take Massive Action – Put lessons learned into play and develop leaders within your organization.

Inspect – Have your fingers on the pulse of the company. Is there a healthy and positive company culture? Is there a vibrant growth-and-development culture?

Modify – Continue to adjust based upon what is measured in company culture.

Engage – Be an integral part of the company culture and be present in the workplace.

Notes

The most important thing I ever learned in business was to know and understand the numbers. Your income statement and balance sheet tell the history and current financial position of your company. How can you plan or make decisions without knowing where you've been and where you are? It takes capital to grow your business. Are you raising it from profits made? If you need to go to the bank, where are you getting the financial information to support your case?

— Ben Stark

Chapter 11

DO YOU WANT TO CRASH AND BURN?

You're flying a small aircraft across the Kansas countryside using visual flight rules. This means you're flying the plane based on visual cues from the landscape and the position of the sun. The weather is clear, you're beneath the clouds, and you have a clear view of your surroundings and the terrain below.

A storm descends. Clouds, rain, and fog make it impossible to orient yourself to the ground below. No worries. You switch to instrument flight rules. This means, without the aid of visual reference, you fly the plane based on instrument readings such as airspeed, altitude, and heading.

As an owner and manager, you need to operate the company at all times under instrument flight rules because, as with aircraft navigation, you can't always see what's going on around you.

For instance, a quick look at how much money you have in the bank simply tells you how much money is there. It doesn't inform you of payroll, accounts payable, or taxes owed. And the busyness of a hot summer season doesn't tell you if you're making or losing money on any particular week.

As a pilot flying the business toward your end game, it's critically important to use instrument flight rules. Fail to do so and it's almost guaranteed: You will crash and burn.

Flying by instrument flight rules is about managing your business via the income statement, the balance sheet, and the cash-flow statement.

You're not in Kansas anymore. You need to know and manage your business by the numbers.

ARE YOU MAKING MONEY? OR ARE YOU LOSING MONEY?

Is your business making more than it's spending? In other words, are you making a *profit*?

If your answers are:

- ★ I'm not sure what it costs to run my business
- ★ I'll let you know when I look at my bank account
- ★ I'll let you know towards the middle of next month
- ★ I don't know
- ★ Yes, but barely
- ★ Nope

Then one, you're not alone, and two, it's time to get serious about managing your business by the numbers.

Ben: *The most important thing I ever learned in business was to know and understand the numbers.* Your income statement and balance sheet tell the history and current financial position of your company. How can you plan or make decisions without knowing where you've been and where you are? It takes capital to grow your business. Are you raising it from profits made? If you need to go to the bank, where are you getting the financial information to support your case?

GET EDUCATED

It took Ben four years of applied effort to learn the numbers. His education consisted of taking classes, learning from successful contractors, and working with his financial documents week in and week out, month in and month out. This wasn't a process that he enjoyed. He might even describe it as something he forced himself to do.

While the learning curve is different for everyone, here's the thing: The time Ben spent in developing his financial acumen is the most important thing that he ever did in business. It paved the way for his financial success!

Do you hear that drilling, clanking, and banging? That is us pile-driving a ten-story footer into the sublevels of your brain. It supports this message: Commit to, learn, and know your numbers. Do this and you'll be ahead of ninety-five percent of your competition.

If you typically struggle to learn important topics like financial management, think about WHY you are doing it. Think about your end game and think about the people you're leading and supporting. The act of committing to and taking massive action inspired by your purpose gets stuff done.

EDUCATE YOUR MANAGERS

It's a special moment in a technician's career when the refrigerant troubleshooting light goes on. They've been told that certain high or low refrigerant readings are bad. Due to experience, they have an idea of where to look in the system for the problem, much the way a non-mechanic reacts to a check-engine light.

Prior to the light going on, the tech has had some type of trade education. Let's assume that, in vocational school, they couldn't grasp the dynamics of the refrigeration circuit and its relationship to external forces, both in the system and in the environment. Now, someone meets the technician at their level. They care for and believe in the tech. They take the time to teach and explain it so that the tech understands. The tech's confidence soars as they now have a true understanding of how external forces affect the refrigeration circuit.

As we discussed in "Key Performance Indicators" a key performance indicator (KPI) is a measurable value that demonstrates how effectively a company achieves *key* business objectives. Most operational KPIs are based on the income statement.

Actual KPIs are equivalent to refrigerant gauge readings. To truly understand the dynamics surrounding KPIs, managers must understand the income-statement numbers and where they come from.

Profitability provides options. Focused attention on our financials increases our options. For me, having options is about service, service to customers and coworkers.
— Chris Hunter

CERTIFIED PUBLIC ACCOUNTANT

Retain the services of a Certified Public Accountant (CPA). A CPA has met state licensing requirements. When it comes to your money, do you really want to trust an individual who isn't state licensed? In addition, secure the services of a CPA who has experience working for contractors and understands the nuances of the business.

SEVEN KEY FINANCIAL AREAS

We're going to briefly describe these seven financial areas. There's a lot more we could talk about here, but it falls outside of the scope of this book. For a more in-depth education and additional information, contact the Go-Time Success Group.

1. **Chart of Accounts**
2. **Income Statement**
3. **Departmentalization**
4. **Balance Sheet**
5. **Cash-Flow Statement**
6. **Breakeven**
7. **Capital and Lines of Credit**

Chart of Accounts

The *chart of accounts* is a list of accounts a company uses to record transactions on its general ledger. It's organized by the balance sheet and income statement accounts, respectively.

Income Statement

Also known as the *profit-and-loss,* or *P&L,* statement, the *income statement* documents revenue, costs, profit, and loss for a specific period of time. It's a financial report card and the primary financial tool for running your company. Basically, it documents income and the costs it takes to generate that income.

Many KPIs are based on individual line-items from the income statement. A KPI is established and then monitored month to month based on income-statement data. Take labor percentage for example. This is the percentage of labor costs against revenue. Labor costs and revenue are found on the income statement and the percentage is easily generated.

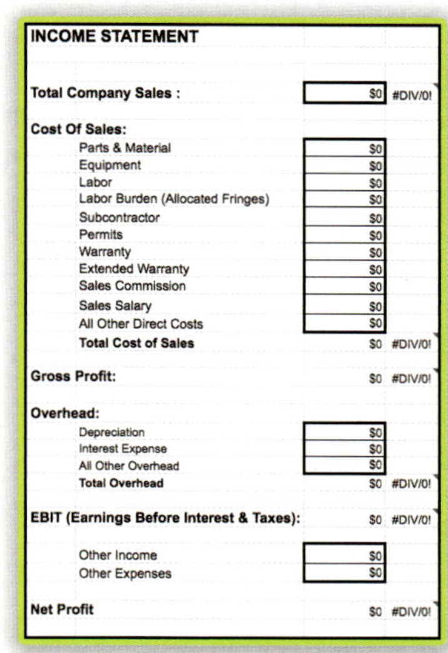

INCOME STATEMENT

Total Company Sales :	$0	#DIV/0!
Cost Of Sales:		
Parts & Material	$0	
Equipment	$0	
Labor	$0	
Labor Burden (Allocated Fringes)	$0	
Subcontractor	$0	
Permits	$0	
Warranty	$0	
Extended Warranty	$0	
Sales Commission	$0	
Sales Salary	$0	
All Other Direct Costs	$0	
Total Cost of Sales	$0	#DIV/0!
Gross Profit:	$0	#DIV/0!
Overhead:		
Depreciation	$0	
Interest Expense	$0	
All Other Overhead	$0	
Total Overhead	$0	#DIV/0!
EBIT (Earnings Before Interest & Taxes):	$0	#DIV/0!
Other Income	$0	
Other Expenses	$0	
Net Profit	$0	#DIV/0!

The process of comparing income-statement numbers and generated performance percentages to KPIs is called *benchmarking*. A differential represents either improved or lagging performance. This gap is an action item to be addressed by the owner and managers. Ben and Chris review their income statements monthly.

Additional Income-Statement Usage

Banks and Vendors – Your ability to obtain lines of credit from the bank and vendors depend on your ability to operate profitably. Consistent profits are more desirable than losses.

Investors and Buyers – The income statement is a roadmap for managing finances during a specific period of time. Manage it wisely and your company will be attractive to potential investors and buyers. Even if you have no intention of selling your company, it's best to operate it as if you intend to.

Departmentalize

Companies break down financial data by department to better understand how each department contributes to company sales and cost of goods sold. Overhead is assigned to each department in relation to consumption, or divided up between departments.

> **Ben:** Why departmentalize? If you put all your cost of goods sold and overhead in one bucket, and sales in another bucket, how can you tell which departments are profitable and which are operating at a loss?

Balance Sheet

The *balance sheet* demonstrates a company's financial position at a specific moment in time. It's a snapshot of your company's finances on one day, as opposed to the P&L which covers a span of days, weeks, months, or even years. It lists assets on one side of a sheet, and liabilities and owner's equity on the other. It's called a balance sheet because assets should always equal liabilities plus owner's equity.

The balance sheet is a big picture tool that allows the owner to gauge the health of their company. It answers these types of questions and many more:

- ★ Is there enough money to pay bills?
- ★ Is there a problem with collections?
- ★ Are there issues with inventory?

Ben and Chris review their balance sheets once per month.

Like the income statement, the balance sheet is a window into how a company operates financially. It informs banks, vendors, and prospective buyers and investors.

BALANCE SHEET

Assets:		
Current Assets:		
Cash		$0
Accounts Receivable		$0
Inventory		$0
All Other Current Assets		$0
Total Current Assets		$0
Fixed Assets:		
Total Fixed Assets		$0
Less Accumulated Depreciation		$0
Net Fixed Assets		$0
Other Assets Total:		$0
Total Assets		$0
Liabilities:		
Current Liabilities:		
Accounts Payable		$0
Current Amount Due on Notes Payable		$0
Maintenance Agreement Reserve		$0
Warranty Reserve		$0
All Other Current Liabilities		$0
Total Current Liabilities		$0
Total Long Term Liabilities:		$0
Total Liabilities		$0
Net Worth:		
Total Net Worth (Equity)		$0
Total Liabilities & Net Worth		$0

Cash-Flow Statement

Known in proper accounting terms as *the statement of cash flows, the cash-flow statement* illustrates cash and cash equivalents coming in and out of a company during a specific time period; in the contracting industry it usually measures one week.

Due to the accrual method of accounting used by most contractors, sales reported might not have been collected. And costs and expenses reported might not have been paid. Tracking cash and cash equivalents in and out on a weekly basis is a critical exercise for helping owners pay bills and run a healthy company.

Ben and Chris review their cash-flow statements weekly.

Breakeven

Every month a company has overhead (fixed expenses), like rent, insurance, salaries, and utilities, that must be paid whether or not trucks are on the road. *Breakeven* is the point in the month when the total sales equals the fixed expense amount. Some successful companies navigate by weekly and even daily breakeven points!

A sale's amount includes desired profit, a portion paid to the company's fixed expenses, and cost of sales, which includes cost of equipment, material, labor, labor burden (taxes, insurance, worker's compensation, etc.) and other job-related costs such as commissions and permits. A clear picture of these costs is found on the income statement under *cost of sales and expenses*.

The earlier in the month a company can fill the fixed-expense bucket, the more flexible it can be in pricing for the month's balance. Reduce pricing when it's slow, raise prices when it's busy.

> **Gross Profit** – *Gross profit* equals sales minus cost of goods sold. For instance, if a job sells for $100, but labor is $40 and material is $20, the cost of goods sold is $60. 100 minus 60 equals 40. The gross profit on this job is $40.
>
> **Gross Margin** – *Gross margin* is defined by percentage; the gross-profit dollars divided by the sales dollars. For instance, if a job sells for $100 and has costs of $60, the gross profit is $40. 40 divided by 100 equals a 40% gross margin.

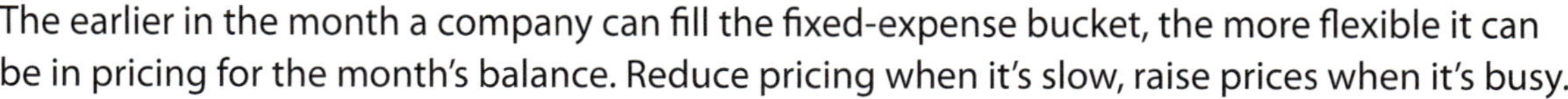

Do not save what is left after spending, but spend what is left after saving.

— **Warren Buffett**

Margin and Mark-up

Margin and *mark-up* are often confused. Let's say a contractor desires a 40% gross margin. With costs of $60, and a target of 40% gross margin, coworkers often multiply $60 X 1.40. This equals $84 and an incorrect gross margin.

Example:

A furnace installed sells for $12,000. Direct costs are equipment, labor and burden, and materials; the total equals $7,200 or 60% of the total sale. The $4,800 left over is the gross profit. In gross margin it's 40%.

So if a company's fixed expenses are $15,000 per month and the gross margin is 40%, breakeven is $15,000 divided by 40%. 15,000/.4 = $37,500

This means our company must do $37,500 in business before it can begin to make a profit.

Chris: If you cut $2,000 of fixed expense per month, how much will it bring down your breakeven?

$15,000 - $2,000 = $13,000. 13,000/.4 = $32,500. So by cutting $2,000 of fixed expense per month, you need to sell and deliver $5,000 less to start making a profit.

Wow! What if you then cut direct sales cost by 2% to bring your gross margin up to 42%? $13,000/.42 = $30,952 breakeven each month. We're getting better—more efficient and more likely to make a profit.

Capital and Lines of Credit

It's imperative that you have enough capital and secured lines of credit to operate your business.

Ben: If you have the opportunity to purchase a thirty-year-old base of service customers from another company, will you be in a financial position to do so?

Building capital starts with smart service and replacement-system pricing. Build profit into your gross margins. I recommend the first ten percent of profits go back into the company for growth and asset expansion. Additional profits are for owner share and coworker bonuses, with managers receiving a higher allotment for their management skill and effort.

Establish a good working relationship with a banker or lender. The intent is to turn the relationship into a long-term partnership. As each year passes, ask for an extension on your line of credit. My goal is to add $50,000 a year. I use this line of credit to buy assets and pay them off in three to six months. Do this and after several years you'll have accumulated enough capital and leverage to negotiate acquisition opportunities.

Have a security net in place. My rule of thumb for operating capital is to have ninety days of cash on hand to cover all overhead expenses. After the September 11, 2001 attacks it took about seventy-five days before the economy loosened up for cash to begin to flow once again in the business. This would have put us in a hole and in the vicinity of bankruptcy had we not been properly capitalized.

Chris: Do you know when you need to get a line of credit? When you don't need one. When you do need a line of credit, no banker will give it to you. Or, if they do, you'll need to put your house up for collateral.

The biggest mistake I see owners making is getting a line of credit and using it to survive. Ben knows the right way to do it. A line of credit is not designed to bail you out of reckless spending or flawed pricing models (The best resource for pricing today is Matt Michel's book *The Power of Positive Pricing*). If your finances are a mess, good luck trying to obtain a line of credit. But if you do, you are asking for serious trouble! Understand your numbers and the *why* behind using a line of credit.

MANAGEMENT

Use a purchase-order system for purchasing. Perform job costing to break out costs on equipment, material, and labor. Provide income statements to each department manager showing sales, direct job costs, and expenses assigned to respective departments. Hold departmental managers accountable to performance metrics and establish KPIs for coworkers based on their specific department.

BEN'S KPIs

KPIs are so important that we devoted an entire chapter to them. Ben is known in the industry for developing a set of KPIs that he says are a leading factor in his overall success. We include them here to highlight their direct correlation to the income statement. He uses this list monthly to guide his company.

- ★ Service labor ≤ 20%
- ★ Maintenance labor ≤ 18%
- ★ Residential replacement labor ≤ 9%
- ★ Sales-closing rate ≥ 40%
- ★ Company gross margin ≥ 45%
- ★ Replacement equipment + materials ≤ 35%
- ★ Maintenance equipment + materials ≤ 10%
- ★ Service equipment + parts ≤ 18%
- ★ Total marketing cost ≤ 10%
- ★ Total operating expenses ≤ 35%
- ★ New club memberships added to base each day ≥ 3.5

As we mentioned earlier, KPIs change based on a multitude of factors, such as company growth. Be sure to adjust KPIs based on your present reality and desired outcome.

Chris: Each month, my managers knew they had to produce so much gross profit dollars to pay our overhead. It's a static amount that they must hit before bonuses are eligible. The following is a sample report, generated by ServiceTitan, that our managers received each day.

DAILY MANAGERS HUDDLE

	Today	WTD	Last Week	MTD	Last Month	YTD
Service Requests	64	256	382	326	2022	10663
Jobs Cancelled	17	43	60	51	307	1370
Jobs Completed	57	282	343	306	1879	10020
Revenue	$29,569.00	$170,975.00	$209,800.00	$183,193.00	$1,124,793.00	$5,943,029.00
Job Avg	$519.00	$606.00	$612.00	$599.00	$599.00	$593.00
Job Avg No. Estimates	$720.00	$879.00	$864.00	$865.00	$773.00	$851.00
Goal	$61,782.00	$308,910.00	$432,473.00	$432,473.00	$1,915,239.00	$13,592,018.00
Pace		$239,365.00		$811,282.00		$9,860,025.00
Estimates	16	88	101	95	428	3048
Recalls	3	27	41	32	204	791
No Charges	8	64	76	70	483	2517
Conversion Rate	72%	69%	71%	69%	77%	70%
Replacement Rate	4%	6%	6%	6%	5%	5%

BOOKKEEPERS GONE WILD

You're probably familiar with this phenomenon: Buy a new car and suddenly you see the same model everywhere. Fortunately, you don't have to get ripped off by a bookkeeper to see that financial embezzlement happens more often than you think. Simply read an article on it or talk with other business owners and the next thing you know, every car on the road is a Ford Pinto. And it can happen with business partners too.

Chris Performed the Following Processes to Ensure Proper Bookkeeping Practices:

★ Inform the entire staff of cross-checking, verification, and audit-trail inspections.

★ All incoming mail was delivered to my home. Some companies have all bank and financial mail sent to the owner's homes.

★ We had separate accounts for payroll and operations.

★ Early on, I was the only person to sign checks. As we grew we had two people signing.

★ The coworker who input invoices did not have permission to sign checks.

★ I set alerts on credit cards to text me with every purchase over fifty dollars.

★ Proper expense reporting was key. Division managers monitored their own department financials. When incentivized by gross or net profits, I guarantee your managers will question any charge that looks off.

★ Be strategic and set up different permissions in the accounting software and bank accounts.

★ Carefully examine each division's income statement. Look for fluctuations in gross margins. Dig in and investigate the problem.

> *Beware of little expenses.*
> *A small leak will sink a great ship.*
> *— Benjamin Franklin*

Goal – Set a goal to learn how to read, analyze, and take massive action on the income statement, the balance sheet, and the cash-flow statement.

Observe – Take basic financial classes, or take a class that exceeds your current level of knowledge. Study and learn how successful contractors manage their financials.

Take Massive Action – Apply what you learn. Start with a small segment if you must, but put action into play.

Inspect – Check the results of your action. Also, be sure to carefully examine your financial documents each month.

Modify – Continue to hone your processes and procedures. Make basic adjustments if necessary.

Engage – Continue to work the process and answer the questions that your financial documents reveal.

Notes

Although I didn't realize it at the time, the effort we put into developing Super Techs to deliver superior customer service was critical to claiming our market on the pegboard and critical to the stool's seat. See how that's reflected here in what it means to be a Super Tech in our company:

★ *You commit to doing it better than anyone else. This requires investing in training and personal growth.*

★ *You go the extra mile. Do the extra thing on a call, volunteer to help others, and look for ways to go the extra mile.*

★ *You build up your team. Have a great attitude and heart for the work we do together. Teamwork makes the dream work!*

— Chris Hunter

Do customers evangelize your business? If so, why? What goes into your product and service that compels them to spread the word?

While it's possible that one of your coworkers did something heroic for the customer, more than likely it was a collection of smaller things that added up. A friendly and helpful call taker. Prompt service from a well-groomed, knowledgeable, and caring technician who fixed the problem. A technician who was thoughtful enough to inquire about health problems and articulate enough to present knowledgeable airside solutions.

★ Whatever generates positive word-of-mouth is marketing.

★ Whatever goes into making it possible to generate positive word-of-mouth *is marketing*.

So it stands to reason, whatever an owner puts into their company to make it attractive, desirable, and of value to customers and coworkers is marketing.

Marketing isn't just something a company does. Marketing isn't just a department down the hall. Marketing permeates every cell of your company's DNA. *Marketing is who you are.*

Think along these lines, put attention, care, and detail into the living structure and the customer-facing framework of your company, and you'll never have to worry about "getting the word out" again.

WHO IS YOUR MARKET?

Hint: It isn't everyone who has a pulse.

Not everyone in your market is your ideal customer. For your marketing campaigns to be effective, it's essential to define and focus on the customer who is best suited for your products and services.

The phone company is a perfect example of what happens when there is a lack of marketing focus. When was the last time you used a phone book? There's a good chance that unless a phone book was under the rump of a millennial at the dinner table, the only time they've ever touched one is to throw it away.

Your marketing should speak to the customers you'd choose if you could choose your customers.

Ben and Chris create customer avatars to help laser-focus their marketing efforts. An avatar is a composite representation of your ideal client. An avatar is a hybrid of:

- ★ People with whom you have worked, *and*
- ★ Characteristics of your favorite clients, *as well as*
- ★ Characteristics of the people you derive tremendous satisfaction and enjoyment from working with, *and*
- ★ As importantly, the people who derive satisfaction and achievement from working with *you*.
- ★ Some questions to ask when developing your customer avatar:
- ★ Who are they?
- ★ What is their gender, or what is the gender mix of the group?
- ★ How old are they?
- ★ What do they have in common?
- ★ What is their income level?
- ★ Where do they live?
- ★ What are their goals?
- ★ What are their hobbies?

Ben and Chris routinely ask more than twenty-five questions to develop and define their customer avatars. Reach out to the Go-Time Success Group for more information.

THE THREE-LEGGED STOOL

Ben has been using a perfect analogy for years to describe how interconnected marketing permeates what you do and what you are. He calls it the *three-legged stool*.

One leg stands for TOMA, *Top-of-Mind Awareness* (Also known as *branding*). A second leg is CTA, *Call to Action*. The third leg is called OM, *Opportunity Marketing*. The three legs of the stool are fastened to the seat, which is the human element that holds your company together and is outwardly manifested in the company culture. Together, the three legs support the stool and the seat holds it together. Take one leg away and the stool crashes. Take the seat away and everything crumbles.

Top-of-Mind Awareness (TOMA) — This is the activities, products, and behaviors designed to identify and represent what you want the company to be known for. We want to own the real estate in our market's brain for terms like HVAC, plumbing, and electrical. If a brand is what your customers and prospects say it is, then you'll want to design, create, and behave in ways that embody how you want them to think of you.

Ben puts together a long-range budget that's part of his culture and vision process. It's designed to fuel TOMA activities so the market will grow attached to the company culture. Don't forget, your market also includes prospective coworkers. Ben reviews and adjusts it accordingly each year.

- ★ Vehicle wraps, yard signs, building signage, billboards, signs, logos, website, business cards, and other marketing collateral
- ★ Company equipment/thermostat stickers and magnets
- ★ Company jingle, slogans, unique selling proposition
- ★ URL, web and email presence, SEO, landing page

★ Google Maps, Google My Business Profile; use Google Beacon
★ Home shows
★ Trade journals
★ Neighborhood news outlets
★ TV
★ Facebook and other social media
★ Uniforms and company-branded clothing
★ Company image
★ Coworker image
★ Contractor-branded equipment
★ Community sponsorships—charitable, athletic, and otherwise

Call to Action (CTA) — Techniques, devices, and material that make the phone ring, generate texts, and induce website clicks. Spend it and get it, if you will. The intent is to create opportunities and book calls. Included in your annual marketing budget, CTAs are turned on or off depending on the need for call volume.

All materials and activities are to be consistent with your brand intent.

Short-Term Managed Campaign — Turn on and off as needed

★ Direct mail – spring/fall tune-ups, ongoing replacement offers
★ Outbound call center
★ Social media
★ Pay-per-click, Angie's List, Google Home Services, Home Advisor
★ Email newsletters
★ Radio, cable, network TV
★ Home shows

Long-Term Marketing Commitments — Contractual commitments

★ Long-term ad campaign, Yellow Pages, local best-pick books
★ Manufacturer marketing plans

Must-Have Elements for CTA ads

★ Compelling Text and Headlines
★ Get people thinking
★ Find their concerns, address their needs and wants

Use Colors to Capture Attention

★ Bold, contrasting shades or colors

The Message

- ★ Try not to confuse
- ★ One offer at a time
- ★ Be the expert
- ★ Use headlines to apply focus
- ★ Use humor if possible

The Ending

- ★ Use the end to circle back to ad
- ★ Sincere ending with CTA using time or limited purchase to incentivize
- ★ Bold contact text and company logo

Opportunity Marketing (OM) — This is your internal marketing effort, where your coworkers meet the market face-to-face. It's a low-cost set of systems and processes orchestrated by your coworkers that optimize marketing efforts.

- ★ Call-Center Opportunity Managers
- ★ Call conversion ratio success
- ★ Proactive future scheduling of service and maintenance calls
- ★ Effective management of sales opportunities
- ★ Proactive scheduling of sales leads

Dispatch

- ★ Assigning the right call to the right technician
- ★ Customer service and follow-up
- ★ Effective and action-oriented debrief of service, maintenance, and sales calls

Networking
Small Market With Large Geographical Area and Sparse Population

- ★ Manage social-media content
- ★ Manage home shows, charity events, community outreach, chamber of commerce, Rotary, business-lead groups, and other face-to-face events
- ★ Manage friends-and-family discount programs with coworkers

> *The aim of marketing is to know and understand the customer so well the product or service fits him and sells itself.*
> — **Peter F. Drucker**

Mid-Size Market – All of the above plus cross marketing with other businesses and contractors in town. HVAC, electrical, plumbing, landscape, pest control, etc.

Large Metro Market – All of the above plus the creation of marketing alliances with like-minded contractors.

THE STOOL SEAT

The seat represents all the human involvement, development, and growth that it takes to put a desirable service and product on the street, one that people will talk about with enthusiasm. The utility and strength of the seat starts with an old business axiom: Take care of your coworkers and they'll take care of your customers.

But providing above-average . . .

- ★ pay for the region
- ★ average paid days off
- ★ benefits
- ★ health, dental, and vision
- ★ life insurance
- ★ 401(k) program
- ★ other perks

. . . only gets your company in the door.

To truly take care of your coworkers also means helping them develop their minds, and offering various career pathways, life skills, and overall mentorship.

STOOL ORCHESTRATION

The strength of the stool is three-part, and leadership is the director.

One, the design, implementation, and effectiveness of each leg's marketing activities along with the seat's blend of company benefits and leadership's ability to develop organizational humanity.

Two, management's ability to call on and direct CTA's individual players in unison with TOMA and OM.

Three, leadership's ability to assemble each leg along with the seat to produce a pleasing, rock-solid, reliable stool that will get the job done for decades.

FROM SERVICE TRUCK TO SKILLED MARKETER

How did Chris go from a one-man company to a multi-branch, multi-million-dollar organization? How did he become such a skilled marketing and branding businessman, not to mention the co-owner of a marketing company?

Short answer: The Go-Time formula.

Let's take a deeper look into Chris's story.

Chris: When it came time to name my company, I did what everyone else does: I named it after myself. In hindsight, that was a mistake. At the time, it was all about me, not on what I was doing or who I was serving.

My marketing and branding reflected this. No strategy, no continuity, no thought—just place an ad in the phone book to tell everyone how great I am.

Education creates change. After joining the Service Nation Alliance, I attended the introductory bootcamp. Change was in my near future. A lot of change!

The greatest change for me came on the heels of then-VP of Marketing Robin Jones's talk on a company's brand story. Robin asked, "Why are you in business, who is your customer, what makes you better or different, and why will they call you?"

Robin encouraged us to think of the market like a pegboard. Each spot represents a portion of the market for some company to claim. Once claimed, it's hard for others to claim it. They can try, but they're either playing catch-up or copycat.

People don't buy what you do, they buy why you do it.
— Simon Sinek

Chris: Think about it. You're the go-to company in town for heat pumps. Your brand is the peg inserted firmly into the board. What does that represent to the market? Are you the fastest? Cheapest? Install specialist? Do you have super technicians?

Thinking hard on these questions, I realized that I didn't relate to any of these points. Back at the office, I pored over all our reviews and noticed a recurring theme: We were getting five-star reviews for being fast, professional, not charging overtime, and saving the day when our customers were in need. That was it. Time to claim our market.

The Super Techs were born! We focused on fast, professional service and no overtime fees. This meant we had to be committed to serving our customers. And not committed when it suited us, but committed when our customers needed us the most. To be a Super Tech is a badge of honor for our team.

Although I didn't realize it at the time, the effort we put into developing Super Techs to deliver superior customer service was critical to claiming our market on the pegboard and critical to the stool's seat. See how that's reflected here in what it means to be a Super Tech in our company:

★ You commit to doing it better than anyone else. This requires investing in training and personal growth.

★ You go the extra mile. Do the extra thing on a call, volunteer to help others, and look for ways to go the extra mile.

★ You build up your team. Have a great attitude and heart for the work we do together. *Teamwork makes the dream work.*

As we stated earlier, what an owner puts into their company to make it attractive, desirable, and of value to customers and coworkers is marketing. And to demonstrate how marketing is who we are, the brand we are trying to establish, is also a standard that revolves around our mission: Keep customers comfortable, save customers money, commit to doing it better than anyone else, and honor God with our heart for the work.

Let's Continue Listening to Chris as he Talks About Marketing and Lessons Learned from his Dad

Chris: Once we got a foothold on branding, we needed to learn how to deliver it and make it known. The only real experience I had in building a customer base was watching and learning from my dad as he built a network-marketing business.

After twenty-three years of service with a local corporation he was laid off during a merger. Then he started a network-marketing business providing phone service. I quickly learned that building a client base was all about influence: getting people to know you, like you, and trust you.

He was able to influence people with his enthusiasm and passion—even in the face of criticism of working as a network marketer. His business eventually ran its course, but the relationships and influence that he built provided other lucrative opportunities. People said he was lucky. Maybe he was. He always told me, "The harder you work, the luckier you get!"

His example of building positive relationships and influence has been a powerful North Star in my career.

As a kid playing baseball, my dad would tell me, "If you're going to do it, might as well hit it with all you've got!" This is exactly what we do today as Super Techs. He also said, "Look good, play good!" This speaks to professionalism and displaying and engaging our brand in the community on a consistent basis.

CHRIS BRINGS MARKETING, BRANDING, AND INFLUENCE TOGETHER

Chris: Word of mouth is the best form of marketing. Combine it with digital and social-influencing channels and watch out. Good things start to happen exponentially when the power of digital amplifies one's word of mouth.

If you want your company to grow, you need to invest in branding it. Not the manufacturer, *you.* Create your brand then put it out there.

> ## *Your culture is your brand.*
> ### *— Tony Hsieh*

CHRIS'S TOP SEVEN WAYS FOR IMMEDIATE AND MAXIMUM IMPACT:

Set up your Google My Business listing – This is critical for appearing in the Google Map Pack search results including a local map. It's one of the first things searchers see.

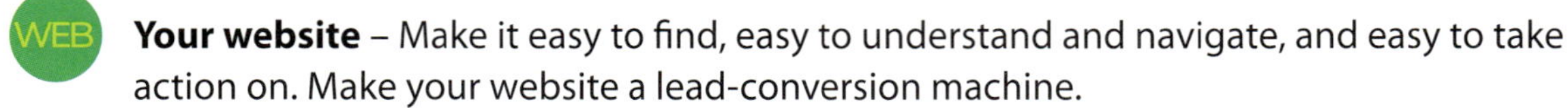
Your website – Make it easy to find, easy to understand and navigate, and easy to take action on. Make your website a lead-conversion machine.

Facebook and other social-media channels – Engagement powers results. Be social! Connect with customers and prospective customers. Connect with prospective coworkers. And connect your company culture and coworkers to the public.

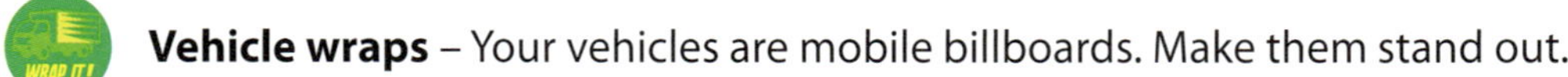
Vehicle wraps – Your vehicles are mobile billboards. Make them stand out.

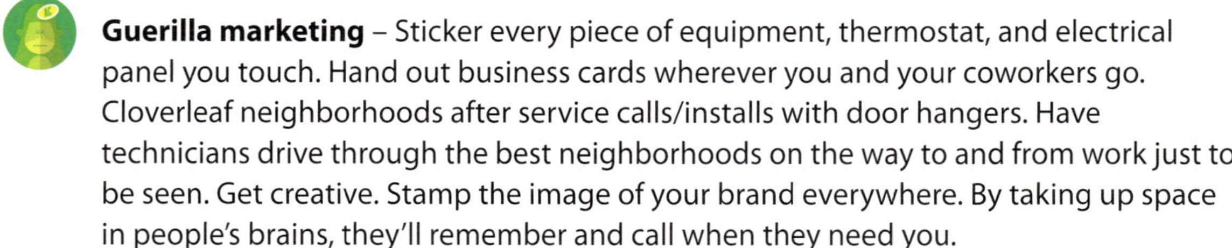
Guerilla marketing – Sticker every piece of equipment, thermostat, and electrical panel you touch. Hand out business cards wherever you and your coworkers go. Cloverleaf neighborhoods after service calls/installs with door hangers. Have technicians drive through the best neighborhoods on the way to and from work just to be seen. Get creative. Stamp the image of your brand everywhere. By taking up space in people's brains, they'll remember and call when they need you.

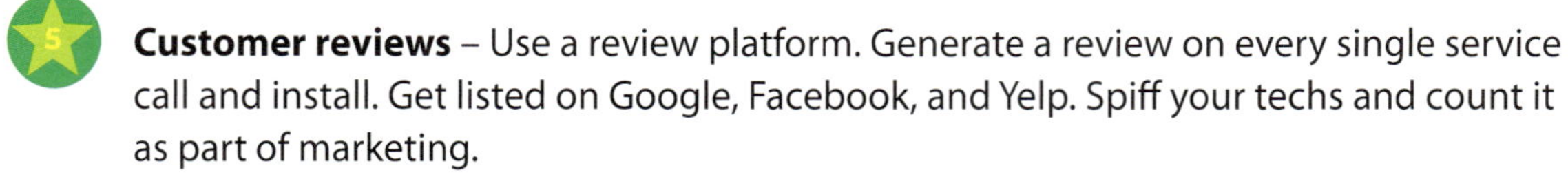
Customer reviews – Use a review platform. Generate a review on every single service call and install. Get listed on Google, Facebook, and Yelp. Spiff your techs and count it as part of marketing.

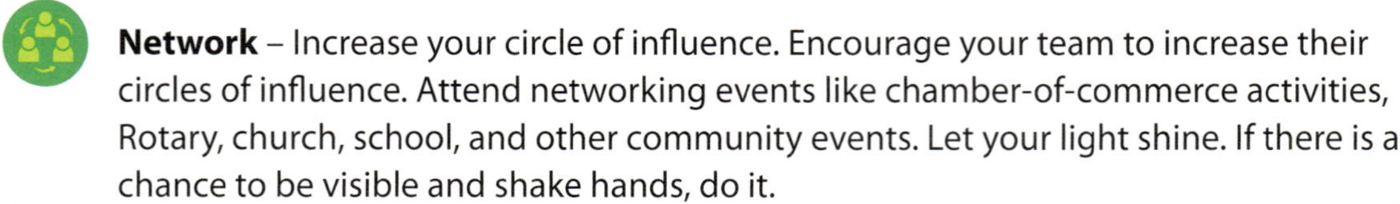
Network – Increase your circle of influence. Encourage your team to increase their circles of influence. Attend networking events like chamber-of-commerce activities, Rotary, church, school, and other community events. Let your light shine. If there is a chance to be visible and shake hands, do it.

YOUR MARKETING: BURN & CHURN OR AN INVESTMENT?

It's important to understand that Call-to-Action marketing efforts like . . .

- ★ Direct mail
- ★ Pay-per-click
- ★ Radio & TV
- ★ Print ads
- ★ Social media CTA
- ★ Billboards

. . . sometimes referred to as *Burn & Churn,* are designed to drive customers to take action *now*. They reflect a spend-it-and-get-it mindset.

Whereas efforts like . . .

- ★ Website
- ★ Social-media TOMA
- ★ Customer reviews
- ★ Vehicle wraps
- ★ Community events
- ★ Search-engine optimization

. . . are TOMA, designed to be a long-term investment reflecting the leadership, consistency, and permanence of your brand.

Both CTA and TOMA are critical to the success of your company. Use a good mix, test your efforts, and track the results.

> *It's easier to make products and services for the customers you seek to serve than it is to find customers for your products and services.*
> — *Seth Godin*

TEST AND TRACK YOUR MARKETING RESULTS

What action did your CTA campaign generate?

Chris: I like to send a free offer or Facebook post to a small group to test the waters. If it works, I know we hit the offer and audience at the right time. If not, it was the wrong message, audience, and/or time.

        We also test different email newsletter headlines and then go with what generates the best results.

Ben: We'll try different versions of various mail-outs like the tune-up letter and go with what works best.

TRACKING

Is your marketing working? A campaign designed to produce system replacement turns over one hundred leads. *Great.* You kept track of the leads. But ultimately, from a tactical standpoint, this type of marketing is designed to produce *revenue*. How many leads converted to sales? What was the total dollar amount in revenue? And was that cost worth the marketing expenditure?

Mrs. Jones calls your office. Betty the CSR asks, "Where did you hear about us?"

Mrs. Jones replies, "Your website, dear."

Really?

Betty: "So you googled something like *air conditioning replacements* and our name came up?"

Mrs. Jones: "Oh no, dear. We've received your flyers in the mail before. I remembered the name because of the ads and I see your trucks in the neighborhood. I just didn't have the number. That's why I googled your company."

Mrs. Jones is responding to your direct mail (and trucks), not your website. It's important for your CSRs to dig into each call and get to the root of how and where people are hearing about your company.

ANNUAL TRACKING

A handful of marketing efforts are successful during a given year and some are not. Be sure to track successful campaigns and the season in which they were run. It wouldn't hurt to record the outside temperature at that time. This way you're not reinventing the marketing wheel each year.

SERVE YOUR CUSTOMERS

This Bible verse, often quoted by Chris, points directly to the Super Tech mission: *Work willingly at whatever you do, as though you were working for the Lord rather than for people.* (Colossians 3:23 NLT)

Note how both Ben and Chris's company missions underscore the desire to serve their customers?

Vision is clearly seeing new opportunity. Achievement requires a plan of action, failures, modification, and amendments.

— Ben Stark

Goal – Develop a customer avatar and run one Facebook marketing initiative.

Observation – Learn how to create a customer avatar. Observe Facebook ads. Ask fellow contractors about their efforts.

Take Massive Action – Create the ad and post it to Facebook.

Inspect – Track the results.

Modify – Continue to develop the avatar and tweak the ad.

Engage – With one solid marketing initiative under your belt, learn the lessons and begin another. Keep repeating the process.

Notes

A selling system is a set of processes and procedures designed to facilitate an organized, consistent, professional, and positive interaction between customer and coworker.

— Ben and Chris

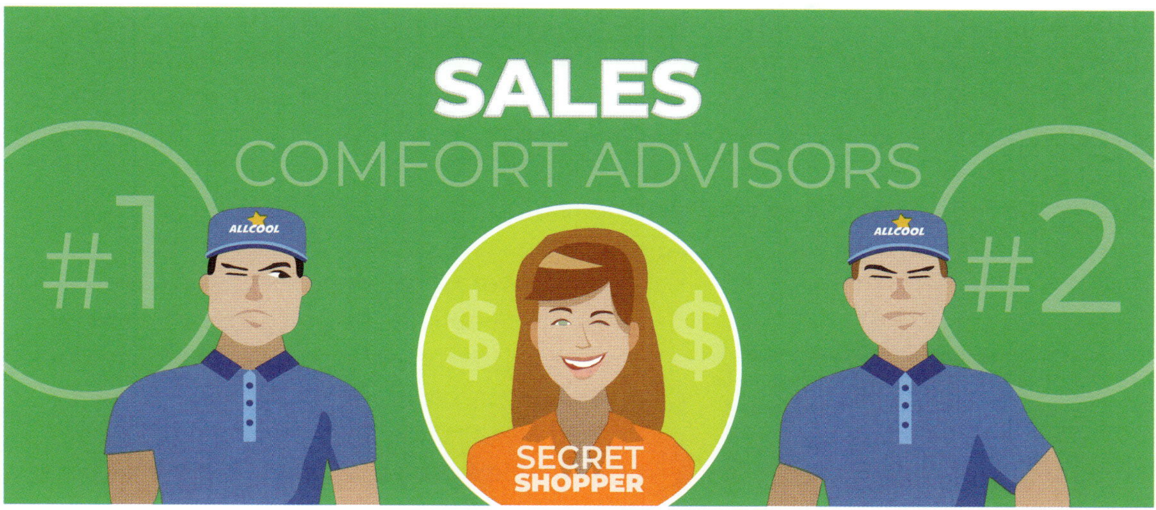

What if your company inadvertently booked two different comfort advisors for the same customer? What if the customer recognized the error, decided to pit one against the other in hopes of getting a better price, and decided not to say anything? Awkward, right?

Noticing that his comfort advisor's closing percentages were in decline, Chris sent two comfort advisors out to the same house at different times on purpose. Using a secret shopper, his intention was to gather intel in hopes of improving his coworker's skills. While it was a great learning experience, it was also awkward.

We're starting this chapter with Chris's story because finding a remedy for declining sales-closing percentages, along with a host of other sales-related problems, is one of the most important things a business owner can do.

We'll Get to That Remedy in a Moment, but First Let's Experience Chris's Pain

SECRET SHOPPING

The secret shopper's name was Julia. Denton was the first comfort advisor to come out and Stan was the second. Here is Julia's assessment as told to Chris:

Denton – Very professional in how he presented himself, although he didn't have shoe covers on. I expected him to, since you told me they wear them. He did a good job looking at everything and then explained what he was looking for. He seemed knowledgeable. He let me know the outdoor unit was only five years old and we didn't need to replace it. The furnace was very old. He told me we needed an air vent downstairs and explained how they'd install it. He gave a few different monthly payment options if we wanted to finance.

Stan – Very professional and wore shoe covers. He found a problem with the water heater. He attempted a repair but did not have the correct material. After checking the electrical panel, he found issues with that as well. He presented a repair price and whole-system replacement price along with new ductwork. He offered financing.

Chris Asked Julia, "What could they have done better?"

Denton – Wore shoe covers. Presented more replacement options. It seemed the option he gave us, for the furnace alone, was based on what he thought we could afford. I felt he was closed-minded. He didn't say anything about the water heater or the electrical panel, so I don't think he even looked at them.

Stan – He presented four different equipment options. He didn't explain why the ductwork needed to be replaced. Denton didn't give us a price on that. He said it would be difficult to get an air vent downstairs and that we should put a window unit in. I asked why we needed to replace the outdoor unit as it was only five years old. He mentioned something about the warranty not being as good with only half a system. I asked if we could keep it. He said yes but he didn't give me a price for that option.

"On a Scale of One to Ten, How Would You Rate Them?"

Denton – I would have given him a nine before Stan came out. But after Stan presented more options, I gave him a five.

Stan – At first a nine. But compared to Denton, he didn't give us an option for the outdoor unit and he didn't think we could put an air vent downstairs. I gave him a five too.

Overall, they were not consistent. It was like they came from two different companies.

"If You Were Going to Buy From Only One, Which Would You Pick?"

They both came at it from different angles. They didn't give me comparable options. I would have gone with Denton because he had the lower price.

Ouch!

It's interesting that Julia gave both comfort advisors a nine when judged individually. But after getting estimates from each, she gave them a five. When neither presented a clear solution, it all came down to price. How many times does this happen when a competitor comes out after our people?

So what is that remedy that Chris spoke of? What can you do in your company to prevent runaway confusion? Answer: Put a selling system into place and use it!

SELLING SYSTEMS

Chris: When studying all of the great home-service companies, I noticed they all had repeatable and consistent selling systems.

A selling system is a set of processes and procedures designed to facilitate an organized, consistent, professional, and positive interaction between customer and coworker. Adhering to a selling system minimizes the conflicting needs-assessment and solutions offered, as we've just seen between Denton and Stan.

Over the years, Ben and Chris developed their own individual selling systems, yet they're very similar. As with many of the processes described in our book, we combined the best of both. Still, a piece was missing. We needed something to bond the system together.

So one day the sales brain trust from the Go-Time Success Group, which includes Ben, Chris, Chuck Morales, and Trapper Barnes, pulled out the blowtorches, steel, and welding compound and bonded away.

> *Sales is an outcome, not a goal. It's a function of doing numerous things right, starting from the moment you target a potential prospect until you finalize the deal.*
> — *Jill Konrath*

C.A.R.E.

The fire, steel, and effort that day produced what is known as the *C.A.R.E. Selling System*. It's beyond the scope of this book to detail it in full, but the following is a brief outline. Contact the Go-Time Success Group for additional details.

C- CONNECT

C stands for Connect, as in *connect with the customer and form the relationship with trust*. Without trust, you don't stand a chance. People buy from those whom they like and trust. From the first point of contact, whether it's from your CSR or technician, it's imperative that your customer is made to feel cared for. Key elements are preparation, execution, and follow-up.

In order to connect with and relate to your prospective customer and become effective in sales, Ben and Chris recommend that your comfort advisors and technicians be trained in a system that helps them understand personality and behavioral styles. A popular system today is the DISC model, a behavioral assessment tool that also provides a common language that people can use to better understand themselves and to adapt their behaviors to others.

Customer Contact

- ★ Whether it's the CSR, comfort advisor, or tech, make a heartfelt first impression
- ★ Tech: Set up lead for comfort advisor
- ★ Sales coordinator/CSR: Send comfort advisor biography in advance to customer

Planning the Sales Call

- ★ Confirm call time and decision-making process
- ★ Come prepared
- ★ Read service-call notes and research customer history (if applicable)

★ Prepare documentation. Bring or ensure digital access to:

> ☆ Customer questionnaire
> ☆ Duct design
> ☆ Heat loss/Heat gain.
>
> ☆ Product guide (for customer)
> ☆ Company folder (for customer)
> ☆ Proposal (for customer)

★ Preplan parking, house approach, and customer greeting
★ Survey the neighborhood. Make notes

Greet Customer

★ Make introductions
★ Build a relationship by finding similar interests
★ First-name basis is best
★ Be prepared for children, dinner preparations, a neurotic dog, any distractions

Connecting and caring for what is best for your customer begins by asking the right questions to identify desires and needs. Take this approach over trying to sell the most expensive system.

A - ASSESSMENT

A stands for Assessment. The assessment begins with questions to the homeowner. This can also be performed via a digital questionnaire prior to visiting the customer's house. An informed comfort advisor can establish a connection with more speed and ease.

★ Perform customer questionnaire (in advance if possible)
★ Sit with customer, share table
★ Define and confirm customer's objectives
★ Define your objectives
★ Build trust through education
★ Review customer's needs

> *Approach each customer with the idea of helping him or her to solve a problem or achieve a goal, not of selling a product or service.*
>
> *— Brian Tracy*

THE DESIGN

With the questionnaire in hand covering the customer's comfort needs and budget, the system design can commence.

- ★ Identify contributing factors
- ★ Involve customer with the process; continue to educate
- ★ Walk through and take pictures throughout the process
- ★ Perform heat loss/gain
- ★ Size equipment
- ★ Perform static pressure testing on ductwork
- ★ Design ductwork
- ★ Show customer best possible way to reduce heat loss/gain
- ★ Demonstrate how to repair previous design flaws
- ★ Cover and offer home-performance solutions

R - RECOMMEND

R stands for recommend. While some recommendations are made during the walk-through, this stage of the CARE process covers the formal presentation and recommendations.

- ★ Presentation starts with ductwork and then moves to air quality and type of system, and covers additional products and services like attic insulation, water treatment, home sealing, etc.

- ★ Present four different systems. Place a star on the most popular system sold in that area. Start with the most expensive system and work from there.

- ★ Lead with payment options to fit their budget, not total system price.

- ★ Identify personality types. Some customers want the best system, some want to be told what to buy, and others want lots of details. We are the experts. So help your customer with the recommendations.

E - EXECUTE

E stands for Execute. This is where the rubber meets the road. You've established a connection with your customer, performed the necessary homework with diligence, and have verbally made your recommendations.

- ★ Ensure decision maker is present
- ★ Deliver proposal at first sales call
- ★ Having prepared for objections, overcome any that arise
- ★ Walk through warranties and financing
- ★ Ask for the sale
- ★ Sign paperwork
- ★ Obtain a down payment
- ★ Schedule the install
- ★ Follow up install/Happy call

Internal Execution

The handoff verbiage here is for the sake of explanation. Most contractors today use some form of digital documentation.

- ★ Handoff sales documentation and financing to appropriate internal personnel
- ★ Handoff job notes including pictures to the install team

Post-Call Follow-Up (if not Sold)

Send a letter or email to prospect and follow up with a phone call.

- ★ Thank prospect for the meeting
- ★ Recap meeting
- ★ Review agreed-upon next steps
- ★ State future intentions

Astute readers will notice that we've used a variation of two Mary Kay Ash quotes so far. Great observation! We feel it's that important.

> *Pretend that every single person you meet has a sign around his or her neck that says, 'Make me feel important.' Not only will you succeed in sales, you will succeed in life.*
>
> *— Mary Kay Ash*

LEAD GENERATION

Lead generation, turnover, and execution are the lifeblood of your company. With your comfort advisors working a well-oiled sales process, data is generated. You know how many calls your comfort advisors must go on to generate *X* amount of dollars. At this point, leads become a numbers game. Generate *X* amount of leads and you'll generate *X* amount of business.

★ Determine daily, weekly, and monthly revenue requirements during your annual success-planning event.

★ Determine how to deal with seasonal swings.

★ Identify potential lead sources.

★ Figure one lead out of every eight demand service calls run. How many calls do you need to run per month for your target amount of leads?

★ Figure one lead out of every thirteen maintenance calls run. How many maintenance calls do you need to run per month for your target amount of leads?

★ Opportunity Managers (CSRs)—follow up tech recommendations. How many calls are required per month to reach your target amount of leads?

★ Call-to-action—How many leads do you need to set your marketing budget for? What is your response and closing rate? Set your target.

★ Internal conversion—The higher your call conversion rate is, the lower your marketing budget is.

★ Set target amount of self-generated leads for comfort advisors.

★ Home show—Measure seasonally or quarterly. Set a goal.

★ Referral program—Fifteen to twenty percent of total leads run. Set goals.

★ Expectations—Goals, KPIs, and expectations should be posted and measured daily.

A PROFESSIONAL SALES FORCE

In today's wild, wild west of HVAC equipment availability, homeowners can purchase equipment themselves, either online or from one of your local distributors, then hire a Slim Shady operator to install it.

Ben: While this is true, a homeowner cannot perform heat loss, heat gain, and ductwork calculations. They are generally not up to date on the latest available technologies. They cannot survey the existing system for compatibility. They do not have the wherewithal to design and put together a new system that works properly, efficiently, and perhaps most importantly, safely. And they'll certainly not be able to obtain any type of warranty.

A professional comfort advisor can assess, calculate, design, educate, and present various options to the homeowner that will help to keep them comfortable and save money on utility bills. The organization will follow up to ensure performance, satisfaction, and make sure club memberships are in place to protect warranties and provide peace of mind.

*We don't rise to the level of our expectations,
we fall to the level of our training.*

— Archilochus

Goal – Establish a selling process.

Observe – Learn from individuals and institutions.

Take Massive Action – Role-play with comfort advisors and put process into play.

Inspect – Examine process to ensure adherence, quality, and consistency.

Modify – Depending upon effectiveness, change steps in process.

Engage – Take it to the streets, delight customers, and continue to refine the process.

Notes

The contractor started his company in the mid-2000s. Business was up, down, and profitability was nowhere to be found. The only consistent thing in his organization was inconsistency. Slugging it out in the summers, getting by in the falls and winters, and holding his breath from January to June. He hung on by a string.

When asked if he did any annual planning he said, "You bet I did. I sat down toward the year's end and looked at my financials. I then said I plan and hope to do better next year."

And how was that working out? "As soon as I got busy, my plan, which was really just a wish, went out the door. I then proceeded to do exactly what I did the year before. And I got the same results. I didn't make any money this year either."

Chris: This was me. Then, in 2012, I attended my first Service Nation Alliance annual success-planning training. At first I was intimidated and overwhelmed. But I found with an open mind, proper guidance, and a systemized approach, I could do it!

And how did *that* work? In 2012 alone, I went from being a non-profit business to one with double-digit profitability. This process continued to add value to my company year after year until I sold the business in 2018. It was a contributing factor in the appeal to private-equity firms and investors.

PLANNING EXPERIENCE

Ben's first annual planning session was in 1992, twenty years before Chris and the Super Techs broke the double-digit net-profit barrier. Ben's companies have maintained at least ten percent net income before taxes since, and average into the mid-teens with an average fourteen percent annual revenue growth.

Ben: Annual planning has been the most important change I made to become a successful business owner!

The most critical point in the planning process is to set the stage for what you want to become. In each year's annual success-planning session, we begin by reviewing, and adjusting if necessary, our vision, mission, and the WHY of why we are in business.

Goal-setting is a must. Goals serve as a challenge to make us better.

INVALUABLE EXPERTISE

Imagine building, developing and refining a concept over twenty-seven years in business. Throw in teaching annual success planning for a number of years and it's safe to say one would qualify as an expert. Consider Ben an expert. Once a student (and always a student), and now a teacher, Chris is also a resident annual-planning expert and instructor. Contact the Go-Time Success Group for more information!

The following is a step-by-step breakdown of the annual planning process that they both teach.

The Game Plan

1. WHY, vision, mission, and core-values statement review
2. Debrief last year — What went well? What didn't? What did you learn?
3. Why us? Weaknesses, external threats, and opportunities
4. Company growth breakdown (the numbers)
5. Manpower — where, when, and how?
6. Recruit/Retain

7. Marketing budget
8. Train/cross train—what, where, and how much?
9. Organizational chart
10. Wish list
11. Action plan — how will we achieve the vision?

WHY, Vision, Mission, and Core-Values Statement Review -
Review your WHY, vision, mission and core-values statements each year. Your WHY will not change and seldom will your core values. The vision and mission, however, might. Update at this time if necessary.

WHY Are You in Business? - What is your purpose, cause, or belief? Why does your company exist? Why do you get out of bed every morning? And why should anyone care?

Vision - With the end game as your destination, the vision is a brief, yet detailed statement designed to develop an internal view of the company's long-term culture and success plan.

Mission - The mission is a statement that describes how the company achieves its vision.

Core Values - The core values are how we carry out our mission. They are guidelines for our behavior and actions.

THE GOOD, THE BAD AND THE UGLY: DEBRIEF LAST YEAR

★ What went well?   ★ What didn't go well?

★ What about people?   ★ What did we learn?

Success starts with a clear vision of the future and a detailed understanding of the past.

— Ben Stark

WHY US? WEAKNESSES, EXTERNAL THREATS, AND OPPORTUNITIES

Why us? is an evaluation of what a company is good at. *Weaknesses* are areas in need of improvement. *External threats* are forces outside of your company's control that leadership needs to be aware of. And *opportunities* are areas of growth, increased revenue, and profits. A growing and striving organization needs to clarify what it's good at, what it needs to improve, to identify external threats, and to optimize opportunities.

Why Us?

Chris and the Super Techs break down what they are good at by location. The following information is from their 2017 success plan, prior to the sale of his business.

Ardmore

1. Reputation - We are very well branded.
2. Fast! We are the fastest to respond. We have the largest group of Super Techs around.
3. One-call solution. We provide HVAC, plumbing, electrical, insulation, drain cleaning, and indoor air quality.

Ada

1. Fast! We are the fastest at responding to needs.
2. Reliable - We do what we say we're going to do.
3. No overtime fees!

Chris's three other locations had similar responses. In sum, the Super Techs provide fast, professional service with no overtime fees. In turn, the company's marketing reflects these strengths, which is the answer to the question, why us?

Weaknesses

In that same 2017 plan, the Super Techs identified a list of weaknesses and then provided actionable solutions. Here are a couple:

Communication - As we continue to grow, communication with our customers and team will be an area in need of continuous improvement.

Solution - Improve our answering service, CSR on-call team, internal Facebook, hire marketing director to coordinate efforts and dedicate a dispatcher to improving communications.

Efficiency - We need to improve in all areas. Improve the service-labor percentage.

Solution - Organizational changes to facilitate more coaching, monitoring, and feedback for areas in need.

Problem-Solving Process

Ben created a problem-solving process that his team uses at this point of the success plan (in addition to using it throughout the year).

- ★ State the problem
- ★ Define the problem
- ★ List or state possible solutions
- ★ State best long-term solution
- ★ Develop an action plan
- ★ Implement the plan—take massive action
- ★ Set time to revisit and follow up the plan

External Threats

Companies face threats from outside of their organizational walls. Examples are the economy, government, weather, and business reputation. Here is how Chris handles two threats in that 2017 success plan.

Chris: In regards to online reviews and Facebook, rant-and-rave pages are a reality. This is a big threat to our reputation. The key is to address the issue quickly with a public, positive statement. Then handle it offline immediately. If you've nurtured and cultivated your customer base, the most enthusiastic customers will come to your defense in public.

Build as many positive reviews as we can so the negative reviews look like a small percentage.

Competition - They are stepping up their game by starting to do what we do. We can overcome this by continuing to be the market leader and not get complacent with our service and progress.

External Opportunities

Opportunities are strewn across your business landscape! It's important to always keep your radar up and be attentive. Examples are business suppliers, brand perception, new technologies, and communications.

Business relationships - We provide an in-depth view on the power of business relationships in the chapter titled *"Transformational Relationships."* For now we use the word suppliers for clarity.

Both Ben and Chris have outstanding relationships with Lennox International, an air conditioning manufacturer.

Ben: Lennox has been a great supporter of Sunny Service and the Five Star Guys organization. They are invested in the growth of each. I can't say enough about the importance of supplier relationships! Suppliers are just the start. It continues with marketing, bankers, fleet management, accountants, and lawyers. All have an impact on our bottom line.

Chris: Lennox and Johnstone (representing Amana), were helpful with annual planning. They provided sales reports, shared trends, offered to bring in consultants, and even fund the offsite location. Clearly communicate with your key suppliers what you are trying to accomplish and, all things considered, it's possible they'll put resources towards your effort.

Your business suppliers can also help create a competitive advantage for your company. For instance, our intention was to put a full-court press on a certain market. Our suppliers offered extra co-op dollars for advertising, discount equipment, or extend a free warranty during seasonal slowdowns.

I recommend involving your key business suppliers during a portion of the annual success planning event. Just be transparent with your objectives and needs, and realize it's a strategic relationship striving for a win-win outcome.

You should keep a working list of opportunities throughout the year and work the list on at least a monthly basis.

Departmental Growth

Departmentalize income statements for service, production/install, and your other departments. A departmentalized income statement focuses on revenue, cost of sales, and overhead for a specific department. Departmentalization allows:

- ★ A detailed evaluation of each department.
- ★ Important data used in evaluating department managers.
- ★ A breakdown of revenue and gross margin contributed by each department.
- ★ A more precise roadmap for improving company performance and profitability.

You'll notice this is the second time we've mentioned departmentalizing income statements. Yes, it's that important!

In success planning, departmental growth is evaluated by looking at last year's and this year's metrics along with percentage of change. A forecast is then based upon this data.

MANPOWER REQUIREMENTS

By way of historical records, a company establishes productivity for each department. For instance, it knows that by averaging three calls and running four techs per day, it will do twelve calls per day. Add in available days to work and you'll know the service call capacity for a given month.

Assign an average ticket amount for demand service and maintenance and the company can project revenue for a given time frame. The same applies for install.

> *By failing to prepare,*
> *you are preparing to fail.*
> *— Benjamin Franklin*

When the company bases what it knows on production, it can calculate manpower requirements to meet projected growth. Set up a spreadsheet and vary average ticket and available manpower to simulate various revenue outcomes.

RECRUIT AND RETAIN

Recruit - Write out your recruiting plans for the year. See the "Recruit, Hire, Retain" chapter.

Retain - What are you consistently doing to cement coworkers' relationships with the company? Are these activities in alignment with your WHY, vision, mission, and values? What are you doing to make your company a desired and best place to work? Detail your efforts for the year.

MARKETING

Are your marketing plans aligned with the company's growth needs? Annual planning is the time to reevaluate, and adjust if necessary, your market, brand, programs, strategies, and budget in order to fuel growth.

Define Your Market - Who will you serve? Identify ideal personas. What are the demographics? What is your market area?

Brand - A brand is a gut feeling about a product, service, or company. It's not what the company says it is, it's what the *public* says it is. Are you working toward a desirable brand?

Branding - The act of communicating your brand to customers and coworkers. It's taking action to drive the opinion that you want the public to have about your product, service, or company.

Programs: Marketing Stool - How will you mix Top-of-Mind Awareness, Call-to-Action, and Opportunity Marketing? (See the "Marketing," chapter).

Marketing Strategies - What's working? What's not working? How can it be fixed? Which ones will you focus on?

Radius Marketing - Focus on a set number of homes within a small radius of a neighbor's system replacement.

Umbrella Marketing - Cast a wide net to build awareness and mental stickiness.

Target Marketing - Market directly to a specific group of people based on a product or specific service.

MARKETING BUDGET

What percentage of total annual revenue should you spend on marketing? Hint: It's related to your desire for company growth.

Established Company	**New Company**
3-5% – Very conservative	5-7% – Very conservative
6-8% – Healthy	8-10% – Healthy
9% and above – Aggressive	11% and above – Aggressive

TRAINING / CROSS TRAINING

Training - Cover all aspects of the business and include all coworkers. How much money should you budget for training? Sufficient training is required for X increments of company growth. Growth can be throttled by marketing. Consequently, start off budgeting half of the marketing budget for training. For instance, if your marketing budget is eight percent of total revenue, budget four percent for training.

The following are a few suggested areas of required training:

* Life-skills
* Service and install procedures
* Technical
* Safety
* Customer service and communication
* Sales
* Leadership
* Management
* Marketing
* Software
* Office and bookkeeping
* Product knowledge

Practice - Professional sports teams practice. You're a professional, so practice.

* Service calls
* Sales calls
* CSR duties

Cross Train - Cross training is one of the most neglected contractor functions today. Each position needs to learn the other one.

* CSR to dispatch
* Service to install
* Maintenance to service
* CSR & dispatch to service
* CSR to bookkeeping and/or data entry
* Service to sales
* Install helper to warehouse

Contact the Go-Time Success Group for training plans and digital calendars. If you're a Service Roundtable member, there is an excellent training calendar called *Training Wizard* in the download section.

ORGANIZATIONAL CHARTS

See the Go Time Success Group for additional organizational charts.

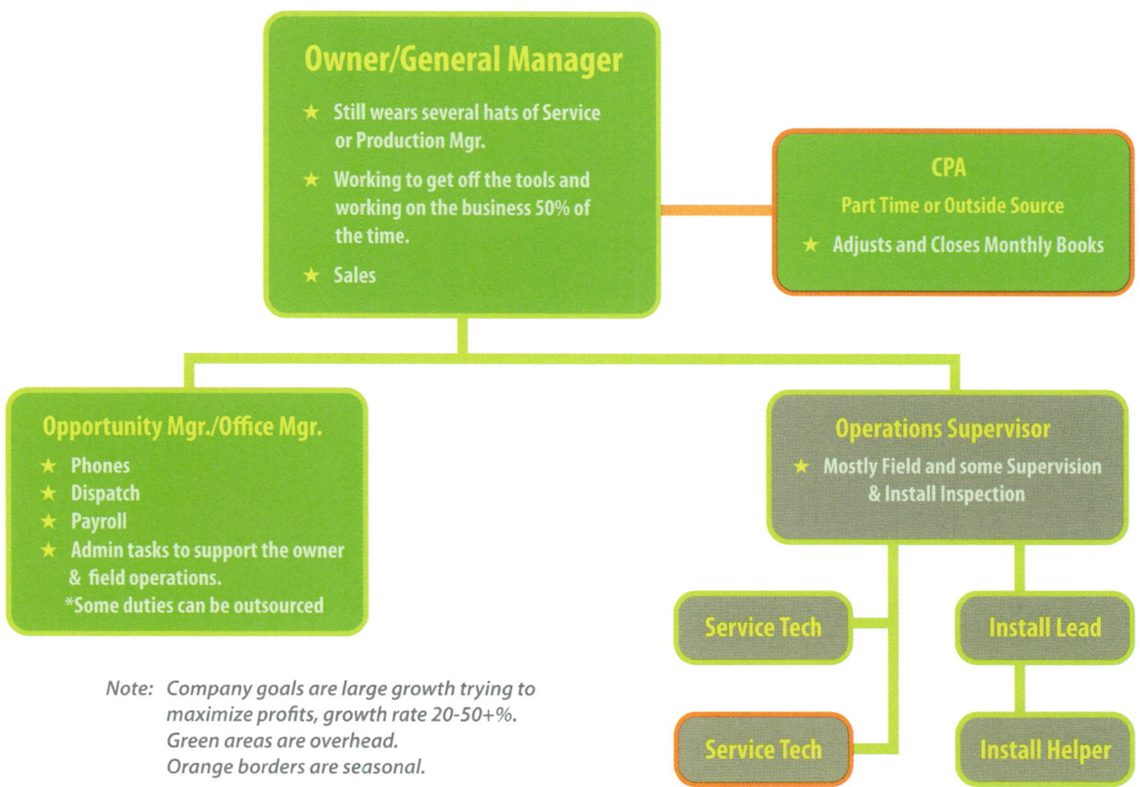

WISH LIST

Document items and budget numbers for company upgrades.

- ★ Facility improvements
- ★ Vehicles
- ★ Equipment, meters, and tools
- ★ Computer software
- ★ Computer hardware
- ★ Training

The best way to predict the future is to create it.

— Peter Drucker

GOALS AND ACTION PLAN

The annual success plan is a living and breathing document. The act of putting your heart and soul into creating one endears you to it. So *use* it—with all your heart and soul. It's a compass and North Star for the year ahead. Don't get lost. Use it.

Chris: One of my leaders was struggling with his department's performance. He came to me asking for advice. The fact is, he had already created and turned in an awesome action plan that, if followed, would have had his department firing on all cylinders. When I reminded him of his efforts I could see the light bulb come on! He reviewed his plan and told me if he hadn't veered from it he wouldn't be in the predicament that he was. He put the time into the success planning process and created a great plan. Problem is he forgot the "T": Take massive action!

Goal – What is your detailed destination? Share with team leaders.

Observe – Understand where you have been. Look for examples of where you want to be.

Take Massive Action – You have the vision; you have the written plan. Now it's time to take massive action! The best ideas and plans never got off the ground until action is taken. I

Inspect – Understand what is going on in the process. Know the facts and review.

Modify – Don't continue to make the same mistakes. Learn, adapt, and adjust. Start over if you have to.

Engage – Define problems and goals. Develop a plan of attack. Take massive action and follow up.

Notes

Do you want to expand? The key is to get your house in order first. Create a repeatable business model. Take action and execute it. You are now one step closer to financial freedom!

— *Chris Hunter*

Chapter 15

Why would a business owner want to purchase another company, add satellite locations, or build out a different trade division?

To fuel the WHY of WHY they are in business!

Every person whose expertise is business purpose will tell you that a critical component of WHY is to be in service to others. Richard J. Leider, author of *The Power of Purpose,* says that at its foundation, purpose consists of growing and giving. As a matter of fact, Leider suggests that if you haven't clearly articulated your purpose, use the default purpose of *to grow and to give* until you do.

Whether or not you have a stated WHY, business expansion allows the opportunity to build wealth and provide professional development for you and your coworkers.

Let's reexamine Ben and Chris's WHY.

Chris: I am in business to achieve my personal mission in life. The business is a tool to help accomplish that. I am in business to create and cultivate. I want to build something great and bring a lot of people with me on the success journey. I am in business to serve others. I am in business to leave a legacy. I am in business to impact the industry that gives so much to my family and my team, for the better. We strive to leave it a little better than we found it!

Ben: I am in business to help design my own destiny and life and to help others grow.

It's impossible for Ben and Chris to fuel their WHY without growing. And because they've chosen to not wait and rely on marketing and good business practices alone, they have acquired other companies, built satellite locations, and added different trade divisions. These are important factors in their success.

> **Ben:**   Growth is the lifeblood of all companies. If you're standing still you're actually in decline. How can you fulfill the promise of a career path to potential team members without a plan for expansion?

WHEN TO EXPAND

Whether you have a WHY or not, it's likely you will find yourself in one of the following categories. Let's listen to Chris describe.

The Blood, Sweat, and Tears Guy - You start your own business with great dreams of success. You run the show, provide a high level of service, and put *everything* on the line. You pour hours and hours into it every week. You went from solving one problem at a time to handling multiple issues every day. You *battle* through hard times and do whatever it takes to keep growing. The entire financial brunt to keep it going is on your back. No one knows this kind of pressure except another business owner. Blood. Sweat. Tears.

If things go well, you start to grow. Then the headaches get even worse. Bringing on more people complicates matters. This is the point where you realize that in order to have more than just a job you need to find a better way.

You join an organization like the Service Roundtable. Then you join the Service Nation Alliance. You learn about systems and processes. You learn that you are far more valuable to your business when you're no longer in the truck. So you start to implement systems and processes. Now, your business no longer runs you, you run it. So, what then? Stay comfortable and coast, or realize the potential of a business that has a very repeatable business model?

The Lose-Your-Best-People Guy - You have a fairly successful business. Your main problem is finding new coworkers and keeping those you have. You invest in training, pay a fair wage, and offer all the standard benefits, but it still seems to be a revolving door. Your best guys have an entrepreneurial spirit and leave to start their own businesses. Now not only did you lose one of your best team members, but gained a competitor who learned about the business from you.

The Trying-to-Stay-on-Top Guy - You're the hometown company that everyone knows. They call you for all of their HVAC and plumbing needs. You dominate the area and customer satisfaction is high. Your market even extends *beyond* your normal service area. But growth is stagnating. In fact, you fight to just maintain what you've done in the past. Staying on top is a *constant* struggle. Successful in your area, you know there are other areas out there that have similar potential. The question becomes, are you looking for opportunities or do you just *hope* things stay the same in the future?

> **Chris:** I just described someone I know very well. Someone who faced all three of these dilemmas. Me!

Let's continue with Chris's thoughts.

The Blood-Sweat-and-Tears Guy - Imagine starting your business again, the one you've worked hard at building, the right way, with systems and processes that *work*. This time, however, the software, pricing, training, and other systems and processes are already in place. Learning by trial and error, learning from your mistakes, you know what to do and what not to do. What a head-start you would have by expanding to another location. It'd almost be like cheating.

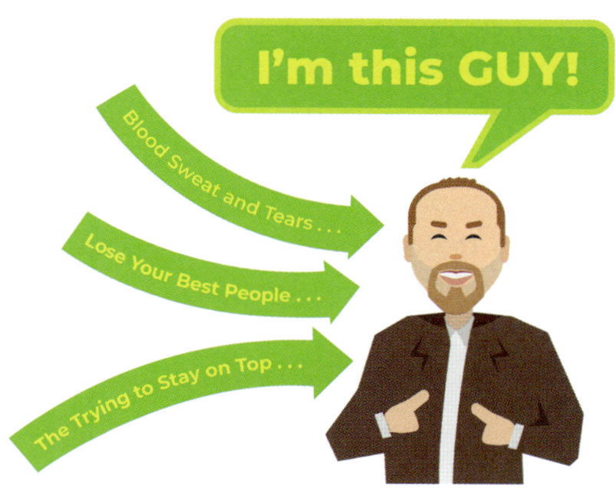

The Lose-Your-Best-People Guy - When it's so hard to find and keep people, why in the world would you want to expand? What if your top guys who have the drive to be business owners could have all the benefits of owning their own business, without most of the headaches that technicians-turned-owners face?

They could have a career path with no cap. You could plug them into a system for success, handle the back-end stuff from a central location, and let them concentrate on growing the new area, doing what they do best: saving customers money, keeping them comfortable, and attending to their safety needs.

> *In this world, you're either growing or you're dying, so get in motion and grow.*
> — *Lou Holtz*

The Trying-to-Stay-on-Top Guy - You started the race yesterday and everyone else starts tomorrow. Your systems and processes are in place. With extreme credibility, you've learned how to dominate a market. Your marketing and presence travels beyond your normal service area. The only thing you're missing is an opportunity to grow. So why not find a similar area and duplicate what you're doing?

So, the bottom line of why to expand? To . . .

- ★ Fuel your WHY
- ★ Build something bigger than yourself
- ★ Enhance the careers and lives of your coworkers
- ★ Help your coworkers achieve their dreams
- ★ Create a lifestyle to help continue fueling your passions

Chris: Do you want to expand? The key is to get your house in order first. Create a repeatable business model. Take massive action and execute it. You are now one step closer to financial freedom!

REDUCE COMPLEXITY!

WHEN NOT TO EXPAND

Chris: While you do not have to wait until everything is absolutely perfect, if your house isn't in order with systems and processes, do not expand. You know those problems you're having now? They'll only increase and get bigger. Also, if you haven't dominated your market or quickly gained market penetration, do not expand. You need to have an efficient business model that is repeatable before trying to expand.

Ben: One of the great things I've learned from watching Chris is how he grew the business by expanding plumbing and electrical departments. When I tried to add plumbing I struggled for three years trying to turn a profit before shutting it down. I think Chris's success was because he focused on the development of people, systems, and processes, while I tried to change the manager to fit what I thought he should be.

SERVICE-MANAGEMENT SOFTWARE

The company's software program must be able to accommodate expansion. If your company requires an upgrade, it's better to change the software and get it up and running smoothly before expanding your operation. Both Ben and Chris's service-management software of choice is ServiceTitan.

If you're a one-person truck or a small company, but have aspirations of serious growth, make sure the right service software is in place as early as possible.

HOW TO EXPAND

Ben and Chris expanded in these directions:

> **Acquisition of Same-Trade Companies** - Purchase existing companies.

> **Acquisition of Other-Trade Companies** - If you're an HVAC contractor, you might consider purchasing a plumbing or electrical company.

> **Expand Geographically** - Move outward to areas to your market.

ACQUISITION OF SAME-TRADE COMPANIES

Ben: Growth through acquisition is a great way to expand the customer base. I have done this over a dozen times. It starts in conversations with your peers, conveying a desire to grow your business. Sharing my desire has brought many people to consider joining forces to become stronger together. It's also developed many lasting relationships that have grown over the years, even if the acquisition didn't develop.

Most every year I send out acquisition letters to my competition; if nothing else it lets them know we are expanding and keeps the pressure on. Ironically, this is *how I sold*

Ben:　*my company* the second time. The purchaser, who was aggressively trying to grow his own business, understood that I, too, was in hot pursuit of growth. After a three-year acquaintance, he decided to buy my company. Needless to say, I think it's important to always be looking at every opportunity to grow.

Chris:　The message, the timing, and the audience are all key. I've acquired two companies and had three basically given to me. Don't discount the one or two-man shops. Some will, for all intents and purposes, give you their customer base. They know about your reputation and they want to join the team and be part of the mission, leaving all of their business frustrations in the rearview mirror.

　　I sought the advice of others, like Ben and Larry Taylor who had purchased companies before. Also, having an acquisition coach to guide you is a must. It's like relying on a Sherpa to climb Mount Everest. They know the lay of the land. One misstep and you'll lose countless dollars!

Considerations

Where will the purchase money come from?

A LINE OF CREDIT

Chris:　I operated for years without a line of credit. As a matter of fact, I wore it as a badge of honor. Then Larry Taylor, a wise advisor, told me the best time to get a line of credit is when I didn't need it, because when I did need it, the banks would be less likely to give it to me if I was in a financial bind.

Small Business Loan - This will require a down payment. There are companies, like Live Oak Bank, that specialize in SBA loans.

Leverage Investors - Perhaps you know people who would be interested in alternative investment strategies. These can be structured in many different ways. Whenever you consider giving up equity, however, be cautious.

Additional Ideas:

- ★ Cash on hand
- ★ Leverage assets
- ★ Short term investment accounts
- ★ Extract from accounts receivable

One of the major factors when purchasing small shops is assessing the value. Chris has found the small business valuation calculator offered to Service Nation Alliance members to be of great value.

Location - Is it more centrally located to your market than your own? Does the owner own or lease the building? If owned, does it make sense to purchase the building?

Consider the amount of change involved between the two different cultures. Ideally, you'd like to acquire a company that believes what you believe. How might your leadership team be affected? What advancement opportunities are possible for your team?

Purchasing a business is not an action to be taken lightly. Do so and your net wealth will more than likely be much lighter. Here are more considerations:

- ★ Integration of financials, including software
- ★ Revenue and profit expectation
- ★ Professionals to involve (lawyer, banker, insurance, etc.)
- ★ Various contracts to sort out
- ★ Update insurance
- ★ Brand transition
- ★ Customer transition
- ★ Coworker transition
- ★ Inventory
- ★ Vehicles
- ★ Equipment
- ★ Cultural; fit and integration
- ★ Update organizational chart
- ★ Update warranties

Are You Ready to Grow?

When you are ready to make a move, hire either a business broker, mergers-and-acquisitions firm, or perhaps your acquisition professional is qualified to assist. We explain the difference in the "Selling Your Business" chapter.

Pre-Due Diligence

So there's a company that you're interested in. Perform pre-due diligence. Like looking at a car before buying, kick the company's tires and look carefully under the hood.

In order to make a sound investment, you need to take the operating, financial, and legal pulse of the company you're considering. Even a pre-due diligence checklist can become comprehensive. The following are just a few items to consider. Involve a professional to help compile a complete list.

- ★ Financial records that comply to generally accepted accounting principles (GAAP)
- ★ Details of one-time expenses and revenue events, add-backs*
- ★ Details of significant pricing and cost changes over a recent period
- ★ Company pricing procedures
- ★ Legal agreements and contracts in place (these are possible liabilities to buyers)
- ★ Bank and credit-card statements
- ★ Vendor agreements
- ★ Accounts payable and receivable records

** Add-Backs, as we explain in the "Selling Your Business" chapter, are expenses that are not part of the everyday cost of operation and sometimes are put back into profits which in most cases gain multiples of profit, increasing value to the seller.*

Perform an evaluation of the company's culture regardless of whether or not you intend to retain the current employees. It's good to understand its environment and how close it is to the culture of your own company.

ACQUISITION OF OTHER-TRADE COMPANIES

Chris: The biggest mistake when adding divisions is doing it too soon. Unless you are very systematized and dominating your market with your primary service, I wouldn't advise going in this direction. Even if you are organized, the addition of another division will be a huge distraction from your primary service. I did it because we had saturated our HVAC market and had less and less room to grow.

Oftentimes you'll need a license holder for the other trade, so look to acquire a company where the owner (license holder) stays on board. I went through two plumbing contractors in the first six months and considered throwing in the towel. They can hold you over a barrel if your contract isn't structured correctly. I highly advise a non-compete or, at the very least, a non-solicitation agreement. Also, the compensation plan for this person needs to be based on production or a flat-fee stipend for the license part.

Chris lays down hardcore realities here that business owners face when adding other trade divisions. Here's another reality if your existing business has been run efficiently and you're dominating the market.

Chris: When we decided to offer plumbing in our main location, something happened that I didn't expect. We made the announcement and were flooded with calls! Our existing customers already knew and trusted us. It was a no-brainer for us to handle the additional services for them.

One major benefit for us was that marketing costs didn't increase much. We simply cross-marketed with Facebook, email, and training the techs.

DEVELOP A PLAN

If the company is fit enough to add a different trade division, it shouldn't be based on a whim during the year. Discuss the possibility in your annual success-planning session. Carefully weigh the pros and cons. Will the new division be a distraction or will it be a profit center? Will your leadership team be able to handle the transition? How will you handle staffing and labor? Plan for it.

That said, healthy and well-operated companies always seem to run into opportunities. Like Ben mentioned above, other business owners are exploring possibilities. You never know when one could come your way. Plan for it.

REVENUE AND PROFIT EXPECTATIONS

Although capital startup expenses can be elevated, your overhead costs are basically covered with the company's baseline service. As with any new business, it's difficult to project revenue and profits for the first six months. Use good business KPIs as you do with your existing business and manage to those expectations.

DEFINE THE MARKET AREA

Chris: Limit your market area to a small circle and expand as you increase labor resources. One issue we had is that in our multiple markets, we were known for fast service. We went

from being able to do calls every day with HVAC, to having to be selective and using a waiting list with plumbing. Start slow and small. Don't take jobs outside of your expertise or comfort zone. Stick to the profitable ones. Let other plumbers chase the difficult ones. There is so much low-hanging fruit with your existing client base. Start there and then expand.

Persona - Identify and describe the desired persona for the new division.

BRANDING

Chris: Our vans are all over town. How would we get people to recognize that we had more to offer than heating and air conditioning? I love what Steve Miles did at Jerry Kelly in the St. Louis market. He designated certain vans to be purple in tribute to the fight against Alzheimer's. This hit home. My wife Nickie's Grandma had Alzheimer's.

So we kept the same logo on all of our trucks, but instead of one color scheme we used purple for plumbing, yellow for electrical, and blue for HVAC. An overall familiar look, but just enough of an eye-catcher to warrant a difference. Stay consistent with your logo. Vary the color scheme.

CULTURAL INTEGRATION

Run coworkers from the acquired company through your onboarding process. Paint the company vision, purpose, growth, and career opportunities. Immerse them into your culture.

ADDING SATELLITE LOCATIONS

Adding satellite locations has been one of the most important keys to Chris's success.

Chris: Everyone in the industry agrees that the two to three-million-dollar company is a sweet spot. Four is the next level, and then five. At five million and above it's a whole different animal and requires an altogether new skill set to run. This is why I decided to invest in a remote location strategy. At the time I sold my business we were in pursuit of that two to three million sweet spot at five different locations. One large company that runs like the smaller ones.

The Two Best Lessons I've Learned From Expansion by Satellite Locations:

No need to repeat lessons others have learned the hard way.
Simple systems and processes are the only way to create something bigger than what you can personally control.

WHERE TO EXPAND

Grow your business in areas with similar markets. Chris uses an excellent analogy to explain his actions.

Chris: If you take a small country school basketball player who is really good, you could put them on any other small country team and more than likely, they would be in the starting five. Now, take that same athlete and put them in a large metropolitan school that has hundreds of kids competing for those five spots . . . they might not even make the team.

This is why I stick to small, similar markets. Once you learn how to win in a similar market, it's very easy to take the same game plan and repeat it.

THE ONE-HOUR MARK

Chris discovered that the best similar markets to expand in are within a one-hour drive from the main office.

Chris: You're more than likely already getting calls from this area and it's peripherally been exposed to your marketing. Especially when you use TV, radio, and social media.

Another advantage of the one-hour metric is shared labor. Remember the old days when you first started your company? With no one to back you, it was hard to take a day off. And with the slow call volume it was hard to add a fulltime install crew.

A one-hour driving distance makes it easy to share labor. We would send an install crew any time we sold a new system in the new area until it grew enough to support hiring its own crew. We'd use our staff to cover the area when the covering technician needed a break.

WHERE IS THE NEED?

Where can you maximize opportunities and minimize costs and risk?

One method is to use a marketing efficiency and effectiveness rating (MEER) report, generated by our friends at Stochastic Marketing. A MEER report scores how effective and efficient your marketing and sales are at turning in new customers and how that compares with contractors who already own companies like yours.

WHO WILL LEAD THE TEAM?

Chris added leaders for the new locations through acquisition and internal growth.

Chris: I had a friend who owned a one-man shop. He had a hard time overcoming the same hurdles most one-man companies face. He loved solving problems and taking care of customers, but he hated the business side.

So I offered him a better way. I made it so he could do what he did best while our office staff handled the back-office duties. By doing this we gained more buying power and actually lowered our overhead expense. Simply by plugging into our system, my friend increased sales by $200,000 over the previous year!

Business owners in situations like this are beaten down, tired, and believe they have no place to go except to keep banging their heads on the wall. Most are happy to join the acquiring company's team for the cost of their assets. And without the headaches, they can infuse their entrepreneurial spirit into your culture and actually make more money for themselves.

Chris thrives on growing leaders. It's a core component of his business purpose.

Chris: My personal favorite is to grow your own leaders. This is also the cure for the company that loses its best people to competitors, or worse, they *become* your competitors.

It's incredibly important to have the right leader in the right location. Immersed in the new community, this person represents your company, its brand, and its culture. Start off with the wrong person and it will set your company back years in that community if you can recover at all!

I take my position of influence very seriously. I am going to make sure you get the proper technical, sales, customer service, and life-skills training. It's rewarding to see someone you've invested in become a leader not only at work, but at home and in their community! Invest in their life, character, and what they do outside of work and it will set you free, releasing you to your highest callings.

WHAT TO LOOK FOR IN POTENTIAL LEADERS

- ★ Same core values
- ★ Displayed leadership ability (not by title)
- ★ Able to handle delegated tasks without unnecessary detailed instructions.
  (This person doesn't need to be babysat. They take the ball and run with it.)
- ★ Entrepreneurial spirit

HOW TO MAKE IT HAPPEN

The next step is to lay the groundwork. Set the vision and identify clear, mutually owned goals, milestones, and deadlines. Specify formal and informal power relationships and lines of authority.

Create a structure and determine what will be handled by the home office versus the satellite location.

Who decides:

- ★ Budget
- ★ Budget approval
- ★ Hiring/Firing
- ★ Purchasing
- ★ Salaries
- ★ Target market and demographics
- ★ Marketing
- ★ Dispatching
- ★ Billing
- ★ Training

COMMUNICATIONS

One of the most critical aspects of home-base and satellite locales is consistent and constant two-way communication. It's essential to create both scheduled and impromptu on-site visits, videoconferencing, and conference calls. Seek out opportunities for phone calls, pictures, joint meetings, get-togethers, celebrations, and encourage a positive atmosphere of teamwork.

> *We cannot limit ourselves to continuing on the path we have already opened.*
>
> *— Amancio Ortega*

COMMUNITY

Plug into the community and network. Create dedicated Facebook and other social media pages for the satellite's community.

Goal – If you're serious about growth, start small and set incremental goals.

Observe – Study and research these various measures of growth. Talk with other owners who have done it. Learn the Go-Time Success way.

Take Massive Action – There are a ton of ways to take action without grabbing a pile of cash from underneath the mattress and running out to buy a business. Start small. Get systems, processes, and your service management software in order. Hire a valuation expert and work from their feedback.

Inspect – Carefully inspect progress.

Modify – Make the necessary changes.

Engage – Repeat the business model that you designed and enjoy the growth.

Notes

Ben/Chris: *What drives ServiceTitan?*

Ara: *Customer success stories*

Ben/Chris: *What better way to indicate the value and potential of a supplier than the customer success stories that they generate!*

He began his career in maintenance working for a company that serviced appliances and HVAC equipment in apartments, condos, and schools

Thinking ahead, a characteristic that would help him blaze a pathway into the future, he wanted a career that would provide a good living. So he invested in a six-week HVAC training course, while attending community college and working during the day.

He had an unusual genetic makeup: a desire to be his own boss; an entrepreneurial spirit; a passion to learn, study, and apply lessons from school, work, and life; the ability to carve positive lessons from failure; the will to experiment, observe, inspect, learn, and modify; and the sense to bring others along on his journey—all were encoded into his DNA.

This sequence of genetic markers overwhelmed his ability to work for someone else. So he sold a car to raise capital and started a business. Ben Stark was now officially an HVAC business owner (By the way, every single description of Ben's genetic makeup can be found in Chris as well).

Like a divining rod in search of water, Ben not only sought out business knowledge and information, he scoured the landscape for credible and effective sources.

One evening, Ben found himself sitting across the dinner table from Gary Anderson of B & B Heating and Cooling at a North Texas ACCA meeting. Gary had just joined Contractor's Success Group (CSG) and encouraged Ben to attend an upcoming function to learn more about the organization.

Ben took that trip to St. Louis with Gary and eventually joined CSG. Although North Texas ACCA had begun to lay the groundwork, Ben says his CSG membership was when he made the transformation from technician to becoming a serious entrepreneur/business owner.

Like Texas Longhorns, no two relationships are the same. From people to people, to people to companies, educational institutions, social media, and beyond, the connections and possibilities are infinite. Organizations like North Texas ACCA, CSG, and folks like Gary Anderson were instrumental in Ben's early career as a business owner.

If not for Ben's determination and drive to improve his business and develop himself as a professional, his star would have faded and his career would never have taken off!

Industry events can be gold mines of opportunity. Ben often describes himself while attending these as "finding myself across the table from __________." Anyone who has eaten dinner at an industry event can say the same thing. But it's what Ben *does* while sitting at the table that separates him from the pack. In between the clink of dinnerware and the chit-chat, Ben uses this precious time to plant the seeds of future relationships.

VENDORS, SUPPLIERS, CONSULTANTS, COACHES, OR PARTNERS?

In trying to name this chapter, we contemplated the above one-word titles. In doing so, we asked, "what do they all have in common?" We finally hit on it. They all need someone else in order to be effective! Wait a minute, *be effective?* Heck, they wouldn't *be* at all without another person. Coaches need clients. Vendors, suppliers, etc., need customers.

However you slice it, dice it, or boil it down, a relationship is involved. But relationships are good and bad, effective and ineffective. Could we simply call this chapter *Relationships?*

To answer this question, we examined the relationships that mean and have meant the most to Ben and Chris throughout their careers. There was at least one common denominator: a positive transformation took place. Due to his relationship with Gary Anderson, a positive transformation took place. Ben had gone from technician to serious entrepreneur/business owner. We describe it as a transformational relationship.

The next question we asked was, "should we separate business and personal relationships in this chapter?" Let's return once more to Ben and that North Texas ACCA meeting. Ben was a member of North Texas ACCA. He meets Gary. Gary suggests CSG to Ben. Ben joins CSG and declares what a pivotal experience it was in his career.

People are a part of ACCA. ACCA holds the meeting. Ben meets Gary. People belong to CSG. CSG puts on a get-to-know-us experience. Ben joins. Why even bother trying to sort out whether it's business or personal? Relationships involve businesses and relationships can be personal. Relationships that make a difference are transformational. Throughout their journeys, Ben and Chris have pursued transformational relationships.

Transformational relationships do not suddenly sprout out of the ground. Seeds must be planted, the ground watered and weeded, along with plenty of sunshine, for the relationship to blossom. We've seen an example of Ben planting seeds here already.

It takes human interaction from both sides to create, grow, and sustain transformational relationships. Ben and Chris gravitate to people and companies that understand this. The intent of each party is that through the exchange of time, information, knowledge, money, education, and goodwill, *both sides prosper!*

We can illustrate this principle with the examples of just a few of the transformational relationships that Ben and Chris have developed over the years.

Suppliers . . .

We use the term *suppliers* to represent companies that furnish the equipment, parts, material, and supplies that a contractor needs to operate their business.

. . . And Professional Services

Professional services cover lawyers, medical doctors, bankers, certified public accountants, financial advisors, educators, coaches and consultants.

There are other entities that fit in this category, companies that perform services on your building, vehicle, technologies etc.

Some corporations, due to legal nuances, are not allowed to refer to what's typically called business partners as business partners, unless there is a legal and binding agreement in place. Therefore, we're not using the term business partners. In addition to suppliers and professional services, we use the term transformational relationships.

> *We make a living by what we get.*
> *We make a life by what we give.*
> — *Winston Churchill*

No matter what term you use, if there is an exchange of time, information, knowledge, money, education, or good will, there is the potential to plant relationship seeds that might one day bud into transformational relationships.

Ben: I approach relationships with professional service providers as a two-way street. I've gained great knowledge from these folks over the years. They've shared information with me that helped to make decisions later on.

I routinely invite professional service providers to attend our annual success planning event and include them in the planning process.

Although some provider's responsibility is to introduce and share information, the better the relationship, the more liberal the scope of the exchange. For instance, guidance I received from one financial advisor prompted me to sell one of my companies on the advent of a declining economy.

I work with bankers to make sure we have at least six months of working capital on hand or a pre-approved loan to protect against unseen forces. We weathered the storm following 9/11 because of this practice.

Our CPA helps us make wise year-end adjustments for tax burden and keeps the company healthy, wealthy, and ready for the ensuing year's planned growth.

Our accountant provides true departmental numbers which allows us to make proper adjustments in training, staffing, and cost-of-goods control.

At first glance, with Ben's relationships, one might think that's what these people and companies are supposed to do. But because Ben treats these relationships with such care, they transcend that transactional barrier to making a real difference in his and his company's life.

BLOODLETTING

Back in the old days, the contractors' philosophy of *getting the most out of the supplier* had a tendency to unmercifully beat up the supplier for the best deal. Of course, the only thing this accomplished was to prod the suppliers to raise their prices that much more. A short-sided approach to relationship building to say the least. In fact, it's the complete opposite.

How Does a Contractor get the Most out of the Supplier Relationship?

TRUST

It starts with trust! Trust takes time to develop. Small acts of integrity, dependability, responsiveness, keeping your word, and respect are the building blocks of a trusting relationship on both sides.

AN ALTERNATIVE POINT OF VIEW

The people on the other side of a business owner's relationship have a different point of view. In order for the relationship to turn transformational, it's critical for the business owner to understand their own wants, needs, and aspirations. We spoke to five people who have truly made a difference in Ben and Chris's careers.

Mike Henson

Mike Henson is the director of strategic alliances for Daikin Industries, Ltd. Mike met Ben in the early 1990s at a Contractor Success Group get-together. At the time, Ben owned Air Experts and Mike was national manager of Amana branch sales. Ben appreciated Mike's outlook on business and business relationships, so he created an open line of communications (he planted seeds).

As fate would have it, shortly after that meeting, the equipment manufacturer that Ben's company was working with cut off their account due to a marketing dispute. Ben's very first call was to Mike Henson. Mike connected Ben with Mike Bush, Amana's branch manager/regional manager for North Texas. Within twenty-four hours, Ben's company was selling a new line of equipment.

Mike Henson maintained that sense of urgency as Ben moved through Air Experts, Service Experts (to which he sold his company), and the launch of Stark Air. Ben still has a business relationship with Mike as he coaches and guides other members of the Five Star Guys who use the Amana products.

> *The business of business is relationships; the business of life is human connections.*
>
> *— Robin S. Sharma*

We Asked Mike: If a contractor's intent is to develop transformational relationships with industry businesses, what should they be looking for in these companies?

Vendors Who:

- ★ Take the time to establish what the customer's specific needs are; not taking a one-size-fits-all approach to the market.

- ★ Demonstrate the ability to embrace productivity-enhancing technology.

- ★ Understand value over cost (unless the customer is dedicated to being the low cost provider in their market).

- ★ Clearly communicate what they need for a successful relationship with the customer (i.e., credit, planning, growth, support, programs, etc.)

- ★ Clearly define their expectations and requirements for a long-term relationship that is defined as win-win.

We Then Asked Mike: What do suppliers look for in prospective customers?

Customers Who:

- ★ Strive to grow their businesses

- ★ Know the difference between value and price

- ★ Want a relationship and not just a transaction

- ★ Are transparent with what their aspirations are and what they need from the business to fulfill them

- ★ Will meet their financial obligations. Suppliers operate on thin margins and should not be the "bank of last resort"

How important are these points? Ben states that he would not be where he is today without Mike Henson. We'd say, pretty darn important!

It's important to note, these are Mike Henson's opinions and not the official position of Daikin Industries, Ltd. The fact that Mike's roots have been so deeply embedded in the Amana/Goodman/Daiken family lineage for so many decades, however, should lend serious credibility to the value of his recommendations.

Steve Wood

Steve Wood is the vice president of sales and marketing for Johnson Supply, an HVAC distribution company serving Texas and Western Louisiana. Ben met Steve in the early 2000s at a Lennox dealer meeting. Steve held many executive senior leadership positions at Lennox International over the years, and he was in a business development position for Lennox in 2009 and 2010 when Ben orchestrated a meeting between him and executives at the Service Nation Alliance. That meeting resulted in Lennox becoming a Service Roundtable Rewards partner.

Did you ever engage with someone for the first time and suddenly feel as if you were in kindergarten and he was a PhD? When it comes to the dynamics of a successful contractor/supplier relationship, Steve Wood has that figurative PhD. Steve is also a John Maxwell Team executive director.

Ben/Chris: What is the primary aim of a supplier?

Steve: To help contractors sell and to look for a contractor who has influence over a large amount of people. How well will a contractor represent the brand and how can they appropriately influence others?

I envision contractors in two different camps. Do they have a vendor mindset? Or do they have a partnership mindset?

Vendor Mindset - Mercenary and transactional in nature, they are driven by the deal. They continually bounce from one supplier to the next exclusively looking for the best deal. In the long run, contractors who continually beat up suppliers on pricing have a way of fading into the sunset. I do not invest in these types of relationships.

Partnership Mindset - They are trustworthy, driven to grow and there's a certainty they will deliver. I invest in these types of relationships.

Note: We appreciate Steve's candor. His company needs to grow. Influential contractors can help him do this. A crisp understanding of this side of the relationship will greatly aid contractors in obtaining maximum resource value from Steve.

> ## The pursuit and engagement of high-quality professional service providers lays the groundwork for uncommon personal wealth.
> ### — Ben Stark

Ben/Chris: What do you look for in a potential client?

Steve: Are they driven by a growth mindset or are they driven to finance a lifestyle?

A growth mindset represents a serious business approach. I don't invest in clients who are driven to buy the next hot boat, condo, or sports car.

A supplier cannot survive on a fixed customer base. Growth must come from increased revenue with existing customers and or an increase in customers.

I am always on the lookout for a flagship customer. These contractors represent the pinnacle of companies in their field. Flagship customers do not get complacent. They continue to grow. Ben and Chris's companies were flagship customers.

Ben: As a serious contractor with a growth mindset, we were the type of client that Steve pursued. Manufacturers and suppliers have money to invest in clients. They will invest in quality leadership, and growth-minded companies. My companies were prime examples.

Ben hits us right between the eyes with the benefits to a contractor who understands the value of being an influential customer—as Steve describes above.

Ben/Chris: Any other recommendations for contractors, Steve?

Steve: Pursue a supplier who will invest in you.

People get promoted at large companies, especially territory managers. Develop a relationship with people above their position. This way you'll have a solid and enabling connection for when they train the next territory manager.

Engage with your suppliers at seminars and industry conventions.

Don't be exclusively price-driven when it comes to suppliers. Focus on the sum total of what they deliver.

Join industry groups like Nexstar or the Service Nation Alliance. They help to bridge the gap of reality to the market. Stay on top of industry change.

Running a successful business boils down to leadership. You can have processes and systems in place, but the organization can outrun you. You need insightful leadership along with a solid leadership structure. You must stay ahead of the game!

Melanie Gentry

 Melanie Gentry is the founder and CEO of Comprehensive Employment Solution. CES is an HR, safety, and compensation management service provider. Ben and Chris have been engaged with CES since approximately 2010. Melanie is known for transcending what is normally expected out of a supplier/contractor relationship and delivering exemplary customer service. One gets the feeling that when dealing with Melanie and Team CES, they would walk across the desert to help their customer!

Ben/Chris: When it comes to the supplier/contractor relationship, what do you see successful business owners doing that others do not?

Melanie: Joining and participating in a contractor-support organization like the Service Nation Alliance.

Ben/Chris: Why would a contractor join an organization like this? What are the benefits?

Melanie: I recommend focusing on the benefits:

The Right Fit - Most business groups have preferred vendors within their communities. Business groups are focused on their members' success. Vendors, therefore, are carefully vetted. The business group is looking for vendors that they believe are capable of enhancing their members' success.

The right business group will help its members find the right vendor to meet their particular needs. The business group helps with the legwork.

Accountability - Members have the power to hold vendors to a higher level than if they were transacting business outside on the open market. Great vendor service starts positive public praise within the community. Poor service will also stimulate public reaction. Vendors do not want this type of publicity.

Trust is the glue of life. It's the most essential ingredient in effective communication. It's the foundational principle that holds all relationships."

— Stephen R. Covey

If a member is having an issue with the vendor, they can bring in the power of the business group to help resolve it.

Access - Members get attention. If a member company needs a product or service developed or an enhancement to an existing one, vendors will be more apt to listen and explore solutions, especially when dealing with a business group. The main reason is that it's not just making developments for a market of one.

Financial Rewards - The business group has buying power. In addition to discounts, most business groups have some type of rewards (or rebate) system.

Insider Knowledge - With acute access to successful members, vendors are in a position to enhance products and services, which often drive down members' costs. Some will develop customized solutions for members that, outside of the buying group, might not otherwise be available.

Skilled-Trades Friendly - Business groups have a tendency to assemble vendors that primarily deal with the home-repair-and-service market. This level of expertise has far-reaching effects that are sometimes overshadowed by the glare of cheap pricing.

Dave Moore

Dave Moore is the Lennox International business development manager for national and strategic accounts. At one point, years ago, Dave was a new territory manager for Lennox, working under Steve Wood. Steve had assigned Dave to Ben's account. Although a rookie at the time, Dave worked to understand Ben's pain points as a businessman. He continues to do that to this very day and that's why we asked him for advice to help contractors do business with their suppliers and to develop and build transformational relationships.

Ben/Chris: What should a contractor look for in their supplier?

Dave: Does the territory manager understand their client's business? Do they:

★ Look at the business through their client's eyes?
★ Understand their pain points and needs?
★ Understand what keeps them up at night?
★ Ask how they can improve their client's life and business?

Ben/Chris: What does a transformational relationship look like to you?

Dave: Set clear expectations up front for both parties. Set goals and work together to achieve them.

Lennox is driven by trust, innovation, and quality. I find that when our customer is transparent, getting all of their cards on the table, and involves me (Lennox) with their long-term plans, I am better prepared and able to deliver tools and resources of impact, those not normally available to clients who are less committed.

Ara Mahdessian

Ara Mahdessian is the CEO and, along with the president, Vahe Kuzoyan, co-founders of billion-dollar service-software giant, ServiceTitan. Chris first met Ara in the early years of ServiceTitan. How long ago was that? Ara was the sales rep and performed the demonstration for Chris.

Ara graduated from Stanford University with degrees in engineering and management science. Vahe graduated from the University of Southern California with a BS in computer science, neuroscience, and business administration and together, the thirty-somethings launched ServiceTitan in 2013. With the budding entrepreneur's age and educational pedigree, one's first notion of them and ServiceTitan is Silicon Valley.

For us, two things differentiate ServiceTitan from the fast-paced tech scene in Northern California. Number one, they're located in Glendale, just north of Los Angeles; and more importantly, two, Ara and Vahe were born in the trades. Their fathers are plumbers.

Ara talks about growing up watching his dad work hard all day and then come home, break out the shoe boxes to pay bills, run payroll, and do paperwork. It was a life of hard work and sacrifice. Once Ara and Vahe met in college and compared backgrounds, they recognized what they had to do: Apply their education, technology, and passion to make the world a better, easier, and smarter place to do business for their fathers and others like them.

> *People do not buy goods and services, they buy relations, stories and magic.*
>
> *— Seth Godin*

It's this forward-thinking connection between technology and passion for the human spirit and family that drove us to seek out Ara for his input on transformational relationships.

Ben/Chris: How does ServiceTitan make a difference with its customers?

Ara: Beyond the products and services we deliver at ServiceTitan, we help our customers with their greatest needs. From recruiting, training, and connecting them with other successful customers to share best practices, we continually look for ways to add value.

We have product experts and implementation managers to get customers set up with our services. Past that, we assign a customer-success manager to each customer to proactively help them throughout the lifetime of our relationship.

Ben/Chris: What drives ServiceTitan?

Ara: We continuously circulate customer success stories in the company.

Ben/Chris: What better way to indicate the value and potential of a supplier than the customer success stories that they generate!

Ara: Customer success stories. We continuously circulate them in the company and at Pantheon, our annual conference designed to strengthen our customer's business potential with takeaways and strategies they can implement right into their business. These stories motivate us to go to work and grow!

Note: When we were interviewing Ara, a customer success story hit his email inbox. We could feel the emotion in his voice as he read it back to us.

Ben/Chris: How else do you work on the relationship?

Ara: We help our customers market better, generate leads, increase service tickets, sell better, and increase closing rates. Customer success equals ServiceTitan success.

Ben/Chris: Where do you see service going in the future?

Ara: Customers expect convenience and trust. We need to bridge the talent gap by creating good customer-service skills, and getting coworkers quickly up to speed. We need to reduce friction within and between the whole ecosystem, from ServiceTitan to all the entities we deal with.

ServiceTitan is participating in the trend that includes big data, machine learning, automation, and AI.

Ben/Chris: What better way to indicate the value and potential of a supplier than the customer success stories that they generate?

TRANSFORMATIONAL RELATIONSHIPS

The following fictitious snippet lives day-in and day-out in our trades.

> *Bob hires on at EZ Breezy as a truck driver. During his first week he meets Marty, a counter guy at Supplies-R-Us. Both Bob and Marty are serious about their craft. They live out the Go-Time Formula and advance within their respective companies. One day in the future, Bob finds himself as the GM at EZ Breezy and Marty is the GM at Supplies-R-Us.*
>
> *Due to their experience and positions, Bob and Marty have significantly more influence today than they did fifteen years ago. Due to their evolving relationship they have significantly more power and resources to effect change and make a difference than they did even two years ago. Relationships that grow, evolve, and stand the test of time continue to open doors and multiply possibilities.*

This True Story is a Quintessential Example.

As we had mentioned, Ara Mahdessian met Chris early on when ServiceTitan was but an infant. Over the years they did more than stay in touch: Chris became a model ServiceTitan user and provided invaluable developmental feedback for the optimization and growth of its software. He even spoke on stage at ServiceTitan's prestigious Pantheon event.

In early 2019, Chris was believed to have stage-four cancer and only a few weeks to live. Ara was the very first person to contact him. He immediately used his influence to connect Chris with the name of a department head in a very prestigious medical institution. As it turned out, that doctor was on pregnancy leave and had only been home two days from the hospital when she took the call. She pulled strings and got Chris into the number-one ranked cancer center in the country!

It turned out Chris does not have cancer. He has a rare but treatable disease that mimics its symptoms.

Ara and Chris continued to develop their relationship and approximately one year later, Ara asked Chris to join his ServiceTitan team. Chris accepted in the second quarter of 2020, opening up a brand-new, exciting chapter in their transformational relationship.

If you think you're too small to have an impact, try going to bed with a mosquito in the room.

— Anita Roddick

WHO IS AT YOUR TABLE?

The next time you meet with a businessperson for the first time or find yourself sitting across the table from someone at an industry event, plant the seeds of possibilities. And then take small steps. Move forward. Be trustworthy. Water the ground. Exchange knowledge. Pull weeds. Conduct business. Turn on the sun. Be dependable, responsive, and respectful. Love your plants. Recognize the transformational relationship for what it is.

Goal – Developing transformational relationships requires time, but you have to start somewhere. Whether you're sitting across the table from someone at an industry event, or calling up a supplier for the first time, view every introduction as a future transformational relationship.

Observe – In addition to our advice here, explore how successful contractors and suppliers approach relationship building. Ask questions and take notes.

Take Massive Action – Take small steps. As you move forward, establish trust and determine if the other party moves past the transactional stage. If so, continue to move forward.

Inspect – Is trust working both ways? Is the other party responsive and dependable?

Modify – Sometimes you have to write the other party off as stuck in the transactional phase and move on. Continue to be both empathetic and forward with your needs. Strive for win-win.

Engage – The goal of your effort is a win for each party. Discuss the positive aspects, and negative if there are any, as the relationship continues to build. Good, transparent dialog is the fuel of transformational relationships.

Notes

An annual cycle like that, even if you are producing ten percent net profit, will not yield uncommon wealth. For that, you need a liquidity event.

And, due to many factors, the wealth in a business can evaporate almost overnight. The thing about a liquidity event is that it sets one and their family up for financial freedom.

Ben taught me this. Grow the business and harvest the wealth out of it. This provides freedom to tackle the next venture. With a security blanket, it frees one's mind from the financial stress. That's what stimulates fear, the fear that keeps people from taking action. Eliminate that and It's Go-Time!

— Chris Hunter

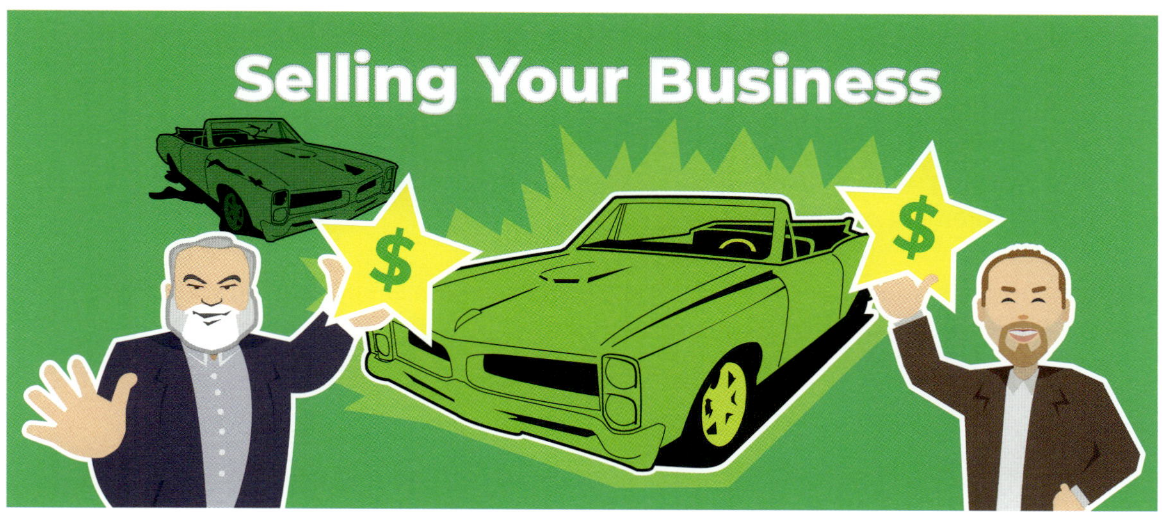

Whoa partner! Don't even think about skipping this chapter! Do you think that just because you're a one or two-man company, or that you finally got out of the truck to start working on the business, this isn't for you? It is. And it might be even more important for you than it is for the guy running the multi-million-dollar company.

Like that 1967 GTO that's been restored with meticulous care to factory specifications in order to get top resale dollars, a business that's in tip-top shape and operating efficiently in all departments will command a top price.

The most effective way to do this is to build your company from the start as if you were going to sell it in the future. (See the chapter "*Begin with the End in Mind*"). Use the tips and information in this chapter as a guide to get your business in shape.

Whether you're just starting out or are the owner of a ten-million-dollar operation, questions about selling your business will surface, both from outside entities and from within.

"Do You Want to Sell Your Business to Us? Are You Going to Sell Your Business?"

EXTERNAL

- ★ A competitor
- ★ Private-equity firms
- ★ Professional partners—lawyer, banker, accountant, financial planner
- ★ Fellow alliance members

INTERNAL

- ★ Family members
- ★ Coworkers
- ★ Moving on to another type of business
- ★ Retirement consideration

Like Ben and Chris, sooner or later all business owners are either approached with these questions, or they arise from thought and planning.

WHY SELL?

Transition to Family - It's time to let the next generation lead.

It's Time to Move on - Perhaps you've lost the passion to own and run a business. Or another opportunity looms on the horizon. Or you need a break and the proceeds of a sale will sustain you until your next venture.

Retirement - Perhaps there is no one to transition the business to. Sell your business so that you can enjoy retirement.

Extract Cash - By selling the business to a private equity firm, the payout an owner receives places them in an uncommon wealth category, but also allows them to stay on and run the business.

Ben: Like most other small companies in our industry, I struggled with weather conditions, economic challenges, and lack of capitalization. Would my company survive another week, another month?

A dependable customer base supports growth and allows reinvestment in the company. This type of stability was my goal, and we achieved it with all of my companies.

I came to a time when I had to make a very important decision: Do I risk the built-up wealth and assets to continue on as an entrepreneurial risk taker? Or is it smarter to move on to a more secure place by selling the company and obtaining what I call uncommon wealth? I chose security. And with the sale of each company came more freedom.

Achieving uncommon wealth is liberating, but it shouldn't be taken lightly. With uncommon wealth comes uncommon responsibility to managing things for the good of all who helped along the way.

While Chris Shares Ben's Financial Thinking, he Adds an Additional Element that Factored Into the Sale of his Company.

Chris: As owners, we take a paycheck. Maybe at year's end we take a percentage of the net profit. If we want to withstand the next year's winter, fuel growth, buy vehicles, and make investments that a growing company demands, we take a small percentage, if any at all.

An annual cycle like that, even if you are producing ten percent net profit, will not yield uncommon wealth. For that, you need a liquidity event.

And, due to many factors, the wealth in a business can evaporate almost overnight. The thing about a liquidity event is that it sets one and their family up for financial freedom.

Ben taught me this. Grow the business and harvest the wealth out of it. This provides freedom to tackle the next venture. With a security blanket, it frees one's mind from the financial stress. That's what stimulates fear, the fear that keeps people from taking action. Eliminate that and It's Go-Time!

That was logical. It was the smart thing to do. From an emotional point, however, I was starting to lose the passion. I didn't want to, it just happened. If I couldn't do it with all my heart, I knew I was doing a disservice to my team, family, and self to continue.

I asked Ron Smith when he knew it was time to sell his company. He said when you no longer have the passion that the business and customers deserve, it's time to go do something else. I listened closely as this was about one year before I was able to pull the trigger and sell my company. It really hit home.

Notice how when Chris approaches an important fork in the road he goes out and seeks counsel. The Go-Time component of "Observe" is hardwired into his DNA and, along with the entire Go-Time formula, a major reason for his success.

There is no success without a successor.

— Peter Drucker

That Other Element that Chris Wrestled with:

Chris: Prior to selling my business there was an overall lid on leadership in my company. Although I passionately pursue the Go-Time formula, am a John Maxwell certified coach, and seek outside counsel, I represent the lid. There was no one else ahead of me in the organization.

I sold to Turn Point, an organization with a higher lid, a higher level of leadership talent. This allows me to grow, which essentially lifts the leadership lid in the entire organization.

WHAT IS WEALTH?

Ben and Chris both use the terms *wealth* and *uncommon wealth*. Let's explore wealth first.

Ben: Wealth is gained as you follow your North Star on the way to your WHY. Learning something from wherever you go, it accumulates as you create value for others, your family, and yourself.

Ben Created a Toolbox Metaphor that Further Explains Acquiring Wealth. (It's Similar to the One we Use in the "Coworker Development" Chapter)

Hand Tools Toolbox: These are the actual tools you use to do the job. Whether it's in the field or office, high-quality tools facilitate quality work efficiently.

Knowledge Toolbox: Pursue education! Keep a business or personal journal to record notes, observations, and ideas along with what you're learning and how to apply it. Reflect on mistakes and failures. Note lessons learned and move on.

Communications Toolbox: Keep dialog simple and continually work to clarify your message. Work to refine ways of communicating and explaining problems to others in pursuit of solution-finding. Role-play between coworkers in all facets of the business. Wealth is accumulated in the people you surround yourself with.

Mindset Toolbox: Critical tools here are attitude, gratitude, and an open mind. Be relentless in maintaining a good and positive attitude! Be thankful to those who've helped and supported you. When it comes to life, business, education, and diversification, keep an open mind.

Chris: Did I have a wealth strategy early in my career? Wealth strategy, exit strategy . . . what was that!? Heck, the only strategy I had back then was a survival strategy! I didn't truly understand the concept of wealth until much later on.

One day you're a tech and you do everything you can to be the best around. Then the next day you own a business and do everything you can to be the best. It's the same thing for wealth, except you need to start much earlier.

Like Ben says, "wealth is not just a number." But it is a part of it. Apply the Go-Time formula. Set a goal. Go out and talk with people. Observe what works for them. Take massive action! Inspect, modify, repeat, and engage!

What is Uncommon Wealth?

Ben: Doorways to uncommon wealth and freedom open each time you sell a well-run and profitable company. Create an investment portfolio by diversifying your proceeds. Real estate, stocks, mutual funds, rental properties, and other companies are options.

Continue to leverage knowledge and industry relationships via the passive sale of knowledge properties (books, websites, royalties, etc.) and consulting.

The key is to find ways, using the Go-Time formula, to continue building personal wealth for the rest of your life.

Chris: After reading *The E-Myth*, I spoke with my eleven-year-old son about the various types of money. There's wage income, produced by working and receiving a paycheck. These funds are important because they fuel other money-making endeavors.

The next is profits. They result from building a team that works within a well-run business.

There's passive income, wealth that's produced even when you sleep (my son liked this one and so do I!). It comes from rent, royalties, etc.

The selling of a business is part of the life journey of the business. It's created, it develops, and it adapts to a new vision and path.

— Ben Stark

Chris: The final one is the ultimate game changer: Equity. The value of a business that, when sold, can create uncommon wealth. Uncommon wealth has the potential to be generational wealth, setting up one's family for decades.

After we talked about the different types of income, my son said, "Dad, I'm going to create several businesses and build equity. Then I'm going to sell them so I can have uncommon wealth!" I smiled. Later that night, I heard him telling my twenty-four-year-old son about the different types of income and how he was going to create equity. Mission accomplished!

ENGAGE WITH A PROFESSIONAL

Ben recently sold his third company and Chris is on his second. Both strongly recommend hiring a professional.

Are you the hunted or the hunter? Because Chris and his company earned national awards like Contractor of the Year, 2016 ACHR NEWS; Best Contractor to Work For; and PHC top 20 Contractors, to name just a few, his company was being hunted.

Chris: To enhance our credibility, we aggressively pursued every award that pertained to our business. Only later did we learn that, by winning all of these awards, we had made ourselves visible and desirable to high-level companies in pursuit of serious growth.

Valuation Specialist - Whether you're the hunted or the hunter, if there's even the slightest notion of selling your business, hire a valuation specialist. Sharp valuation specialists will not only perform a valuation, they'll provide recommendations to increase the company's value.

As you'll see, there are other types of firms and individuals that you can engage with. Some even provide their own valuation services. It's not a bad idea to invest in a third-party entity to give you a non-biased perspective.

Mergers and Acquisition Specialists - A mergers and acquisition (M&A) firm usually deals with companies larger than one million dollars in annual revenue. The M&A has inroads to private-equity groups and corporate entities. As such, they have the ability to keep a seller's name out of the public. M&A deals are usually complex, involve extensive preplanning, and take longer to finalize than a straight-out sale to a single entity. An M&A is usually compensated on multiples of earnings before interest, taxes, depreciation, and amortization (EBITDA).

Business Broker - Business brokers deal with firms valued at less than one million dollars. The broker can assist on both sides of the deal whereas an M&A will work for one or the other. The broker lists companies in public databases. They are compensated on seller's discretionary earnings and/or discretionary cash flow, averaging approximately ten percent of the payout. Their fee is success based, meaning, with the exception of valuation services, they are paid only when your business is sold.

Chris: The business broker or M&A firm will help you obtain maximum dollars for your business. When hiring, perform the same due diligence you would when hiring someone to sell your house. Look at their success record, visit with people who have worked with them, and make sure you have a good feeling about them. You will be spending considerable time together as they assist in what more than likely will be the largest transaction of your life.

TO WHOM SHOULD YOU SELL THE BUSINESS?

Chris looked at four different avenues to sell his business. Let's listen to what was going through his mind as he evaluated each option.

Chris: The first option I considered was selling to my kids and the key people in the company. The problem is they would have been burdened by the debt of the transaction and it would have made it difficult for them to grow the company for years to come. And because they didn't have the money, I would have had to sell at a discount and self-finance all or part of it. This type of deal can lead to internal relationship issues. I didn't want to go down that road.

The second option would have been to try and sell to a competitor or individual. Because we were one of the larger contractors in the area, there weren't many that could afford to acquire us. And even if there was, the culture might not have been a good fit. My objective was win, win, win! Win for my team, customers, and family.

Wealth is not about having a lot of money; it's about having a lot of options.

— Chris Rock

Chris: The third option was to sell to one of the larger groups that are consolidating contractors. The Hunter Super Techs brand is important to everyone in the organization. I had no interest in losing and or changing the brand.

The final option was a private-equity firm. Turn Point Services is the company I chose. Their intention is to leverage local brand equity. It was a perfect fit! We didn't have to change our Hunter Super Techs brand or company culture.

It truly was win, win, win!

The team members saw an instant improvement in benefits with things like a health-care plan that was half the cost, better pay plans, structured growth paths, and equity opportunities for key people.

Our customers won by receiving stronger warranties, more competitive pricing, and the ability to scale to a larger footprint so we can serve even more people.

In addition to our shareholder status in Turn Point, our family was able to take some chips off the table as a reward for all the hard work and investment we had made.

PREPARE COMPANY TO SELL

While we've covered our begin-with-the-end-in-mind approach to operating a business, when a sale is looming in the near future, there are essential steps you must take to optimize the value of your business.

A Pitch Book - Create and prepare a pitch book. This is an elaborate brochure for your company. It includes:

- ★ Company history
- ★ Profile of leadership and company staff
- ★ Company revenue and profitability progression
- ★ Progression demonstrating increase in customers
- ★ Club-membership program
- ★ Growth of staff
- ★ Financial histories
- ★ Vision
- ★ Mission
- ★ Core values
- ★ Business WHY
- ★ Market strategy, including growth opportunities
- ★ Operational strategy
- ★ A progression of annual success-planning documents
- ★ Future business plan
- ★ Pictures showcasing vibrant company culture
- ★ Pictures of company facilities
- ★ Pictures of company vehicles

Service-Management Software - The Hunter Super Techs and Sunny Service both use ServiceTitan. This was an advantage to Turn Point, their acquiring company. And companies already running on the same software will actually pay more for your business. The reason is that there is no conversion cost; everything's compatible with the purchasing company's systems and ready to go on day one.

Another reason to have a high-quality software system is ease of pulling needed data during the due diligence period. Chris gave the auditors his login and they were able to gather what they needed with ease. Without such ease, the responsibility falls upon the business owner to gather and/or calculate the necessary data.

Maximize EBITDA - While it's a standard business practice to maximize earnings, when there is even a notion of selling your company it's time to put on a full-court press. Drive that bottom line! Reduce or cut off any unnecessary expenses. Remember, every dollar saved in expenses is a dollar more to EBITDA, which gets multiplied to drive up the purchase price. This isn't the time to reduce tax liability. Again, every dollar spent is one less dollar of EBITDA.

> **Chris:** Anything that can be depreciated should be. In the past, if I set up a call center, I may have just lumped it into *office expense* or *building maintenance*. This basically cost me the sell-price multiple. If I would have put it in as a capital expenditure and depreciated it, those dollars could have been added back to increase the sale amount.

Add-Backs - An add-back is a one-time and/or owner's expense that is added back to the EBITDA to bolster profits. An add-back is an expense that will not be incurred again. For instance, say you paid one-year membership dues to an organization. After a few months in, you recognize its culture is not a good fit for your company and decide not to renew. These dues can be added back to increase the profits. The bottom line here is to consult with professionals and get a good understanding of what can and cannot be added back. Failure to do so will result in less compensation for your company.

Increase Sales - Keep the hammer down on sales throughout the selling process. A business trending backwards throws up a red flag. Purchasing companies are interested in *growing* companies, not those that stagnate or fall behind.

Collect Accounts Receivable - Like a vibrant service agreement program, one that is the focus of continuous attention and action, working accounts receivable is a mindset that should be part of your business every day. That said, it is particularly important to rein in and collect accounts receivable as you prepare your business to sell. One more thing: You should have little or no accounts receivable in the first place. And that's a mindset, too.

APPROACH PROSPECTIVE BUYERS

While many business owners have built up large networks inside industry associations, the contractor alliance they belong to, and the local market, it generally isn't a large enough base to provide an adequate market for purchases. For that you need to enlist a business broker or an M&A specialist.

Letter of Intent

Following a thorough discussion of an offer along with terms, a buyer issues a letter of intent (LOI), a non-binding, documented expression of the purchaser's intent to proceed with a potential transaction. It includes concise details of the deal; pricing, terms, conditions, obligations, and exclusivity. An LOI un-muddies the water from previous negotiations and discussions.

The LOI outlines the buyer's offer, intent, and expectations in respect to the transaction. It also opens the door for the prospective buyer to perform due diligence, a comprehensive inspection of the seller's operations, finances, and customer base. LOIs come with a deadline and will be null and void if not signed by the expiration date.

Also included in an LOI is a date range in which the seller cannot directly or indirectly solicit, engage in discussions with, and/or negotiate with other prospective buyers.

Once the seller receives the LOI, they begin a process of negotiation with the buyer. When satisfied, the seller signs the document and the buyer proceeds with the due diligence phase.

> **Chris:** I remember getting the call that the LOI was coming by day's end. My heart started racing. I'm talkin' NASCAR! I tried to be patient, but it didn't come by lunch, it didn't come by mid-afternoon, then finally, at zero hour, it hit my inbox.
>
> I anxiously read it. When I saw the offer amount, I knew we were close but not quite where I wanted to be. This was such a period of anxiety. If I accepted it there was a great chance it would happen. Then I would have to begin telling key people on the team. It kept running through my head, "this is happening, this is happening." I would get cold feet, then excited, cold feet, then excited. I didn't sleep all night.

> *Opportunity is a haughty goddess who wastes no time with those who are unprepared.*
> — *George S. Clason, The Richest Man in Babylon*

Chris: I submitted the changes that I requested, and after a couple of days I got another draft that *was* what I wanted. The realization of it all hit me like a freight train. It was Go-Time!

Everything Ben had talked with me about, along with the uncommon wealth, was on the cusp of getting done. What I hadn't thought about, and I'm glad I hadn't, was that only a fraction of people who receive an LOI actually end up closing on the deal. I was one of the lucky ones, though!

DUE DILIGENCE

A buyer performs comprehensive inspection into the seller's operation, finances, and customer base.

Ben: Due diligence is a major fact-seeking process that buyers must perform. The more detailed financials you keep and live with on a day-to-day basis, the smoother the process and the more appealing your company will be. In our first company sale, the due diligence was a major undertaking. I'd never do it again. The second and third times I sold a company I employed professionals. It helped the closing process and, in the long run, it aided greatly in company growth.

With those second and third companies, the process was also much easier because we not only kept meticulous financial records, we lived and breathed them daily. Stark Air, my second company, was designed from the ground floor to build, grow, and sell. Sunny Service, my third company, was an unexpected opportunity created by our reputation and relationships with folks like Chris Hunter.

The key, as we say throughout this book, is to build your company with the end in mind. This strategy has led to success beyond my dreams!

Chris: Due diligence is like a proctology exam. A real pain in the butt that sees all of the uglies! I recommend performing preliminary due diligence either internally or with outside help. Be sure to have a good accounting team; half the stuff in due diligence was above my head, and it might be above yours, too.

The following are major areas of concern and a couple examples of required detail.

General Corporate

- ★ Company organization chart demonstrating reporting structure
- ★ A strengths, weaknesses, opportunities, and threats (SWOT) analysis of the company

Sales and Marketing

- ★ Provide a report detailing marketing and advertising spent over the previous three years
- ★ Provide details on your club-membership programs

Coworkers

- ★ Coworker roster including seniority, compensation, bonuses, and benefits
- ★ List of management resumes and biographies

Financials

- ★ Copies of monthly balance sheets for the previous three years
- ★ A detailed budget for the existing and/or previous year

Customers

- ★ Describe market area of service
- ★ Detail existing install and service warranties

Service-Management Software

- ★ Provide copies of critical operational reports
- ★ Provide call summary detail report

> *Success is not the result of making money; earning money is the result of success — and success is in direct proportion to our service.*
>
> **— Earl Nightingale**

Suppliers

- ★ Copies of supplier contracts and agreements
- ★ A report on purchases from top suppliers from previous three years

Competition/Market

- ★ Provide pricing sheet for standard services offered
- ★ Detail of major local competitors

Property/Assets

- ★ List company vehicles
- ★ Lease agreements and/or property owned

The items listed above are but a fraction of a fraction of the items evaluated and analyzed during the due diligence process.

Chris: Another part of due diligence is an environmental inspection of your facilities. Do not house fuel or dangerous chemicals. There are always questions about refrigerant handling. Make sure your program is in accordance with EPA guidelines.

IS EVERYONE ON THE SAME PAGE?

A prospective buyer will conduct discussions with various key personnel and even the seller's spouse. Companies with a company purpose, vision, mission, and code of values that are embedded in the company culture, that are lived and talked about every day, will have little problem presenting a consistent front and story. This is a critical piece that the prospective buyer will analyze.

IT WORKS BOTH WAYS

The seller should perform due diligence on the buyer. Do an internet search. Read articles, check for reviews, and work your network. Perhaps most importantly, talk with others in the buyer's organization working underneath the executive level. What excites them? What doesn't? Oftentimes the insight you uncover provides a more candid view.

If you're dealing with a private-equity group and plan on investment moving forward, it's imperative to buy into their WHY, vision, mission, and values. Also, ask if they have an exit strategy.

Ben: It's important as a seller to understand the risk incurred with the deal. Seldom do buyers pay one hundred percent cash. Where will the capital originate?

 ★ Personal wealth?
 ★ A bank loan on assets or wealth?
 ★ Private equity backing?
 ★ Some type of shady resource loan?
 ★ Stock options?

What experience does the buyer have in running your company?

What type of risk are you willing to take? What if the buyer decides to flip the company and play a shell game, moving the cash in and out of offshore accounts? In the quest to get its money, the seller could get overwhelmed with legal fees.

If, as a seller, you get the asking price for your company, perhaps you'd be able to withstand the risk of loss. On the other hand, if you offer a twenty-five or thirty percent discount off the asking price *and then* take on the risk of a shady deal, you're asking for stress, anxiety, and a barrel of trouble.

Stock options are a risky deal. Just ask companies that were consolidated back in the mid-to-late nineties. Ben has firsthand experience with this.

On the outset of a company sale, the seller's stocks are X amount of dollars per share. The seller is now at the mercy of whatever whims affect the market. For instance, when Lennox purchased Service Experts, the stock price dropped dramatically. The other consideration when taking stock options is the seller might be locked into either holding that stock for a required period, or limited as to when and how much can be sold.

Chris: This is why it's important to consider a professional broker or a seasoned M&A specialist. It's all a game and you had better know how to play it or find someone who does. Otherwise, as Ben said, "You're asking for stress, anxiety, and a barrel of trouble."

PREPARE FOR CLOSING

Due diligence is complete and the buyer sends a contract to be signed along with these documents:

- ★ Purchase agreement
- ★ Bill of sale
- ★ Employment agreement
- ★ Non-compete document
- ★ Non-solicitation document
- ★ APA disclosure schedules
- ★ Property leases
- ★ Lien releases
- ★ Third-party consents
- ★ Trademark assignments
- ★ Flow of funds

CLOSING DAY

Along with the signed documentation comes a transfer of funds. With cash in the bank, reality sets in!

Chris: One of my first thoughts was, *My life is fixin' to be different!* My team, family, and self had put in an incredible effort to pull this off. It was such a big deal. I was incredibly grateful!

After this powerful first wave of emotion subsided, I thought, *WOW, this must be what Tom Brady feels like the night after winning a Super Bowl.* With victory in hand, he thinks, *Okay, what's next?*

With that, however, it's time to celebrate with family and friends. Enjoy the moment.

It's also a time to reflect. All of your life's work has come to a sort of fruition and a finish line. But, for the entrepreneurial heart, a finish line in one race soon becomes the starting line for the next one. Its Go-Time!

TRANSITION

There are many variables to transition. Like a relay race, the transition is the most important part of the event. A smooth exchange without losing speed is key. This comes with preparation and practice.

In Chris's case, weeks before the close, they began discussing the transition. The Super Techs created a playbook for day one, week one, the first thirty days, and the next thirty days. Relying on checklists, it detailed tasks and responsibilities.

As the transition takes place, if well-planned and done correctly, team members and customers shouldn't feel much different than they would have on any other business day.

Chris: The company leader's final and most important task is getting the team fired up and comfortable with what is taking place. There is no success without a successor.

For the owner who stays on board, things will be different. Not being the final decision maker and working in an environment where you are no longer the boss is challenging and takes some getting used to. Simple things, like being referred to as *the former owner*, can sting. But a great leader who truly cares about their people and the business, will rise above ego and make it happen.

LESSONS LEARNED

Chris: My number-one lesson learned from this experience is that golden opportunities knock only so many times. As a leader, you owe it to your team, family, and self to have your company prepared to capitalize on such an opportunity. When that knock comes, you are confident the house is clean. Open the door and invite that bad boy in!

The second most important lesson: the importance of your company story and reputation! Investors are looking for growing, profitable, clean, well-run, and reputable companies. Positive online reviews and a great Net Promoter Score, which is a tool that measures customer loyalty, are of the utmost importance. Pay attention to what your customers are saying because, essentially, your brand is what your customers say it is.

The money you have gives you freedom;
the money you pursue enslaves you.

— Jean-Jacques Rousseau

Chris: The most surprising lesson we learned was how ServiceTitan helped get a higher valuation for our business. Turn Point places a higher value on companies already using ServiceTitan. Their goal is to have all companies on the same operating and accounting system within ninety days of purchase, so any company already using it saves them a conversion expense. Plus, during the due diligence process, ServiceTitan saved countless hours because its data was easy to access and share.

Looking back on this incredible opportunity, the only thing I would have done differently would have been to start the process earlier.

Goal – Put together a successful plan to achieve the maximum amount of wealth from the sale of your company. Evaluate and rate its sale-readiness.

Observation – Explore how other companies are structured. Talk with contractors who have sold their businesses. Hire an evaluation consultant to assist in the process.

Take Massive Action – Perform due diligence on all aspects of your own company.

Inspect – Evaluate the results.

Modify – Continue to work on bringing all areas up to speed.

Engage – Test your results and have your company professionally valued.

Notes

Notes

Know your numbers and live by them!

— Ben Stark

*The fastest way to get where you want to go is
to duplicate what others did without repeating their
mistakes. Seek advice from trusted advisors and show your
appreciation for their time and effort.*

— Chris Hunter

*Live Your Purpose — While the Freedom's purpose
is to push the boundaries of what is known, to explore,
discover, process, delineate, and Radio-Back the
coordinates of knowledge, wisdom, and ideas to others,
we all have our own, individual purpose.*

*We join the Freedom and her crew to help mobilize
and actualize our own purpose. The Freedom's collective
belief is that transformed lives are major components of
success. We cannot transform lives unless we are living
our own purpose.*

Live your purpose and help others uncover theirs!

— David E. Rothacker

So here we are, almost at the end of the book. We've shared a lot of knowledge and wisdom in these pages, but we haven't summarized it and made it easily accessible. *Until now*. Here are Ben, Chris, and Dave's principles for success .

BEN STARK: BEN'S COMMANDMENTS

Network, Share, and Learn With Other Contractors; Join an Alliance

- ★ Reach out and learn from successful contractors
- ★ Seek out those who are more successful, learn from them, adapt their wisdom to your culture, and put it into action
- ★ Join contractor-support organizations
    - ☆ Sitting across the table at dinners offers countless opportunities
    - ☆ Share success and failure stories

Make Sure You are Properly Funded With Capital and Appropriate Lines of Credit

- ★ Obtain a line of credit even when you don't need one
- ★ Develop a relationship with your banker
    - ☆ Invite banker to your place of business
    - ☆ Routinely ask for business advice
- ★ Plan
    - ☆ Ensure enough capital for the first six months
    - ☆ Make sure you have sufficient capital
- ★ Reinvest a minimum of ten percent of profits back into the company

★ Use your line of credit wisely
★ Use it sparingly
★ Don't depend on it
★ Use it when opportunities come along
★ It's there for future growth

Create a Vision With Detailed Plans Covering Five Years, Ten Years, and an Exit. Write it Down. Share it. Make it Visible

★ Start with an annual success plan

★ Share vision with all, details with leadership and management, include people, create career pathways

★ End game—start, path, and end. Begin with the end in mind. Doesn't have to be a specific time frame

Have a Recruiting Plan to Consistently Attract the Right Coworkers, Including Leaders and Managers

★ Build culture—look good to the outside world

★ Devote thirty percent of time recruiting, retaining, and developing career pathways

★ Hire the right person if they come along. Take that leap of faith and then market accordingly

★ Mentorship, get your people to bring people in, bring people along career path

Invest in and Develop Coworkers

★ Never stop training!!!!!!!!!!!

★ Educate well

★ Be involved in all facets of the company

★ Grow your coworkers as industry assets

★ Discuss where they want to grow and go. Incorporate this in the annual success plan

★ Use your toolboxes
    ☆ Hand Tools toolbox
    ☆ Knowledge toolbox
    ☆ Communication toolbox
    ☆ Mindset toolbox

★ Teach coworkers life skills. Focus on the whole individual and help them to build wealth

Create a Market-Development Plan With Focused Market Penetration; Expand as Needed to Achieve Revenue Growth. Market for Acquisitions.

- ★ Focused market penetration—a market you can grow into, choose desired zip codes, develop one market at a time
- ★ Marketing plan
    - ☆ Know and understand the available media
    - ☆ Continuously develop it
    - ☆ Use direct mail as a lead into social media and the local community
    - ☆ Establish marketing budget. Implement, test, use feedback, modify
- ★ Track your marketing. Go with what works. Continue to analyze and try stuff out
- ★ Send acquisition letters to competition

Develop a Sales Force Superior to Your Competition's by Using Successful Sales Systems

USE THE CARE SELLING SYSTEM

CONNECT **A**SSESSMENT **R**ECOMMEND **E**XECUTE

- ★ Be consistent

Develop Departments That use Systems and Defined Processes to Deliver Consistent Service. Use Outside Trainers to Build Trust and Success With Your Systems

- ★ Separate departments and establish systems/processes for all
- ★ Put these processes in writing. Train relentlessly
- ★ Bring in outside trainers to enhance and support your message
- ★ Ensure trainers are compatible with your culture
- ★ Use various sources to bring in multiple ideas and information

Control Labor Costs and Price Your Service to Achieve Desired Profit and Margins

- ★ Place labor costs in correct departments to better understand costs
- ★ Strive for twenty percent or less service labor
- ★ Strive for nine percent or less install labor
- ★ Pricing—incorporate overhead in each department
- ★ Set appropriate gross margins for various departments
- ★ Profit—double-digit percentages for sustained growth
- ★ Control with proper financial management

Consistently Expand the Customer Base and Pursue Ways to Lock in Your Customers

- ★ Customers are the lifeblood of your company
- ★ Secure customers with club memberships
- ★ Keep customers involved by reaching out to them
- ★ Expand market areas and territory
- ★ Target correct areas

Insist on High-Quality, Detailed Accounting that Allows Your Company to Take Tax Advantages. Show Non-Recurring Expenses. This Makes the Company Attractive to Buyers

- ★ Employ on-site bookkeeper
- ★ Hire off-site professional CPA
- ★ Meet quarterly with CPA
- ★ Strive to bolster your endgame and create wealth
- ★ Understand true profit in relation to year-end activity designed to drive down taxable income

Know Your Numbers and Live by Them

- ★ Know and understand your overhead, sales-closing, and labor percentages and cost of goods sold
- ★ Place numbers in a simplistic and easily viewable format
- ★ Look at numbers on a consistent basis
- ★ Take action before anything gets out of hand
- ★ Pay attention to the small stuff monthly
- ★ Delegate KPI monitoring to department managers
- ★ KPIs change depending on many factors; adjust accordingly

Try New Things. Don't be Afraid to Fail. What if You Don't Fail?

- ★ Change happens
- ★ Make notes in a journal. Look back on old successes
- ★ Learn from failures
- ★ Tweak, modify, and make adjustments
- ★ It's not a failure until you quit

CHRIS HUNTER: CHRIS'S SUCCESS PRINCIPLES

David Heimer, senior vice president of Service Nation, Inc., once asked me, "If you had the opportunity to go back and talk to yourself when you were first launching your company, what advice would you give?"

That was a great, reflective exercise. It helped me to flush out these very important success principles. They are universal, applying to anyone in any business at any point in their career.

It's Go-Time!

Know your WHY

What is your purpose in life? What is your purpose for being in business? Sadly, most people never seek answers to these questions. They live a life of busyness, a rat-race quest to find the ever-elusive cheese. There is no purpose and passion in the hunt. Just get up every morning and do it again. Who wants that?

To know your purpose is to get up each morning with intent! It's the most important key to success in life and business! It fuels each day with meaning, and the built-up momentum powers you through, over, and around obstacles.

Your coworkers, customers, and potential customers need to know WHY your business exists. People gravitate to those who believe what *they* believe.

As a business leader, you need to communicate a single vision clearly, creatively, and continually, ensuring your coworkers are on the same page. Demonstrate to your coworkers how achieving company goals through meaningful work will also help them to achieve their own goals.

When looking back on our lives, we want our work to represent more than a rat chasing cheese. We want to look back on a life of significance, meaning, and impact. We want to have made a difference in other people's lives.

Always Do What's Right and You'll Never be Wrong

Integrity is doing the right thing even when no one is looking. Integrity is the only foundation from which to build your company, team, and organization.

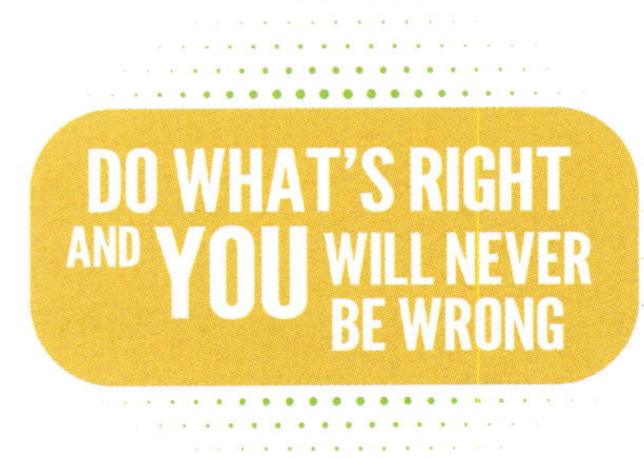

Seek Advice From Those Who Have Been There and Done That

The fastest way to get where you want to go is to duplicate what others did without repeating their mistakes. Seek advice from trusted advisors and show your appreciation for their time and effort.

Hire Above You and Get Out of Their Way

It takes a secure leader to empower the team. Empower the team. Delegate authority and not just tasks. Delegating authority creates leaders; delegating tasks creates followers.

Invest in Your Team

Train your team for technical, sales, life and character skills, and for leadership.

One is way too small of a number to achieve greatness. In order to reach meaningful goals, you need to build a team. Team-building is your greatest investment. Success is built from people's knowledge over product knowledge. Structure your training to reflect this.

It's far more meaningful and rewarding to increase your team's leadership levels, better their home lives, and improve their finances. Seek out knowledge and programs that add value to your team.

Invest in Yourself

Your organization will never be better than your leadership level. This is why business owners plateau at one, three, or five million dollars in annual revenue. If you want to succeed, you must take the time, put in the effort, and invest in your education. Develop your own personal-growth plan and adhere to it with diligence.

Brand Yourself

In order for people to buy from you, they have to hear about you, right? How are they going to hear about you unless you tell them?

Word of mouth coupled with intentional marketing is the most effective way to go to market. To grow your company, you must invest in branding it. Not the manufacturer, YOU! Create your brand and put it in front of the right people.

Here are my top five ways to maximize your effectiveness:

1. Facebook - Be social and commit to using the paid ad feature as part of your advertising budget.

2. Vehicle wraps - Your vehicles are rolling billboards. Invest in quality wraps and designs. Make them stand out.

3. Yard signs - Put them out whenever you can. People will soon assume that you are everywhere.

4. Website with reviews - Use a program that can generate a review on every call you go on. Spiff your techs and count it as part of your advertising budget.

5. Networking - For some, this is hard to do, but it pays the largest dividends. Let your light shine. Increase your circle of influence by going to networking events, church programs, community events, school programs, etc. If there is an opportunity to be visible and shake hands, do it. Involve your whole team.

Give

Whatever you want more of, give more of that.

- ★ Respect
- ★ Better communication
- ★ Gratitude
- ★ Teamwork
- ★ Love
- ★ Grace

Give and it will be given to you. A good measure, pressed down, shaken together and running over, will be poured into your lap. For with the measure you use, it will be measured to you.

— Luke 6:38 NLT

Don't Let a Negative or Unethical Person Stay too Long

Fill your team with people who add value, not those who take it away. Every time I let a negative person go, I always wish that I had done it sooner. Have ZERO tolerance for unethical behavior. It's a virus that will infect other team members. Be a bad-attitude assassin.

Create a Repeatable Model

Once you learn the power of systems and processes, you will unlock the potential for personal freedom and uncommon wealth!

In order to grow and make your company attractive to potential buyers and investors, create and use simple processes and systems.

Rest and Celebrate

The work/life ebb-and-flow is the most overlooked thing in our industries. In the end, it won't be the hours we worked that made a difference. Our true impact will be made on relationships we developed and a well-lived life.

DAVE ROTHACKER: THE STARSHIP FREEDOM'S CODE

 I traveled a much different path than both Ben and Chris. When they were toiling away in a service truck, I was toiling away in a grocery store. I finally started working for an HVAC contractor as a truck driver at the age of twenty-eight. Approximately one year later, I moved into service operations and have had roles in installation, service, operations, and general-management positions for the balance of my contractor career.

We brought the internet into our family home in 1996. By '97 I was writing online. Back then, because corporate America did not understand the internet and I didn't want to get in trouble, I wrote my articles anonymously. Readers thought I was a company owner, CEO, or consultant. I wasn't any of these. I was a service manager. Due to the favorable reaction I received, I saw no reason to clear the air.

The more I was able to write and influence the influencers online, the less satisfaction I was able to derive from my role as a service manager. So I continued to write and in the process created a fictional world that used metaphors to illustrate my ideas and thoughts.

The theme behind my intent was that of a community venturing out to explore new worlds—as in, explore other industries, particularly what was working on the edge of the technology, education, marketing, leadership, and social-science fields. Collectively, we would delineate and distill the intelligence and use it to advance business knowledge in the skilled trades.

The Road

For as long as I can remember, I have viewed my activity in life as traveling down a Road. I wanted to learn about those who had been there and done it and I wanted to pass along the knowledge, wisdom, and ideas to others. The goal was to inform others about the road ahead while at the same time learning myself.

On my imaginary Road, those ahead can actually be behind those behind. A classic example was the industry leaders back in the '90s who, while they had advanced business knowledge about HVAC and plumbing, they had little knowledge of how the internet worked. Consequently, on my Road there is no authoritative hierarchy. Another real-world example: An apprentice that I worked with was one of the most talented leaders I've ever met.

In 2003 I bolted *The Wizard of Oz* onto my vision of the Road and came up with the metaphor *Oz is the Yellow Brick Road*. It simply means it's more about the journey than the destination. In fact, with each step forward, along with the dynamics and people who we meet on the Road, it's highly probable that the destination will change.

The Starship Freedom

In 1998, author extraordinaire Dan Holohan provided me with my first opportunity to write on an industry website (Prior to that I'd written anonymously at various places within Yahoo Finance). I wrote short articles and posted them on The Wall, Dan's website at the time.

The Wall allowed my two partners, Steve Merker and Tom Steiger, to build our voice and sea legs. Due to nasty trolls, Dan had to take The Wall offline temporarily toward the end of 1998. Consequently, Steve, Tom, and I launched AREA51HVAC to provide a place for The Wall's community to meet while Dan took care of business.

AREA51HVAC was a community for industry professionals to gather and exchange knowledge, information, and ideas. Members came from all corners of the HVAC industry. We had CEOs, high-level executives, middle management, technicians, installers, engineers, truck drivers, floor sweepers, media . . . the list was seemingly endless.

It was at this time that I created the imaginary Starship (the name Freedom didn't come until much later) and used it to represent not only my Road, but to board and house industry professionals as we traveled through space on the way to the edges of business reality as we knew it. Here is how I described her at the time:

> *She travels at speeds beyond human comprehension. Her size fluctuates according to her occupants. Her structure is metamorphic, ever-changing as it incorporates the new technologies and business ideas of those on board. The Starship is a vehicle built to vaporize boundaries and limitations. She will take us to the very brink of our imaginations. And with but a glimpse of visions to be, she engages the afterburners, blasting us forward, screaming to shatter the barriers of conventional thinking and complacency. How can a ship accomplish such noble tasks you ask? Because her fuel is the collective passion of those on board. The passion to learn, share knowledge, information, and ideas. Through this collaborative effort she reaches destinations impossible for one human being or alien.*

The Starship Freedom's crew are like-minded, like-valued and possess a growth mindset. We are wired to push the boundaries of what is known to explore, discover, process, delineate, and radio-back the coordinates of knowledge, wisdom, and ideas to others traveling through space. Sometimes our transmissions are the product of combining elements of what we're discovering with our own new thoughts and ideas.

Although we shut the site down in 2004*, the Freedom's activities never ceased coursing through my mind, body, and soul. This is how I approach purpose, transformational leadership, and my writing in general. The following is the code that governs the Freedom on her missions to the edge of the Universe.

The Starship Freedom's Code

Do the Right Thing - Our foundational belief. Our mission is collaborative. Consequently, trust is essential. In order to be trustworthy, each individual needs to do the right thing.

Pursue the Growth Mindset - The desire to grow emotionally, spiritually, and intellectually is the human fuel of the Freedom. One cannot fly on the Freedom without the passionate desire to grow!

Be Curious - Curiosity fuels exploration and leads to discovery. It's the flint that sparks the tinder that explodes into an all-out fire of growth and possibility.

Create - Because the Freedom flies on the fringes we are exposed to many different high-level elements, some from our industries, most from without. Whether it's ideas, thoughts, or physical manifestations, we are in a position to combine these disparate elements and create something new and different.

Radio-Back - Radio-Back is the act of relaying the coordinates of our discoveries and creations to those traveling behind. Ours is not a reporter's voice; it's that of a guide. Our syntax is leadership driven.

Connect Others - As solar systems come and go, we continually meet like-minded and like-valued people. Whether we connect them to our mission or connect them with each other, we believe it's good for the Universe.

Inspire Others - You cannot board and fly even a single mile on the Freedom and not be inspired. The emotion overwhelms your consciousness, stimulates your heart, and ignites the act of inspiring others!

Live Your Purpose - While the Freedom's purpose is to push the boundaries of what is known, to explore, discover, process, delineate, and Radio-Back the coordinates of knowledge, wisdom, and ideas to others, we all have our own, individual purpose.

We join the Freedom and her crew to help mobilize and actualize our own purpose. The Freedom's collective belief is that transformed lives are major components of success. We cannot transform lives unless we are living our own purpose. Live your purpose and help others uncover theirs.

My Own Purpose Is: To inspire fellow travelers to connect with their purpose and pursue transformational leadership. To connect with knowledge, ideas, and others so that they'll be more effective transformational leaders.

The Starship Freedom: www.gotimesuccessgroup.com/the-starship-freedom/

Tom Steiger brought the AREA51HVAC experience back to life in 2020. It serves today as an RSES chapter in Northeastern Ohio. Steve Merker passed away January 30, 2013. He is presently building an AREA51HVAC community in Heaven.

Don't go around saying the world owes you a living. The world owes you nothing. It was here first!

— Mark Twain

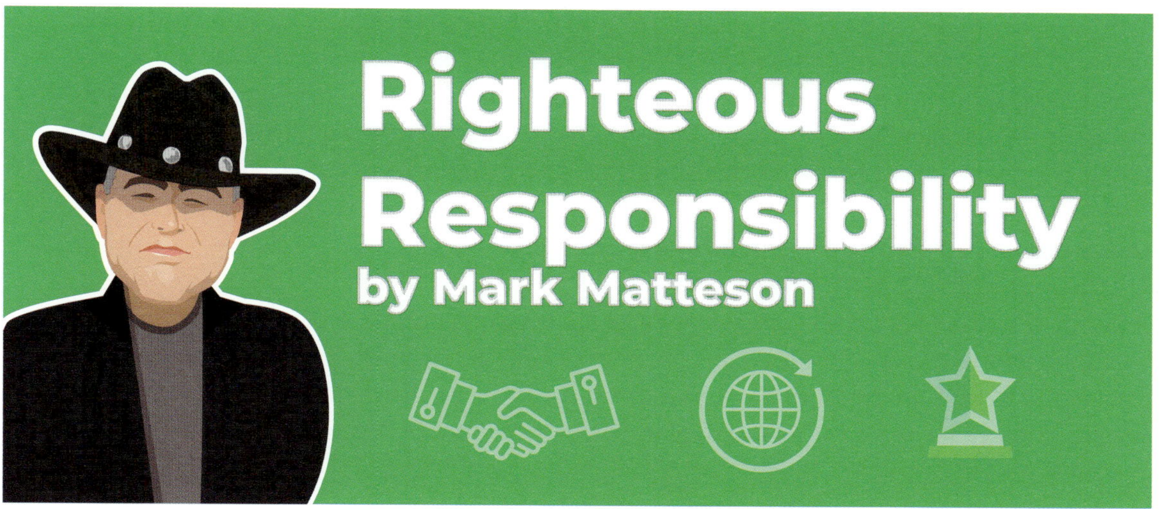

Mark Matteson had been a subtle but guiding and instrumental force in Ben and Chris's career (Dave's too)! Whether it's been through his books, articles, monthly EZine Street newsletter, or personal discussion, Mark has been an eternal source of encouragement and guidance.

If the three of us have heard it once, we've heard it a hundred times: "When are you going to write a book?" Or, "Have you started that book yet?" What you're holding in your hands right now is our answer to Mark's question.

We know for a fact that many of you have been on the other side of Mark's book-writing question. To that we say, dig in and start today. Set a goal and deadline, take small steps and work a little on it every day.

— David E. Rothacker

One of my literary heroes is Samuel Clemens, aka Mark Twain. A few years ago, I checked *Visit Mark Twain's Connecticut home* off of my Lifetime Goals List. I savored every nook and cranny. They had to kick me out. I bought a coffee cup, covered with his pithy aphorisms and memorable quotes, to remember the visit. He had the unique ability to convey a principle, with a humorous twist, in a few short words. Proverbs with a pun. His insights have stood the test of time.

Here are some timeless tips from the master:

★ Humor is mankind's greatest blessing. Against the assault of laughter, nothing can stand.

★ Anger (and resentment) is an acid that can do more harm to the vessel in which it is stored, than to anything on which it is poured.

★ Don't go around saying the world owes you a living. The world owes you nothing. It was here first!

In my late twenties I read Dr. Ken Olson's *The Art of Hanging Loose in an Uptight World*. Dr. Olson advised, *Stop playing the Blame Game! It's time to assume 100% responsibility for my life and business. My problems are my own. I believe people can change. I must take personal responsibility for changing; decide what it is I want to change, then examine all the barriers and resistance that exist in the path of that change. Be ready to pay the price and to work hard until . . .*

Today I choose to embrace Righteous Responsibility.

Legendary author, consultant, and sage Peter F. Drucker spent most of his life in Claremont, California where he was a professor in the nearby college. He wrote dozens of books that are considered classics in the business community. He wrote an article for the *Harvard Business Review* many years ago entitled "Managing Yourself**.**" He begins by saying:

> *History's great achievers—a Napoleon, a Da Vinci, a Mozart have always managed themselves. That, in large measure, is what makes them great achievers. And we will have to learn to develop ourselves, which means knowing how and when to change the work we do. Most people think they know what they are good at. They are usually wrong. More often, people know what they are NOT good at, and even then, more people are wrong than right. One cannot build performance on weaknesses, let alone something one cannot do at all.*

Feedback analysis is the key. It was invented in the fourteenth century by an otherwise totally obscure German theologian and picked up a hundred and fifty years later by John Calvin and Ignatius of Loyola. The commitment to this process explains the incredible performance and results that this habit produces and why Calvinism and the Jesuit order came to dominate Europe within thirty years.

Practiced consistently, this simple method will show us within a fairly short period of time where our strengths are. Put yourself where your strengths can produce results.

In order to assume one hundred percent *Righteous Responsibility* for your life and business, ask and answer the following questions:

1. What are my strengths? (What is the best and highest use of my time?)

2. How do I work? (In what ways do I work best?)

3. What are my values? (What are my ethics?)

4. Where do I belong? (What is the best seat for me on the bus?)

5. What can I contribute? (How might I make the greatest contribution to my organization?)

We shouldn't waste time improving areas of low competence. It takes far more energy and work to improve from incompetence to mediocrity than it takes to improve from first-rate to excellent.

In Daniel Coyle's extraordinary book *The Talent Code* he advises his readers to adopt three simple strategies to take your skill to the next level:

1. Decide to master the skill that provides the most contribution and value to your organization. In other words, "Ignition . . . blast off!"

2. Commit to two hours of daily *Deep Practice* on the primary skills that will make the biggest difference.

3. Continue to invest in *master coaching*, that is, learning from mentors who have the specialized knowledge to assist you in becoming great at your work.

Mark Twain was right. The world owes us nothing. We may pay the price in advance for what we want in life and business. I call it *Righteous Responsibility*. What do you call it?

Remember the words of William Penn:

I expect to pass through life but once. If, therefore, there be any kindness I can show, or any good thing I can do to any fellow being, let me do it now, and not defer or neglect it, as I shall not pass this way again.

Age is an issue of mind over matter.
If you don't mind, it doesn't matter.
— Mark Twain

Your Takeaway Notes

One Action You Will Take

Notes

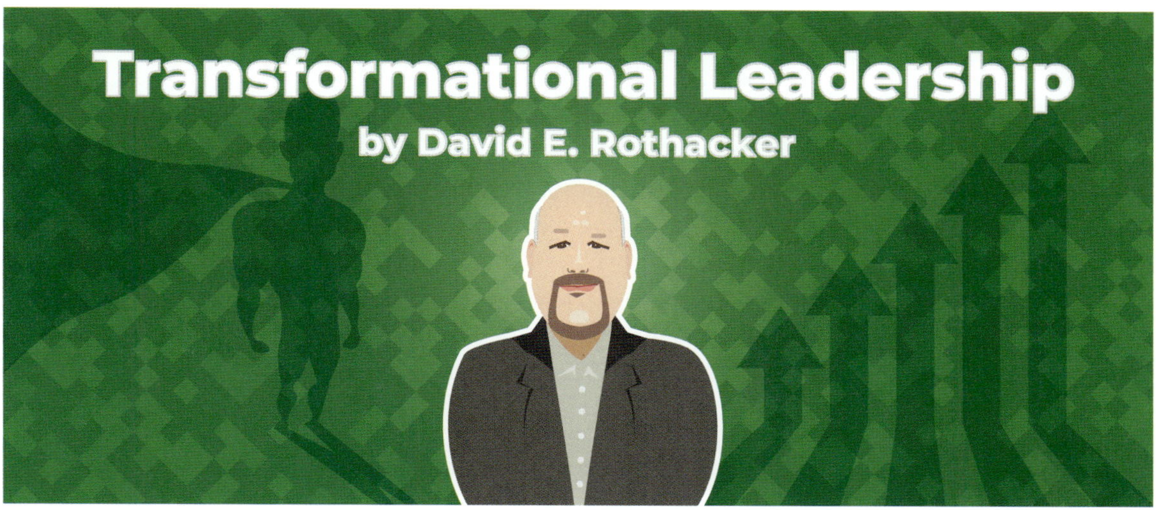

"I can't get buy-in. I've been over and over it. I just can't make our people________!"

Fill in the blank. From systems to processes to procedures to training, the message isn't getting through to your coworkers. Short of hypnotizing them, what can you do?

> *I am about ready to close shop and go work for someone else! I would hire a body if they walked through the door. I can't get anyone to even walk through the door. Labor shortage? No, labor outage!*
>
> *— Average Struggling Contractor*

Do you struggle to attract and keep quality coworkers? Let's check in on one of the most accomplished leaders today.

JOHN C. MAXWELL

John C. Maxwell has more years in leadership teaching and experience than most of us have been alive. Let's take a look at a lesson in his treasure-laden archive.

Maxwell founded the non-profit organization EQUIP along with his brother Larry in 1996. In 2003, the brothers set a goal to train one million leaders in countries around the world.

EQUIP hit that mark five years later. By 2013 they had trained five million leaders worldwide. A serious problem, however, began to surface. Although these leaders had been through the highest quality training, they were not making an impact; they were not making a positive difference in the lives of others.

It's About Being Intentional

Maxwell's leadership team was perplexed. After significant debate and soul-searching, they figured it out.

> "The training we had done was educational, not transformational. We had focused on the lesson we taught more than the lives we hoped to change."

> ". . . giving leaders training does not make them transformational in the lives of others. They don't automatically make an impact, they do not automatically become transformational in the lives of others. They don't live out intentional significance."

Think Back in Your Life

Did a manager, coach, teacher, or parent ever make a difference in your life?

In addition to lessons learned, it was how they made you *feel* that was important. They saw something that led them to foster and grow a belief in you. They knew that you not only had the mind to make things happen, you also had the heart.

Their belief in you supercharged the lesson and, more importantly, your life.

TRANSFORMATIONAL LEADERSHIP

If your actions inspire people to dream more, learn more, do more and become more, then you are a transformational leader. You influence people to think, speak, and act in ways that make a positive difference in their lives and the lives of others. —John C. Maxwell

What is the difference between trained leaders and transformational leaders?

Trained Leaders	**Transformational Leaders**
✔ Understand the how behind leading	★ Understand the why behind leading
✔ Have a career	★ Have a calling
✔ Love leading	★ Love the people they lead
✔ Are educated	★ Are educated and transformed
✔ Are of influence today	★ Are of influence today and tomorrow
✔ Teach people	★ Teach and inspire people
✔ Direct people	★ Direct and inspire people
✔ Connect intellectually	★ Connect intellectually and emotionally

Our Industries Do Not Have a Labor Shortage, They Have a Leadership Shortage

People not only want to work for transformational leaders, they want to be a part of what they're a part of. Envision the coworker who passionately believes in their owner and what the owner believes. Imagine being on the receiving end of all that a transformational leader has to give. Picture and feel the potential. This coworker is making an impact and a difference in the world. They love their work.

What are the chances these coworkers go on about their lives outside of work and NOT tell anyone!? Zero. Even if they didn't verbalize their delight, their family, friends, and acquaintances will see it and feel it in their actions.

Educator

Transformational leaders realize more educational options are necessary than traditional trade schools, so they've taken on the role of educator. Whether it's a CSR, bookkeeper, plumber, technician, or installer, they have the ability to take an inexperienced applicant off the street, school them, and get them started on productive work. Their education never really ends.

The transformational leader has now increased their pool of potential labor into an ocean.

Community Asset

The transformational leader's company becomes known within the community. It:

- ★ Is a beacon of hope and light
- ★ Has a vision, mission, and culture that people embrace
- ★ Makes a positive difference in the community
- ★ Lives its beliefs every day
- ★ Cares about its people and families
- ★ Cares about coworker growth and development
- ★ Inspires coworkers as they become beacons of hope and light
- ★ Reinvests in its people and the community

There are only two ways to influence human behavior:
You can manipulate it or you can inspire it.

— Simon Sinek

IT'S TIME TO TAKE MASSIVE ACTION

We can transform our industries! One educated and inspired leader at a time who, with intention and resolve, inspires and makes a positive difference in the lives of others. Then it's up to those who recognize the stimulating results transformational leaders produce. Study these leaders and emulate their practice. Take massive action and be the change you so passionately wish to see!

Transformational leaders have their lights on, and they want to help others turn theirs on.

— *John C. Maxwell*

You can't read too many books . . . But you can read too few.
— *Jim Rohn*

MUST READ

HVAC Spells Wealth: How to Build and Manage a Highly Successful HVAC Residential Retail Business and Dominate Your Market,
by Ron Smith

More and New HVAC Spells Wealth: A Companion, Update and Follow-up to the Best Selling Book HVAC Spells Wealth,
by Ron Smith

Invest Your Heartbeats Wisely: Practical, Philosophical, and Principled Leadership Concepts for Business and Life,
by Theo Etzel

The Power of Positive Pricing: How Much is Your Pricing Costing You?, by Matt Michel

Soaring With Eagles: The Life and Legacy Of Frank J. Blau Jr.,
by Ellen Rohr and Helena Bouchez

Where Did the Money Go?: Accounting Basics for the Business Owner Who Wants to Get Profitable,
by Ellen Rohr

Never by the Book: Overcome Obstacles to Build a Life of Wealth and Fulfillment,
by Kelly Schols

The E-Myth HVAC Contractor: Why Most HVAC Companies Don't Work and What to Do About It,
by Michael E. Gerber and Ken Goodrich

Why Won't They Pay Me What I'm Worth?,
By Rodney Koop

Freedom From Fear: The Story of One Man's Discovery of Simple Truths That Lead to Wealth, Joy and Peace of Mind,
by Mark Matteson

Freedom From Fear Forever: Len's Last Lessons,
by Mark Matteson

A Simple Choice,
by Mark Matteson

Be Bodacious: Put Life in Your Leadership,
by Steven D. Wood

Proposition Selling: How to Create Extraordinary Success in Business-to-Business Sales,
by Tom Piscitelli and John Sedgwick

The Courage to be Profitable: Get and Stay Profitable in Less Than 30 Minutes a Month,
by Ruth King

Building a Big Small Business Brand: How to Turn Your Brand into Your Most Valuable Asset,
by Dan Antonelli

Patterned after Excellence: Pursuing Truth in Work and Life,
by Brigham Dickinson

No matter how busy you may think you are, you must find time for reading, or surrender yourself to self-chosen ignorance.

— *Confucius*

CHRIS HUNTER'S RECOMMENDATIONS

The Maxwell Leadership Bible,
by John C. Maxwell

The 21 Irrefutable Laws of Leadership: Follow Them and People Will Follow You,
by John C. Maxwell

Intentional Living: Choosing a Life That Matters,
by John C. Maxwell

Get Your Business to Work!: 7 Steps to Earning More, Working Less, and Living the Life You Want,
by George Hedley

17 Indisputable Laws of Teamwork: Embrace Them and Empower Your Team,
by John C. Maxwell

Build an A-Team: Play to Their Strengths and Lead Them up the Learning Curve,
by Whitney Johnson

When Work and Family Collide: Keeping Your Job From Cheating Your Family,
by Andy Stanley

A Stake in the Outcome: Building a Culture of Ownership for the Long-Term Success of Your Business,
by Jack Stack

The Resolution for Men,
by Stephen Kendrick

The Purpose Driven Life: What on Earth am I Here for?,
By Rick Warren

Not all readers are leaders, but all leaders are readers.
— Harry Truman

BEN STARK'S RECOMMENDATIONS

How to Win Friends & Influence People: The Only Book You Need to Lead You to Success,
by Dale Carnegie

The Greatest Salesman in the World,
by Og Mandino

Emotional Intelligence: Why it can Matter More Than IQ,
by Daniel Goleman

The One Minute Manager,
by Kenneth Blanchard, Ph.D. and Spencer Johnson, M.D.

Traction: Get a Grip on Your Business,
by Gino Wickman

The Richest Man in Babylon,
by George S. Clason

The Great Game of Business: The Only Sensible Way to Run a Company,
by Jack Stack

Built to Last: Successful Habits of Visionary Companies,
by Jim Collins and Jerry I. Porras

Raving Fans: A Revolutionary Approach to Customer Service,
by Ken Blanchard and Sheldon Bowles

Emotional Intelligence 2.0,
by Travis Bradberry and Jean Greaves

You are the same today as you'll be in five years except for two things, the people you meet and the books you read.

— Charlie "Tremendous" Jones

DAVE ROTHACKER'S RECOMMENDATIONS

Grit: The Power of Passion and Perseverance,
by Angela Duckworth

Give and Take: Why Helping Others Drives Our Success,
by Adam Grant

*What Color Is Your Parachute? 2020: A Practical Manual for Job-Hunters and
 Career-Changers,*
by Richard N. Bolles

Start With Why: How Great Leaders Inspire Everyone to Take Action,
by Simon Sinek

*It's the Manager: Gallup Finds That the Quality of Managers and Team Leaders
 is the Single Biggest Factor in Your Organization's Long-term Success,*
by Jim Clifton and Jim Harter

*Change by Design, Revised and Updated: How Design Thinking Transforms
 Organizations and Inspires Innovation,*
by Tim Brown

Creative Confidence: Unleashing the Creative Potential Within Us All,
by Tom Kelley and David Kelley

Drive: The Surprising Truth About What Motivates Us,
by Daniel H. Pink

The 8th Habit: From Effectiveness to Greatness,
by Stephen R. Covey

Flourish: A Visionary New Understanding of Happiness and Well-being,
by Martin E. P. Seligman

*The Book of Beautiful Questions: The Powerful Questions That Will Help You
Decide, Create, Connect and Lead,*
by Warren Berger

*I think books are like people, in the sense that they'll turn up
in your life when you most need them.*

— Emma Thompson

Give the gift of knowledge! Gift a book today!

Acknowledgements

We'd like to thank David Thompson for his creative services and illustrations. David's patience and determination to get it right is a tribute to his work and is so much appreciated.

Thanks to Jason Liller for his masterful work on cleaning up our language and editing the book. Ours was a two-year-plus project and Jason was with us every step of the way offering guidance, tips, and suggestions.

Thanks to Dillon Phipps of the Go-Time Success Group for his organizational talents.

Matt Michel, CEO of Service Nation, Inc., is the beacon of light who not only brought our ships into the Service Nation harbor, but other members as well who recognized the power of our community to grow and develop their people and companies. Thanks, Matt!

David Heimer, COO of Service Nation, Inc., is a combination of master architect, chessman, and human bonding agent. David has done many quiet, positive things over the years that have added to the incredible cohesion of both the organization and our lives.

The three of us are Advisory Board (AB) Mentors within the Service Nation Alliance. ABs are contractors who are serious about driving profitable growth at their companies while guiding the growth and development of their people. Meeting with these folks each week is like a saline drip for the soul. They are why we do what we do.

The following are our ABs, past and present:

> Ben: AB1, AB2, AB23
>
> Chris: AB7, AB6, AB9, AB57, AB18, AB25
>
> Dave: AB10, AB16, AB9
>
> A huge thanks to each and every member from these ABs!

A special thanks to Mark Matteson for his thoughtful contributions to the world via his books, talks, and website, and for his encouragement to each of us, collectively and individually, to write this book.

Go-Time Success Group Clients—The Go-Time Success Group evolved from the process of writing this book. Our clients are our rock, our reason, and our purpose. As evidenced in one of Chris's favorite Proverbs: "As iron sharpens iron, so one person sharpens another," our clients have made us stronger! Thank you!

Ben: *This book is for all of the great women who helped build and support the home-service industry. The moms, wives, sisters, and daughters who work in the industry, and also the ones who support us from home. You are the backbone that keeps our families going with your support. Many thanks, without you none of this is possible.*

My personal thanks to my mother, Arteth Stark, who as a young lady worked in the factories supporting the war effort, a single mom raising four children who sometimes worked three jobs to support us. She set a great work ethic for me to follow. My Grandmother, Emma Stark, who taught me keep my head up, shoulders back, look people in the eye, and keep a positive attitude. My two great aunts, Addie and Sydney, both old-maid school teachers who taught me to learn something from everyone I met: "You can learn their wisdom, or learn their mistakes."

I look back at the thousands of people I have visited with for almost fifty years and, somehow, everyone is supported by family and friends.

Let's not forget the technician: One who is in their truck before sunup, in extreme weather, and not home until hours after dark. The tech endures the elements that he is trying to protect us all from. The 140-degree attic and the 20-degree rooftops in a snow storm, they risk health, safety, and time spent with loved ones to provide our communities with a craftsman service. They suffer heat burns, frost burns, heat strokes, fall injuries, driving accidents, cuts, infections, viruses, and so much more. Not many earn what they deserve, but they will provide a needed service for just a smile, a handshake, and a thank you!

I'd like to thank Chris Hunter and Dave Rothacker for all the time spent working on our book.

I'd also like to thank all the industry acquaintances who have selflessly shared successes and failures for the benefit of all who listen; and the teachers, coaches, consultants and leaders who are too many too list.

Chris: *First I'd like to thank God for directing my steps. I would have never dreamed of taking the path that I did, but now looking back, I wouldn't have dreamed of taking a different one. I'd like to thank all of my mentors and fellow contractors who I learned from. Ben Stark was by far the most influential mentor in my journey. Iron sharpens iron, and I'm truly sharper today because of you. I want to thank my family for giving me the support to take the challenge of building an organization. Nickie and my kids lived on this rollercoaster with me 24/7/365. Without their support, none of it would have been possible. The team at Hunter SuperTechs needs a big thank you! The core group of leaders would run through a brick wall for me and I would for them as well. I could not have done it without them. I'd also like to thank Dave Rothacker. Without you, we would not have had this book, this legacy, recorded in ink. I am truly thankful for all the help in capturing our thoughts, lessons, and beliefs in words.*

Dave: *I view life as a traveled road (or Star Trail). And living is what we do on the road. I am grateful for all of the travelers I've met and been influenced by along the way.*

Thanks to Ben DiMarco. At fifteen years old, Ben was my first protege. Today, he is a few months shy of fifty and we've been connected at every step of our individual journeys. When it comes to engaging the growth mindset and fusing technical and business expertise, Ben is unequaled. His drive and determination to separate himself from status-quo HVAC companies is a light that drives my own efforts.

Thanks to Tom Steiger and Steve Merker, my partners in AREA51HVAC.Com. It was a great ride and opportunity to live out our authentic selves—even though we used aliases.

Thanks to Dan Holohan for giving me my first chance to write for people in our profession. Dan recommended the book Writing the Natural Way in the late nineties and it's my number-one book recommendation on the subject of writing.

Thanks to Rosa Say for inviting me into her leadership and management community. Rosa's blend of the high-level executive and Hawaiian culture provided a dynamic learning ground for many leaders, including myself.

Thanks to Farida Stino for her guidance and direction. Sometimes a person comes into our life, who, like a boulder, alters the flow of a river, altering the course of our lives. Farida not only altered the flow of my river, but also strengthened it.

Thanks to Matt Michel. Although we also included Matt in our collective thanks, he was personally instrumental for my long-time association with the Service Nation, Inc. From the proverbial paper-napkin first look at what the Service Roundtable might be, today, Matt has been a warrior against the status quo and, within the industry, I know of no greater honor.

Thanks to Larry Taylor. To me, Larry embodies the essence of what a leader is. Larry's teachings about an old man going down the highway and building bridges will forever be lodged in my psyche, and it embodies what I aspire to be. Google Will Allen Dromgoole's The Bridge Builder and read it yourself.

A special thanks to members of the Service Nation Alliance. It's because of you and your passionate effort to develop and grow that I didn't abandon the HVAC industry. You rekindled and fueled my faith.

A fist-pumping, slam-dunking, spike-the-football-in-the-endzone thanks to Ben Stark and Chris Hunter! Ben and Chris gave me a chance to write their evolutionary tale from technician to entrepreneur to creators-of-wealth. I'm not bad at conjuring words, but I have no words to describe the honor I have felt along our two-plus-year journey to write this book.

Ben and Chris have a deep and passionate desire to make this book a gift to the industry. A gift to give back to the industry for all it has done for them. And a gift of possibility to others who have a burning desire to run successful home-service companies. I pray that what I've done here is worthy of such noble aspirations.

And finally, my reasons for being…

Thank you to my daughters, Victoria Rose Orban and Carla Marie Rothacker, along with your families. Your journeys to be strong, loving, caring moms and successful career professionals are a continuous source of strength and inspiration to me. I love you to the Moon and back!

And then there's my soulmate and adversary, errr, partner. Since 1975, we've been arguing over who gets to be Kirk and who has to be Spock. Thanks are not sufficient here, Rosemary. You are my anchor! That twenty-five-year journey that we took as managers in different fields, coming home every night and discussing business and people, was a once-in-a-lifetime experience.

Your ability to run our home and raise our girls while successfully managing a large bank still boggles my mind. Neither I or 99% of the other men out there could do that. And while I aspired to be a tenth of the manager you were, I also aspire to be a tenth of the writer you are. Throw in the fact that you've actually read more books than I have and I really might have to sit behind you on the bridge of the Enterprise. You are my forever and forever love!

Biographies

Ben Stark: *I was born and raised in Fort Worth, Texas, graduated Grand Prairie High in 1975, and attended Eastfield College. I am husband to Kim, Dad to our five children, and Papa to seven grandkids.*

My forty-two years in the home-service industry began with a job as a service tech; by 1985 I owned my own business. I launched Air Experts, StarkAir, Outlook Tx, Sunny Service, and partnered in the Go Time Success Group. I successfully sold three of the companies and continue to operate the others.

Chris Hunter: *I am a Christ follower, husband, father, Go-Paw and family leader. As a founder of the Hunter Super Techs and the Go Time Success Group, I am a business leader and advocate for the trades. My wife Nickie and I have three great kids and lots of family in Oklahoma and Texas.*

I get my business and life philosophies from the ultimate instruction manual, the Bible. In Colossians 3:23 it says, "whatever you do, work at it with all your heart as to The Lord and not to men." That type of mentality is what led me to seek out the best to learn from, assemble the best teams I could, and always look for ways to better serve.

David E. Rothacker: *I am an author and guide for 21st century Lewis and Clark leaders, commander of the Go Time Success Group based Starship Freedom, and a passionate autodidactic fueled by a growth mindset.*

I am a certified John C. Maxwell coach, recipient of the Service Roundtable Servant Leadership award and twenty-five plus year veteran in HVAC management.